Contemporary Directions

KOREA RESEARCH MONOGRAPH 27

INSTITUTE OF EAST ASIAN STUDIES
UNIVERSITY OF CALIFORNIA • BERKELEY
CENTER FOR KOREAN STUDIES

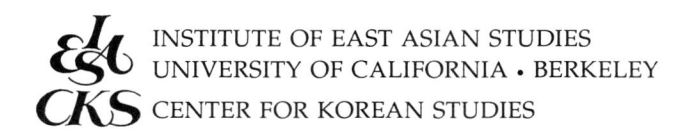

Contemporary Directions
Korean Folk Music Engaging the Twentieth Century and Beyond

EDITED BY
Nathan Hesselink

A publication of the Institute of East Asian Studies, University of California, Berkeley. Although the Institute of East Asian Studies is responsible for the selection and acceptance of manuscripts in this series, responsibility for the opinions expressed and for the accuracy of statements rests with their authors.

Correspondence and manuscripts may be sent to:
Ms. Joanne Sandstrom, Managing Editor
Institute of East Asian Studies
University of California
Berkeley, California 94720-2318
E-mail: easia@uclink.berkeley.edu

The Korea Research Monograph series is one of several publications series sponsored by the Institute of East Asian Studies in conjunction with its constituent units. The others include the China Research Monograph series, the Japan Research Monograph series, and the Research Papers and Policy Studies series. A list of recent publications appears at the back of the book.

Library of Congress Cataloging-in-Publication Data

Contemporary directions : Korean folk music engaging the twentieth century and beyond / edited by Nathan Hesselink.
　　p. cm. — (Korea research monograph ; 27)
　In part translated from Korean.
　Includes bibliographical references and index.
　Contents: The historical development of Korean folk music / Song Bang-song — The traditional opera of the future? : ch'angguk's first century / Andrew P. Killick — On the road with Och'ae chilgut : stages in the development of Korean percussion band music and dance / Nathan Hesselink — Some westernized aspects in Korean folk songs / Sheen Dae-cheol — The development of the construction and performance techniques of the kayagum / Lee Chaesuk — "Recycling" an oral tradition transnationally / Chan E. Park — Korean folk songs for a contemporary world / Keith Howard — The script, sound, and sense of the Seoul Olympics / Margaret Dilling.
　ISBN 1-55729-074-1 (alk.paper)
　　1. Folk music—Korea—20th century—History and criticism. I. Hesselink, Nathan. II. Series.

ML3752.5 .C66 2002
781.62'957—dc21

2002020745

Copyright © 2001 by The Regents of the University of California.
Printed in the United States of America.
All rights reserved.

In memory of Margaret (Marnie) Walker Dilling

Contents

Acknowledgments viii
Introduction 1
1. The Historical Development of Korean Folk Music 5
   Song Bang-Song
2. The Traditional Opera of the Future?
   Ch'anggŭk's First Century 22
   Andrew P. Killick
3. On the Road with "Och'ae Chilgut": Stages in
   the Development of Korean Percussion Band Music
   and Dance 54
   Nathan Hesselink
4. Some Westernized Aspects in Korean Folk Songs 76
   Sheen Dae-Cheol
5. The Development of the Construction and
   Performance Techniques of the *Kayagŭm* 96
   Lee Chaesuk
6. "Recycling" an Oral Tradition Transnationally 121
   Chan E. Park
7. Korean Folk Songs for a Contemporary World 149
   Keith Howard
8. The Script, Sound, and Sense of the Seoul
   Olympic Ceremonies 173
   Margaret Dilling
Index-Glossary 235
Contributors 259

Acknowledgments

This undertaking began as a one-day symposium and concert titled "Korean Folk Music Engages the Modern World" held on the University of California, Berkeley, campus in May of 1999. The event would not have been possible without the generous support of a number of institutions: the U.C. Berkeley Center for Korean Studies, the Korea Foundation, the Intercultural Institute of San Francisco, the Korean Consulate General, the Korean Youth Cultural Center, and the Korean Zither Musicians' Association. Special thanks are extended to Lewis Lancaster, Jonathan Petty, Joanne Sandstrom, Lee Chaesuk, Susie Lim, Sung Ki-Ryun, and Lee Ki-Woo, who all gave unselfishly of their time and energy at various stages along the way. I also wish to acknowledge the hard work and graciousness of the original symposium presenters and performers, as well as the additional authors and translators of the solicited papers that make up this volume. Margaret Dilling's chapter is being published posthumously and was made available to me by John MacAloon.

Introduction

It is perhaps inevitable at the close of a century to stop and ponder not only our place in history but the way in which we define ourselves and meaningful activity taking place around us. This volume is largely an attempt to address and answer the question What is Korean folk music? or, perhaps more important, What is the *nature* of Korean folk music? Definitions of "folk" in the West have been problematic at best. The concept within musicological circles was initially associated with "primitive" or nonindustrial communities (Wallaschek 1970; Lomax 1968), a lack of formal education (Herzog 1936), and traditions that are untouched, stable, communicated almost exclusively by oral means, and without the "benefit" of a notational system (McClean 1983; Anon. 1954). Various components of these older perspectives resurface in the definition of "folk(life)" provided in the 1976 law passed by Congress creating the American Folklife Center: "Generally these expressions are learned orally, by imitation, or in performance, and are maintained or perpetuated without formal instruction or institutional direction" (cited in Bartis 1990:1).

Despite recent activities of the center to return the "folk" to contemporary experiences—as well as criticism leveled by (ethno)musicologists at the more negative connotations of this term (perhaps most eloquently stated in Blacking 1987:2)—there remains the lingering feeling that folk music must somehow be linked to an anonymous past, a feeling evident among large segments of music revival movements (Livingston 1999:75). This issue is further confounded when entering the field of Korean musicology. Traditional music is commonly divided between *kugak*, often translated as "court music" or "classical music," and *sogak/minsogak*, or "folk music." Folk music in the Korean context, however, encompasses local and rural traditions as well as semiprofessional and professional urbanized genres, "music whose sources and materials lay in the lowest social classes, but which was developed to a professional level by career musicians from the same low classes" (Provine 1975:1). Branches of Korean folk music grew under the dual influences of oral and literate transmission (Walraven 1994:121–41; Song Bang-song 1974), and today this music can be found in formalized school and institute settings taught in Korean and Western notation (see Kim Kisu 1983 as an example). An ongoing debate by Korean musicologists over the past three decades includes the additional question of whether or not certain genres of "folk music" shouldn't fall rather under the (equally dubious) category of "art music" (Pak Such'ŏl 1993:20–22; Song Pangsong 1985:318–75; and Chang Sahun and Han Manyŏng 1975:35–38).

The first issue this collection grapples with is the common perception that Korean folk music is purely simple, unrestrained, fast, and emotional, distinctions that seem to reappear in the literature every year (see Han Myung-hee 1998:4–6 as a classic example). What will become immediately apparent in a reading of the various chapters is the depth and range of this music. While energetic and adrenalin-inducing performances are certainly prominent aspects of Korean folk music, particularly so in percussion band music and dance (*nongak/p'ungmul*) and shamanist musical traditions, there are equally contemplative, reserved, and sublime forms of expression often found in genres such as *sanjo* (solo instrumental suites) and, to a lesser extent, *p'ansori* (narrative song). Establishing boundaries for the manner in which someone is allowed to listen to and appreciate this music only results in a grave disservice to all. The second and perhaps more contentious issue that will be faced is the even more pervasive argument that "folk" must be linked to the past. One only needs to reflect historically, however, to discover that the folk music of any particular period in Korea was that era's *contemporary* music. Folk music was marked by constant evolution and adaptation through the borrowing, mixing, and developing of styles, processes existing not only in the past but continuing on down to the present day. It is really a story of engagement—engagement with society in all of its various guises. This volume examines this special relationship largely in the context of the twentieth century.

Underlying the various approaches and subject matter of the chapters that follow are common themes that bind this work together into a coherent whole. All the authors make connections with, or draw parallels to, folk traditions (though many Koreans and others would not readily identify all of these genres as "folk"); all deal with creativity, change, and the place of professionalism; and a large number of the authors examine the role and aftereffects of preservation and the cultural asset system. Subthemes include historical concerns, particularly with the struggle to define "tradition" (chapters by Song, Killick, Lee, Park, Howard, and Dilling), colonialism under Japanese rule (Song, Killick, and Sheen), the social context of the performance, including influences from the West (Song, Hesselink, Sheen, Lee, Park, and Howard), the place of mass media and recordings (Hesselink, Sheen, Howard, and Dilling), the development of musical fusions (Hesselink, Howard, and Dilling), and the idea of cultural identity, intimately linked to nationalism (Sheen and Dilling). A certain tension between folk and more "elite" forms of performance art in Korea is also felt throughout the various contributions.

What is (the nature of) Korean folk music? In the absence of new terminology, we will for the purposes of this volume expand on existing concepts and vocabulary. Korean folk music will be defined more by its essence—a process in motion—than by title or genre. It will not be bound by instrumentation, method of transmission, an established canon, a particular socioeconomic class, level of education, or even manner in which it is perceived. Korean folk music will, however, be understood as musical activity that hails from a collective folk past, yet strives for or is open to change, embracing the here and now.

References

Anonymous. 1954. "Proceedings of the Seventh Conference of the International Folk Music Council, Sao Paulo, 16–22 August." *Journal of the International Folk Music Council* 7:6–46.

Bartis, Peter. 1990 [1979]. *Folklife and Fieldwork: A Layman's Introduction to Field Techniques.* Washington, D.C.: Library of Congress.

Blacking, John. 1987. *"A Commonsense View of All Music": Reflections on Percy Grainger's Contribution to Ethnomusicology and Music Education.* Cambridge: Cambridge University Press.

Chang Sahun and Han Manyŏng. 1975. *Kugak kaeron* [An introduction to traditional music]. Seoul: Han'guk kugak hakhoe.

Han Myung-hee [Han Myŏnghŭi]. 1998. "Korean Music: Harmony with Nature." *Koreana* 12.4:4–9.

Herzog, George. 1936. *Research in Primitive and Folk Music in the*

United States. Washington, D.C.: American Council of Learned Societies.

Kim Kisu. 1983. *Tanso kyobon* [A manual for the *tanso*]. Seoul: Segwang ŭmak ch'ulp'ansa.

Livingston, Tamara E. 1999. "Music Revivals: Towards a General Theory." *Ethnomusicology* 43.1:66–85.

Lomax, Alan. 1968. *Folk Song Style and Culture*. Washington, D.C.: American Association for the Advancement of Science.

McLean, Mervyn. 1983. "Preserving World Musics: Perspectives from New Zealand and Oceania." *Studies in Music* 17:23–37.

Pak Such'ŏl. 1993. *O.K. kugak* [O.K. traditional music]. Seoul: Chagŭn uri.

Provine, Robert C. 1975. *Chŏnbuk nongak changgo changdan* (Drum rhythms in Korean farmers' music). Seoul: Shinjin munhwasa.

Song, Bang-song [Song Pangsong]. 1974. "Korean Kwangdae Musicians and Their Musical Traditions." *Korea Journal* 14.9:12–18.

Song Pangsong. 1985. "Chosŏn hugi ŭi ŭmak" [Music of the latter Chosŏn dynasty]. In *Han'guk ŭmaksa* [A history of Korean music], ed. Yi Haerang. Seoul: Taehan min'guk yesulwŏn.

Wallaschek, Richard. 1970. *Primitive Music: An Inquiry into the Origin and Development of Music, Songs, Instruments, Dances and Pantomimes of Savage Races*. New York: Da Capo Press. Reprint of first edition published in London, 1893.

Walraven, Boudewijn. 1994. *Songs of the Shaman: The Ritual Chants of the Korean Mudang*. London and New York: Kegan Paul International.

ONE

The Historical Development of Korean Folk Music

SONG BANG-SONG

Korean traditional music today is conveniently categorized into two branches: music that was performed in the court and music that was performed for commoners outside of the court during the Chosŏn period (1392–1910). The former is commonly called court music (*kungjung ŭmak*), the latter, folk music (*minsok ŭmak* or *minsogak*). This chapter is a survey of the development of folk music from a historical perspective.

A New Phase of Folk Music after the Seventeenth Century

Music of the Chosŏn period from the seventeenth century onward changed drastically as a result of invasions by the Japanese (1592) and the Manchus (1636). These two wars caused changes in every aspect of the local politics, economy, society, and culture. Naturally, music could not escape such influences. As a result, these two wars became a dividing point of the five hundred years of the Chosŏn period into early and late Chosŏn. Music from roughly the seventeenth century to the nineteenth century is therefore described as part of the late Chosŏn period (1592–1910).

The prominent rise of folk music is the distinctive aspect of music history of the late Chosŏn period. After the seventeenth century, there are two noticeable changes in folk music: the development of vocal music and the development of instrumental music. These developments were accomplished by the performance activities of salons for music ensembles (*p'ungnyubang*) and folk entertainers (*minsok yenŭngin*). *Kagok* (long lyric song) and

Translated by Serra Miyeun Hwang.

similar such vocal music, as well as the orchestral ensemble suite *Yŏngsan hoesang* and other related instrumental music are the representative music of such salons. *P'ansori* (folk dramatic song), *minyo* (folk song), and other such vocal music, along with *sanjo* (solo instrumental suite) and similar instrumental music, belong to the musical culture of folk entertainers.

The music salon tradition was developed by a nascent middle class composed of music lovers called *kagaek* (*kagok* singers) and *yulgaek* (instrumentalists). *Kagaek* sang and *yulgaek* accompanied them on the *kŏmun'go* (6-stringed plucked zither); together they are called *p'ungnyugaek* (music salon participants). These music lovers of the late Chosŏn period did not hold high government official posts but were cultured intellectuals who held technical professions, such as physicians or translators and interpreters. These middle-class intellectuals were wealthy enough to enjoy such activities of the music salon; they contributed a great deal to the music history of the period by leaving various scores for *kŏmun'go, kagok,* and the ensemble suite *Yŏngsan hoesang.*

In contrast, folk entertainers such as the *kwangdae* (professional folk entertainers) belonged to the lowest segment of society. They could not settle in one place, but rather had to tour from one village to the next. Unlike the middle-class *p'ungnyugaek*, professional folk entertainers were not educated. Therefore, their musical traditions, including performance techniques, had to be transmitted orally—"imparted by lips, taken in by heart" (*kujŏn shimsu*). As a result, the history of *p'ansori* and related vocal music is based on fragmented documents composed by intellectual audiences of the *p'ansori* performance.

New Developments in Vocal Music of the Late Chosŏn Period

There are three varieties of vocal music of the late Chosŏn period: (1) the music of the salon—*kagok* (long lyric song), *kasa* (narrative song), and *shijo* (short lyric song); (2) *p'ansori* (folk dramatic song) of the *kwangdae;* and (3) *minyo* (folk song) and *chapka* (literally, "miscellaneous song") of the common folk. *Kagok, kasa,* and *shijo* are closely related to poetry in Korean literature, and today these three are commonly called *chŏngga* (literally, "proper song").

In addition to the oral tradition, *p'ansori* performed by *kwangdae* was transmitted by documents recorded by a new class of educated aristocrat *kwangdae* (*yangban kwangdae*) in the nineteenth century. Shin Chaehyo (1812–84), the best-known aristocrat *kwangdae*, left texts for six *p'ansori* repertories (*madang*) out of a total repertoire of twelve. Poor documentation makes it difficult, however, to trace the historical development of orally transmitted *minyo* (folk song) of the common folk and *chapka* of professional singers.

The Historical Development of Kagok, Kasa, *and* Shijo

The history of *kagok*, a song form composed of five sections, developed in close relationship to earlier vocal pieces by the names of "Mandaeyŏp," "Chungdaeyŏp," and "Saktaeyŏp" of the Chosŏn period. "Mandaeyŏp," one of *kagok*'s forerunners, is contained in the oldest extant manuscript, the *Kŭm hapchabo* (*Kŏmun'go* tablature) of 1572, while "Mandaeyŏp" and "Chungdaeyŏp" were discovered in the *Yanggŭm shinbo* (Yang's new *kŏmun'go* handbook) of 1610, the *Hyŏn'gŭm tongmun yugi* (Classified records on the *kŏmun'go* in Korean literature) of 1620, and the *Kŭmbo shinjŭng karyŏng* (Newly revised *kŏmun'go* handbook) of 1680. The music of "Chungdaeyŏp" and "Saktaeyŏp" is recorded in older manuscripts such as the *Kŭmbo shinjŭng karyŏng*, the *Paegunam kŭmbo* (Paegunam's *kŏmun'go* manuscript), the *Han'gŭm shinbo* (Han's new *kŏmun'go* manuscript) of 1724, the *Yŏndae sojang kŭmbo* (*Kŏmun'go* manuscript preserved at Yonsei University Library), and the *Shinjak kŭmbo* (Newly compiled manuscript for the *kŏmun'go*). The above are all presumed to be from the late seventeenth century to the early eighteenth century.

According to the treatise *Sŏngho sasŏl* (Essay collection by Sŏngho) by the "practical learning" (*shirhak*) scholar Yi Ik (1681–1763), "Mandaeyŏp" was not sung during the reign of King Yŏngjo (1724–76) because of its extreme slow tempo. Few people liked "Chungdaeyŏp," which was only slightly faster than "Mandaeyŏp"; "Saktaeyŏp" was the most popular. In other words, "Mandaeyŏp" of early Chosŏn disappeared in the early eighteenth century, and "Chungdaeyŏp" was popular in the seventeenth century but declined in popularity by the eighteenth century. From the eighteenth century onward, "Saktaeyŏp" was the favorite among music salon participants (*p'ungnyugaek*), and it was this "Saktaeyŏp" that is the origin of existing *kagok* today.

The appearance of three variations of "Saktaeyŏp" in the late seventeenth century has been confirmed in the *Kŭmbo shinjŭng karyŏng*. These new variations of *kagok*, known as "Ch'osudaeyŏp," "Isudaeyŏp," and "Samsudaeyŏp," are the most representative of the eighteenth century. Because these variations were so favored by the singers (*kagaek*) and instrumentalists (*yulgaek*) of the music salon, collections of *kagok* texts appeared as song books in the eighteenth century. During the reign of King Yŏngjo (1724–76), singer Kim Ch'ŏnt'aek's *Ch'ŏnggu yŏngŏn* (Eternal songs of Korea; 1728) and Kim Sujang's *Haedong kayo* (Songs of the eastern sea) were the best-known song text collections of this type.

According to the preface of the *Ch'ŏnggu yŏngŏn*, Kim Ch'ŏnt'aek was the best-known singer and Kim Sŏnggi the best-known *kŏmun'go* accompanist of the music salon of the early eighteenth century. Kim Ch'ŏnt'aek was not only a famous singer but also a poet who composed fifty-seven new *shijo;* Kim Sŏnggi composed eight *shijo*. All of their poems can be found in the *Ch'ŏnggu yŏngŏn*. These men contributed greatly to the development of *kagok* by performing and writing with others in the most famous music salon of them all, the Kyŏngjŏngsan kadan (Music salon of respected arbor mountain).

At the end of the eighteenth century, according to the *Yuyeji* (Section on amusing arts) edited by Sŏ Yugu (1764–1845), many variations of *kagok* had been introduced. "Nongyŏp," "Urak," "Kyerak," and "P'yŏnsudaeyŏp" are representative variations of the *nong, nak,* and *p'yŏn* types of *kagok*. New variations in particular such as "P'yŏnsudaeyŏp," "P'yŏllak," or similar such *kagok* were based on *sasŏl shijo* (narrative *shijo*), not *chŏnghyŏng shijo* (standard *shijo*), and because of this the music underwent a change from a 16-beat *kagok* rhythmic cycle (*changdan*) to a 10-beat rhythmic cycle.

Kagok of the nineteenth century was transmitted in old manuscripts such as the *Samjuk kŭmbo* (Samjuk's *kŏmun'go* manuscript), Yun Yonggu's (1853–1939) *Hyŏn'gŭm oŭm t'ongnon* (Introduction to the *kŏmun'go*'s five tones), and the *Hakp'o kŭmbo* (Hakp'o's *kŏmun'go* manuscript). Many *shijo* that were sung to *kagok* variations in the music salon of the nineteenth century can be found in singers An Minyŏng and Pak Hyogwan's songbook *Kagok wŏllyu* (Fundamental styles of *kagok;* 1876). A new *kagok* repertoire also came into being in the nineteenth century—pieces such as "Soyongi," "Ŏllak," and "Panyŏp" were new variations of "Isudaeyŏp," and variations such as "Ŏllong," "Ŏnp'yŏn," and "Hwan'gyerak" were new variations of the *nong, nak,* and *p'yon* styles.

The history of *kasa*, a song form that is a branch of *chŏngga* (proper song) together with *kagok*, is not clear, but it is assumed to have surfaced around the eighteenth century or late Chosŏn period. *Akchang kasa* (Song texts of *akchang*), *Kogŭm kagok* (Past and present *kagok*), *Ch'ŏnggu yŏngŏn* (1728), and *Namhun t'aep'yŏngga* (Namhun's peaceful song) are writings conveying the texts of *kasa*. Among the existing twelve *kasa*, the texts of "Chukchisa," "Ch'unmyŏn'gok," "Yangyangga," and "Ŏbuga" are found in the *Ch'ŏnggu yŏngŏn*. The history of sung *kasa* is, therefore, assumed to have existed at the latest since the early eighteenth century.

The *Samjuk kŭmbo* is the oldest *kŏmun'go* score conveying the music of *kasa*, and it is assumed to be a product of the early nineteenth century. This old manuscript contains the *kŏmun'go* parts to the pieces "Sangsa pyŏlgok," "Ch'unmyŏn'gok," "Kil kunak," "Maehwagok," "Hwanggyegok," and "Kwŏnjuga." It has been confirmed in this source that *kasa* were accompanied by the *kŏmun'go* as with *kagok* in the nineteenth century, though today they are accompanied only by the *changgo* (hourglass drum). Among the existing twelve *kasa* repertories, "Paekkusa," "Chukchisa," "Suyangsan'ga," "Yangyangga," and "Ch'ŏsaga" are estimated to have been sung beginning in the late nineteenth century since they are not found in the *kasa* repertoire of the middle nineteenth century. The tradition of *kasa* of the late Chosŏn period was carried through to the present era by the master singer of *kagok* Ha Kyuil (1867–1937) and the master singer of *kasa* Im Kijun (1868–1940).

The history of the three-section form of song known as *shijo* is estimated to have first appeared during the reign of King Yŏngjo (1724–76), an assumption based on Shin Kwangsu's *Sŏkpukchip* (Literary collection by Sŏkpuk). This work recorded that the singer Yi Sech'un, who appears in the *Kwansŏ akpu* (Music section of the western province), added rhythmic cycles (*changdan*) to *shijo* for the first time. The oldest manuscripts of *shijo* are Sŏ Yugu's *Yuyeji* and Yi Kyugyŏng's (1788–?) *Kura ch'ŏlsa kŭmjabo* (Manuscript for the Western dulcimer). *Shijo* from these two manuscripts are proven to be the origin of existing *Kyŏngje p'yŏng shijo* (Seoul-style ordinary *shijo*). It would not, therefore, be wrong to say that *p'yŏng shijo* was sung to a three-section form from the late eighteenth century or early nineteenth century.

From this point on, *p'yŏng shijo* was enjoyed by singers in music salons as it developed different variations: *chirŭm* (high pitch) *shijo* and *sasŏl* (narrative) *shijo* are examples of these variations. The first section of *chirŭm shijo* is sung in a loud and high voice as the *tugŏ* (male singer) does in *kagok* repertories. The text of *sasŏl shijo* is sung in three sections, similar to the pieces "P'yŏnsudaeyŏp," "Ŏnp'yŏn," or "P'yŏllak" of *kagok*.

As *Kyŏngje shijo* became popular in the capital, Hanyang (present-day Seoul), singers from various provinces produced *shijo* with their own regional flavor, called *hyangje* (country-style) *shijo*. The representative *hyangje shijo* of the different provinces include *Yŏngje shijo* of Kyŏngsang province, *Wanje shijo* of Chŏlla province, and *Naep'oje shijo* of Ch'ungch'ŏng province. *Kyŏngje shijo* and the various regional *hyangje shijo* that have been performed by singers with *changgo* accompaniment in music salons (*p'ungnyubang*) of the capital as well as other provinces continue on to the present day in these same settings.

The Historical Development of P'ansori

P'ansori was developed as a vocal genre by professional folk entertainers known as *kwangdae* in the late Chosŏn period. In contrast to *kagok, kasa,* and *shijo, p'ansori* texts are based on more worldly stories. But to understand the history of *p'ansori*, it is first necessary to introduce the history of the *kwangdae*.

It was confirmed in the *Koryŏsa* (History of the Koryŏ dynasty) that the word *kwangdae* was originally used for a mask or mask drama during the Koryŏ period (918–1392). In the early Chosŏn period (1392–1592), however, the word *kwangdae* was used for a person who acted with a mask, or to designate an actor (*kwoeroe*). In the later Chosŏn period (1592–1910), the word *kwangdae* was used for folk drama groups made up of talented performers. This drama was composed of mask dances, acting, acrobatics, dance, and music. Such entertainment groups were executively managed through government offices such as the Kwangdaech'ŏng (Office of *Kwangdae*) and the Chaeinch'ŏng (Office of Entertainers). According to Shin Chaehyo's *Kwangdaega* (Song of the *kwangdae*), the word *kwangdae* began to mean a professional *p'ansori* singer at the beginning of the nineteenth century. Folk entertainers or the *kwangdae* of *p'ansori* both belonged to the lowest segment of Chosŏn society. They existed as homeless, itinerant troupes traveling throughout the various provinces.

The first literature on *p'ansori* is Yu Chinhan's (1711–91) *Manhwajip* (Essay collection by Manhwa), which transmits the "Song of Ch'unhyang" ("Ch'unhyangga") in two hundred sentences of Chinese characters. *Manhwajip* is, therefore, written evidence proving that the "Song of Ch'unhyang" was sung by *kwangdae* before the eighteenth century. Following the *Manhwajip*, Song Manje's poem *Kwanuhŭi* (Viewing an actor's performance), also in Chinese characters, confirms that all twelve *p'ansori* repertories had already been performed by *kwangdae* in the early nineteenth century. At that time, the twelve repertories were "Ch'unhyangga" (Song of Ch'unhyang), "Shimch'ŏngga" (Song of Shim Ch'ŏng), "Pak t'aryŏng/Hŭngbuga" (Song of the gourd/Song of Hŭngbu), "T'okki t'aryŏng/Sugungga" (Song of the rabbit/Song of the underwater palace), "Hwaryongdo/Chŏkpyŏkka" (Song of the Hua-yung road/Song of the red cliff), "Paebijangjŏn" (Tale of Paebijang), "Onggojipchŏn" (Tale of a stubborn person), "Pyŏn'gangsoe t'aryŏng" (Song of Pyŏn Kangsoe), "Changkki t'aryŏng" (Song of the cock-pheasant), "Musugi t'aryŏng" (Song of Musugi), "Katcha shinsŏn t'aryŏng" (Song of the false hermit), and "Kangnŭng maehwajŏn" (Tale of the Kangnŭng plum).

From among these twelve repertories, Shin Chaehyo recorded six: "Ch'unhyangga," "Shimch'ŏngga," "Sugungga," "Hŭngbuga," "Chŏkpyŏkka," and "Pyŏn'gangsoega." Only "Pyŏn'gangsoega" has not survived to the present day; the remaining pieces have been passed down through Yi Sŏnyu's *Oga chŏnjip* (Complete collection of five *p'ansori* songs; 1933).

The surviving pieces emphasize different aspects of Confucianism. For example, filial duty to one's parents is emphasized in "Shimch'ŏngga," chastity of husband and wife in "Ch'unhyangga," loyalty to the king in "Sugungga," sense of duty in friendship in "Chŏkpyŏkka," and love between siblings in "Hŭngbuga." This is the reason these five pieces have survived until today.

In the beginning stages of *p'ansori's* history, U Ch'undae, Ha Handam, and Ch'oe Sŏndal were the famous *kwangdae*; among them, U Ch'undae was mentioned in Song Manjae's *Kwanuhŭi*. Kwŏn Samdŭk, Mo Hŭnggap, and Song Hŭngnok—all of whom are mentioned in Shin Chaehyo's *Kwangdaega*—were the next generation of famous *p'ansori* singers in the early nineteenth century. In addition, Shin Manyŏp, Hwang Haech'ŏng, Ko Sugwan, Kim Kyech'ŏl, Song Kwangnok, and Chu Tŏkki were also famous singers in the early nineteenth century. These singers were often compared to famous Chinese poets—for example, Song Hŭngnok to Li Po (701–62), Mo Hŭnggap to Tu Fu (712–70), Kwŏn Sain to Han Yü (786–824), Shin Manyŏp to Tu Mu (803–52), Hwang Haech'ŏng to Meng Chiao (751–814), Ko Sugwan to Po Chu-i

(772-831), Kim Kyech'ŏl to Ou-yang Hsiu (1007-72), and Song Kwangnok to Wang Wei (669-739).

These great *p'ansori* singers left distinctive melodies representative of a characteristic singing quality or technique (*tŏnŭm*) to their followers. Kwŏn Samdŭk's *tŏnŭm* known as *sŏllŏngje*, which creates an energetic and vigorous feeling, was passed down in the "Chebiga" (Swallow song) of "Hŭngbuga." Mo Hŭnggap, who sang on Nŭngna Island in the midst of the Taedong River at the invitation of the governor of the city of P'yŏngyang, left his *tŏnŭm* in the "Ibyŏlga" (Farewell song) of "Ch'unhyangga." Yŏm Kyedal, who was famous for a cheerful feeling known as *kyŏngdŭrŭm*, left his *tŏnŭm* in the "Shipchangga" (Song of whipping by ten sticks) of "Ch'unhyangga." Ko Sugwan's *tŏnŭm* is found in the "Sarangga" (Love song) of "Ch'unhyangga," while Kim Kyedal's *tŏnŭm* is found in Shim Ch'ong's birth scene in "Shimch'ŏngga." The master singer of *p'ansori*, Song Hŭngnok, not only created the *chinyang* rhythmic cycle (*changdan*) but also a newly improved *u* mode (*ujo*) and *kyemyŏn* mode (*kyemyŏnjo*); he is also famous for creating a sorrowful sound similar to the effect of a ghost crying. All of these singers who appear in the *Kwangdaega* were active in the early and mid nineteenth century.

Although most of the famous *p'ansori* singers were from Chŏlla province, there were some famous singers from Kyŏnggi and Ch'ungch'ŏng provinces as well. These singers created characteristic musical traits of their own provinces—*tongp'yŏnje* (eastern style), *sŏp'yŏnje* (western style), and *chunggoje* (upper-central style) are the primary divisions of *p'ansori*. The character of *tongp'yŏnje* melody (*karak*) is energetic and grand, and it mainly uses the *u* mode. Most *tongp'yŏnje* singers are from the cities of Kurye, Unbong, and Sunch'ang, which are to the east of the Sŏmjin River in Chŏlla province; Song Hŭngnok is considered the best *tongp'yŏnje* singer. Singers from the cities of Kwangju, Naju, and Posŏng, to the west of the Sŏmjin River, developed *sŏp'yŏnje*. *Sŏp'yŏnje* frequently uses the *kyemyŏn* mode, and its character is melancholy, elaborate, and flavorful; *sŏp'yŏnje* is also called *kangsanje*. Pak Yujŏn is considered the best *sŏp'yŏnje* singer. Most *chunggoje* singers are from Ch'ungch'ŏng and Kyŏnggi provinces; Yŏm Kyedal is considered the best *chunggoje* singer. The singing style of this area is as emotionless as the recitation of a telephone book.

Because of the rise of singers from the fallen aristocrat and intelligent middle classes, a new horizon of history opened up for *p'ansori* in the second half of the nineteenth century. Local aristocrat Kwŏn Samdŭk was the most famous *yangban kwangdae*. Chŏng Ch'unp'ung was a *yangban kwangdae* who passed the primary state civil service examination. Shin Chaehyo, who was keen on *p'ansori* theory, also belonged to this class of *kwangdae*. These men not only wrote their notes in Chinese characters for the *p'ansori* text, but were responsible for transmitting the five *p'ansori* repertories that laid emphasis on the Confucian doctrine of *samgang oryun* (three bonds and five relations) to the following generations.

During the reign of King Kojong (1864–1907), there were famous *p'ansori* singers such as Pak Mansun, Song Uryong, Kim Sejong, Chŏng Ch'unp'ung, Chang Chabaek, Yi Nalch'i, Chŏng Ch'angŏp, Kim Chonggŭn, and Han Songhak. Among these men, Pak Mansun, Song Uryong, Kim Sejong, and Chang Chabaek were *tongp'yŏnje* singers; Yi Nalch'i and Chŏng Ch'angŏp were *sŏp'yŏnje* singers; and Kim Chonggŭn and Han Songhak were *chunggoje* singers.

Song Kwangnok's son Song Uryong was famous for "T'okki t'aryŏng" (Rabbit song). Song Hŭngnok's pupil Pak Mansun was loved by King Kojong's father because of his outstanding "Ch'unhyangga." His *tŏnŭm* is conveyed in the "Mongyuga" (Dreaming song) of "Ch'unhyangga." Shin Chaehyo's trainee Kim Sejong was especially knowledgeable in the theory and performance practice of *p'ansori*. His *tŏnŭm* is conveyed in the "Ch'ŏnja twip'uri" (Finishing song of a thousand Chinese characters) of "Ch'unhyangga." Yi Nalch'i studied with Pak Yujŏn, who was the originator of *sŏp'yŏnje*. Yi Nalch'i sang "Sae t'aryŏng" (Bird song) uniquely well, and his *tŏnŭm* is passed down in the "Chat'an'ga" (Grieving song) of "Ch'unhyangga." The *yangban kwangdae* Chŏng Ch'unp'ung, who was very good at singing "Chŏkpyŏkka," imparted his *tŏnŭm* to the short song (*tan'ga*) "Sosang p'algyŏng" (Eight landscapes of the Hsio-hsian region). Chŏng Ch'angŏp's *tŏnŭm* is found in the part of the scene in "Shimch'ŏngga" where the head monk of the Mongŭn temple comes down. Kim Sejong's disciple Chang Chabaek sang "Ch'unhyangga" well, and his *tŏnŭm* is found in "Chŏkpyŏkka."

According to the proverb *Il kosu i myŏngch'ang* (first the drummer, second the singer), the *kosu* is as important as the singer in a *p'ansori* performance. In the nineteenth century, several famous *p'ansori* singers started out as drummers; Song Hŭngnok's younger brother Song Kwangnok and Chu Tŏkki were the most famous of these. Their tradition of *kosu* techniques was transmitted by Han Sŏngjun in the twentieth century.

P'ansori's musical aspects can be summed up as the melody of the singer and the rhythm of the drum accompaniment. The character of the vocal line depends on the use of the *u, p'yŏng, kyemyŏn, kyŏngdŭrŭm,* and *sŏllŏngje* modes (*cho*). In the case of rhythmic cycles (*changdan*), there are *chinyang, chungmori, chungjungmori, chajinmori, hwimori, ŏnmori,* and *ŏtchungmori*.

The melodies of the *u* and *p'yŏng* modes that originated from *kasa* or *shijo* bring out a grand and peaceful atmosphere. The melody of the *u* mode is used in the "Kin sarangga" (Long love song) of "Ch'unhyangga," while the melody of the *p'yŏng* mode is used in the "Ch'ŏnja p'uri" (Song of the thousand Chinese characters) of "Ch'unhyangga." *Kyemyŏn* mode brings out a melancholy and compassionate atmosphere and is found in Hŭngbu's wife's "Kanan t'aryŏng" (Poor song) of "Hŭngbuga." *Kyŏngdŭrŭm* originated in Kyŏnggi province folk song (*minyo*); its musical traits are light and cheerful. The most representative melody of *kyŏngdŭrŭm* can be found in the episode where Yi Toryŏng comforts Ch'unhyang in "Ch'unhyangga." *Sŏllŏngje,* created by the famous *p'ansori* singer Kwŏn Samdŭk, is energetic and vigorous. The most representative musical example of *sŏllŏngje* can be found in the episode where Nolbu is going to catch the swallow in "Hŭngbuga."

The slowest *p'ansori* rhythmic cycle (*changdan*) is the 24-beat *chinyang,* which is composed of four groups of six beats. The *chinyang* rhythmic cycle is used for peaceful and lyrical passages, as in the "Chŏksŏngga" (Song of the red wall) of "Ch'unhyangga." *Chungmori,* a 12-beat (12/4) cycle, is employed for either the reciting of a serene situation or a lyrical melody. *Chungjungmori,* which is slightly faster than *chungmori,* is a 12/8 cycle used for joyous dancing parts. The fast 12/8 *chajinmori* is used in dramatic scenes, such as the entrance of the royal inspector in "Ch'unhyangga." These *p'ansori* musical traits have been embellished throughout the past two centuries by famous singers.

Tan'ga, Chapka, *and* Minyo

Tan'ga is a short song that *p'ansori* singers sing before they start the main portion of the performance. It is generally accompanied by *chungmori* or *chungjungmori* rhythmic cycles. The first literary record of *tan'ga* is found in Shin Chaehyo's *Kwangdaega* (Song of the *kwangdae*); here he introduced thirteen pieces of *tan'ga* in all.

After Shin Chaehyo's *tan'ga* a variety of *tan'ga* were performed by famous *p'ansori* singers. The most representative repertoire of *tan'ga* includes such pieces as "Man'go kangsan," "P'yŏnshich'un," "Chin'guk myŏngsan," "Changbuhan," "Chukchang manghye," and "Sosang p'algyŏng."

In the late Chosŏn period, folk entertainment troupes known as *sadangp'ae* traveled from village to village singing and dancing. *Sŏnsori* or *ipch'ang* (literally, "standing song") was a type of vocal music the *sadangp'ae* developed. Because this music's main repertoire consisted of the song "San t'aryŏng" (Mountain song), the name of the group who sang *sŏnsori* became *san t'aryŏng p'ae* (a *san t'aryong* troupe). At the end of the nineteenth century, the fathers of *Kyŏnggi ipch'ang* were Ŭi T'aegi and Shin Nakt'aek. The *Kyŏnggi ipch'ang* tradition was imparted by singers such as Yi T'aemun, Ha Sunil, and So Wanjun in the twentieth century. *Sŏdo ipch'ang* was introduced to Seoul by *naltangp'ae* (a folk entertainment group) of P'yŏngyang in 1908, and it was transmitted by Mun Yŏngsu and Yi Chŏnghwa at the Wŏn'gaksa Theater.

At the end of the Chosŏn period, a new branch of vocal music called *chapka* was created by professional singers. These singers were commoners who lived outside of Seoul's South Gate (Namdaemun: present-day Yŏngsan-gu, Ch'ŏngp'a-dong area); their *chapka* was later known as *Kyŏnggi chapka*. At the end of the nineteenth century, Ch'u Kyoshin, Cho Kijun, and Pak Ch'un'gyŏng were the best *Kyŏnggi chapka* singers; during the Japanese occupation (1910–45) famous singers included Pak Ch'unjae (1877–1948), a pupil of Pak Ch'un'gyŏng, and Ch'oe Kyŏngshik (1874–1949) and Chang Kyech'un (1868–1946), pupils of Cho Kijun. Their *chapka* tradition was imparted by such singers as Yu Kaedong, Chŏng Tŭkman, Kim Sunt'ae, Yi Chinbong, Muk Kyewŏl, and Kim Okshim.

At the end of the nineteenth century, *Sŏdo chapka* was introduced by Hŏ Tŭksŏn and Kim Kwanjun, and it was transmitted to Kim Oksŏn through Kim Ch'ilsŏng. *Namdo chapka* was introduced by Shin Pangch'o at the end of the reign of King Kojong. It was transmitted by Chang P'an'gae and Kim Chŏngmun during the colonial period; its main repertoire consisted of "Hwach'o sagŏri," "Poryŏm," "Sŏngju p'uri," and "San t'aryŏng."

In the 1920s, Pak Ch'unjae, Mun Yŏngsu, and Yi Chŏnghwa were famous *Kyŏnggi chapka* and *Sŏdo chapka* singers. In the 1930s, Yi Chinbong, Kim Ogyŏp, Kim T'aeun, and Ku Taegam were famous *chapka* singers. During the colonial period, Yi Kŭmok, Yi

Yŏngsanhong, and Kim Ogyŏp were famous *Sŏdo ipch'ang* singers; and Kang Namjung, Kim Ch'uwŏl, Shin Kŭmhong, Yi Hwajungsŏn, and Pak Nokchu were famous *Namdo chapka* singers.

There is no doubt that *minyo* (folk song) was one of the most representative vocal musics "imparted by lips, taken in by heart" by the commoners outside of the court during the Chosŏn period. However, there are no literary records that can trace the history of *minyo*. According to the early-twentieth-century literature, traditional *minyo* can be divided into two categories: the first is sung by commoners in their daily life and is called *t'osok minyo;* the second is sung by professional *minyo* singers for the theater or various media and is called *t'ongsok minyo*.

The most representative *t'osok minyo* are "Moshimnŭn sori" (Sowing song), "Kimmaegi sori" (Weeding song), and "Pyŏbegi sori" (Harvesting song), which are all farming songs (*nongyo*); "Paennorae" (Boat song) and "Nojŏnnŭn sori" (Rowing song), which are fishing songs (*ŏyo*); "Sangyŏ sori" (Bier song) and "Talgujil sori" (Pounding song), which are funeral songs; and "Pet'ŭlga" (Loom song) and "Mulle sori" (Spinning song), which are women's songs. This repertoire of *t'osok minyo* is believed to have a long history; therefore *minyo* from the late Chosŏn period should be considered a continuation of this older tradition.

The Historical Development of Instrumental Music in the Late Chosŏn Period

Instrumental music of the late Chosŏn period can be divided into three branches: instrumental ensembles developed by *kŏmun'go* players in music salons, solo instrumental music developed by professional touring entertainers, and communal instrumental ensembles passed down by farmers. *Yŏngsan hoesang* is the representative piece of the first type, while *sanjo* (literally, "scattered melodies") is the representative solo instrumental piece of the second type. And *nongak* (farmers' music) is what farmers have been engaged in for generations throughout its long history.

The Historical Development of Yŏngsan hoesang

Yŏngsan hoesang (an orchestral ensemble suite) is composed of nine movements in the form of a suite. It is divided into three types depending on the instrumentation or the musical mode employed. The first type is called *Hyŏnak* (string ensemble music) *yŏngsan hoesang* and is centered on the string instrument the *kŏmun'go.* Another name for this type of *Yŏngsan hoesang* is *Chunggwangjigok* or *Chulp'ungnyu.* The second type is for wind ensemble and is called *Kwanak* (wind ensemble music) *yŏngsan hoesang;* it is also called *P'yojŏngmanbangjigok* or *Taep'ungnyu.* The third type transposes *Hyŏnak yŏngsan hoesang* down a fourth to a new pitch center and is called *P'yŏngjo hoesang*—its poetic name is *Yuch'oshinjigok.* The broad meaning of *Yŏngsan hoesang* includes all three types of ensembles, but in a narrower sense the title indicates only the string version (*Hyŏnak yŏngsan hoesang*). The existing string version is a suite composed of nine movements: "Sangnyŏngsan," "Chungnyŏngsan," "Seryŏngsan," "Karak tŏri," "Samhyŏn hwanip," "Hahyŏn hwanip," "Yŏmbul," "T'aryŏng," and "Kunak." It was not until after the seventeenth century that these movements were formed into suites.

Among these three types of *Yŏngsan hoesang, Hyŏnak yŏngsan hoesang* has the longest history; it was developed by music salon participants (*p'ungnyugaek*) who came from the middle classes. *Kwanak yŏngsan hoesang,* however, has been transmitted mainly as musical accompaniment to court dance. *P'yŏngjo hoesang* took form the latest; therefore the history of *Yŏngsan hoesang* is discussed with a focus on the string version.

In the early Chosŏn period before the Japanese and Manchu invasions, *Yŏngsan hoesang* was a vocal piece accompanied by a string and wind ensemble; it had the text *Yŏngsan hoesang pulbosal* (Buddha and bodhisattvas meet at Spirit Vulture Peak). After the wars, the text was removed and the work became a purely instrumental piece. At that time, the oldest score that conveyed the music of *Yŏngsan hoesang* was the *Kŭmbo shinjŭng karyŏng* (Newly revised *kŏmun'go* handbook; 1680). The music in this old manuscript corresponds to the existing music of "Sangnyŏngsan." Variations of *Yŏngsan hoesang,* however, began to appear in the eighteenth century.

The first variation, called *Yŏngsan hoesang kapt'an,* was recorded in the *Ŏŭnbo* (Ŏŭn's manuscript; 1719); today it exists as "Chungnyŏngsan." Other variations appeared in the *Han'gŭm shinbo* (Han's new *kŏmun'go* manuscript; 1724) including *Yŏngsan hoesang hwanip* and *Yŏngsan hoesang cheji.* It has been confirmed in Sŏ Yugu's *Yuyeji* that more new variations of *Yŏngsan hoesang* were produced in the late eighteenth century.

Pieces related to *Yŏngsan hoesang* that appear in the *Yuyeji* are as follows: "Yŏngsan hoesang" is the origin of the existing "Sangnyŏngsan," "Seryŏngsan" exists as "Chungnyŏngsan,"

"Yŏngsan hoesang ich'ŭng cheji" exists as "Seryŏngsan," "Yŏngsan hoesang samch'ŭng cheji" exists as "Karak tŏri," "Samhyŏn hoeip" exists as "Samhyŏn hwanip," "Samhyŏn hoeip ijang tu" and "Sajang tu" exist as "Hahyŏn hwanip," and "Yŏmbul t'aryŏng" and "Yukcha yŏmbul" exist as "Yŏmbul hwanip"; it has been proved that the rest of the pieces are sources of the existing "T'aryŏng" and "Kunak." Therefore, the form of the now existing *Hyŏnak yŏngsan hoesang* became nearly complete in the late eighteenth century and early nineteenth century.

In the nineteenth century, various names of *Yŏngsan hoesang* movements appeared in works such as the *Samjuk kŭmbo* (Samjuk's *kŏmun'go* manuscript), the *Hyŏn'gŭm oŭm t'ongnon* (Introduction to the five tones of the *kŏmun'go*; 1886), and the *Hakp'o kŭmbo* (Hakp'o's *kŏmun'go* manuscript). Titles that appear in the *Hyŏn'gŭm oŭm t'ongnon* include "Ponyŏngsan," "Chungnyŏngsan," "Seryŏngsan," "Karak hwanip," "Sanghyŏn hwanip," "Hahyŏn hwanip," "Yŏmbul," "T'aryŏng," and "Kunak," pieces that almost match the existing nine movements of *Yŏngsan hoesang*. This similarity shows that the current *Yŏngsan hoesang* completed its suite form in the late nineteenth century.

The Historical Development of Sanjo

If *p'ansori*, which was developed by professional entertainers known as *kwangdae*, is the crowning achievement of all vocal music in the late Chosŏn period, then *sanjo*, which was also developed by these entertainers, is the core of all instrumental solo music of the nineteenth century. We must, therefore, search for the origins of *sanjo* in the folk entertainments of the *kwangdae*, such as *shinawi* (instrumental ensemble for shamanistic rituals) or *p'ansori* of the late Chosŏn period, because *shinawi* and *p'ansori* were both used in shamanistic religious rituals (*kutp'an*) of that time, and both were developed in close relationship to the *kwangdae* who were husbands of female shamans (*mudang*).

Shinawi ensemble music, which is played in shamanistic rituals, is mainly performed on the *p'iri* (double-reed wind instrument), *chŏttae/taegŭm* (large transverse flute), *haegŭm* (2-stringed bowed fiddle), *changgo* (hourglass drum), and *ching* (large hand-held gong), though occasionally instruments such as the *kayagŭm* (12-stringed plucked zither), *ajaeng* (8-stringed bowed zither), *t'aep'yŏngso* (double-reed wind instrument with a funnel), and *t'ongso* (long end-blown flute) were added to the ensemble. *Shinawi* ensemble music often employs rhythmic cycles (*changdan*) such as *salp'uri, chajin salp'uri,* and *tosalp'uri;* in Chŏlla province, musicians also use *anjinban, tŏngdŏkkungi, kukkŏri, chungjungmori,* and similar such cycles. It has been assumed that *sanjo* began during the late Chosŏn period when a shaman's husband who performed *shinawi* came up with "scattered melodies" (*hŏt'ŭn karak*) by putting *p'ansori* melodies and rhythms on a string instrument. Scales or modes such as *ujo, p'yŏngjo,* and *kyemyŏnjo,* which bring out the distinctive melodic traits of *sanjo,* as well as typical *sanjo* rhythmic cycles such as *chinyangjo, chungmori, chungjungmori, ŏnmori, chajinmori,* and *hwimori,* all coincide with names of *p'ansori* scales and rhythmic cycles. Because of this type of musical similarity, we believe that *sanjo's* historical appearance was formed under the influence of *p'ansori.*

Kim Ch'angjo (1865–1920) created *kayagŭm sanjo* in the late nineteenth century by systematizing the improvisational music of the shaman's husband and by employing *p'ansori* rhythmic cycles and melodies on the *kayagŭm.* Other famous *kayagŭm sanjo* players of the late nineteenth century include Han Sukku, Yi Ch'asu, and Shim Ch'angnae. Following in Kim Ch'angjo's footsteps, Paek Nakchun (1884–1934) created *kŏmun'go sanjo* in the early twentieth century. *Taegŭm sanjo* was created by Pak Chonggi during the colonial period, *haegŭm sanjo* by Chi Yonggu, *p'iri sanjo* by Yi Ch'ungsŏn, and *ajaeng sanjo* by Han Ilsŏp.

Kim Ch'angjo's *kayagŭm sanjo* developed into schools of *sanjo* with distinctive styles through famous performers such as Han Sŏnggi, Ch'oe Oksan, An Kiok (1905–48), and Kang T'aehong (1894–1968) during the colonial period. The Han Sŏnggi school of *kayagŭm* was independently transmitted to Kim Chukp'a, the Ch'oe Oksan school to Ham Tongjŏngwŏl, and the Kang T'aehong school to Wŏn Okhwa. Yi Ch'asu's *kayagŭm sanjo* was transmitted to Pak Sanggŭn (1905–49), and Shim Ch'angnae's *kayagŭm sanjo* was passed on to his son, Shim Sanggŏn.

Paek Nakchun's *kŏmun'go sanjo* diverged into different schools by transmission through the performers Shin K'waedong (1910–78), Kim Chonggi, and Pak Sŏkki. Among the existing *kŏmun'go sanjo* schools of Shin K'waedong and Han Kaptŭk, Han's school is a result of transmission from Pak Sŏkki's *kŏmun'go sanjo.* Pak Chonggi's *taegŭm sanjo* was transmitted to Han Pŏmsu through Han Chuhwan; today Kang Paekch'ŏn and Kim Kwangshik *taegŭm sanjo* also exist. Chi Yonggu's *haegum sanjo* was transmitted to Chi Yŏnghŭi, with Yi Ch'ungsŏn's *p'iri sanjo* being passed on to Chŏng Chaeguk.

The Tradition of Nongak

Nongak (farmers' music) is the oldest kind of instrumental music outside of the court. From the pre-Chosŏn period, however, *nongak*'s performance was handed down orally as part of farming life, not by professional entertainers. It is difficult, therefore, to look into the history of *nongak* of the late Chosŏn period in any detail because of the lack of written materials.

In general, a *nongak* band was composed of a *kkwaenggwari* (small hand-held gong), *ching* (large hand-held gong), *changgo/changgu* (hourglass drum), *puk* (barrel drum), *nabal* (valveless long trumpet), and *nallari/t'aep'yŏngso* (double-reed wind instrument with a funnel); its music was called *nongak*. Depending on the region, *nongak* is also called *kut, maegu, p'ungjang,* or *p'ungmul,* but most recently *p'ungmul* is more generally favored. *Nongak* can be divided into four types according to the occasion under which it is performed: *p'an kut* (entertainment-oriented performance), *ture p'ungjang kut* (communal labor performance), *kŏllip kut* (fund-raising performance), and *maŭl kut* (village ritual performance).

Maŭl kut is performed as supplication for the village's safety and prosperity; it is also called *tangsan kut* because it is performed at the *tangsan* or shrine of the local deity. *Kŏllip kut* was performed to collect rice or money from each household for the village's communal expenses. *Ture p'ungjang kut* was played during communal labor, such as rice sowing and weeding; this was typical *nongak* activity before the Chosŏn period. The *p'an kut* was performed by ritual groups or fund-raising groups as entertainment; it is the predecessor of what is played these days at the National Folk Arts Competition (Chŏn'guk minsok yesul kyŏngyŏn taehoe). Although these four types of *nongak* have been transmitted since the late Chosŏn period, *ture p'ungjang kut* is considered the oldest *nongak* of all.

Folk Music's Present and Future since Korea's Liberation

Korean traditional music has been divided into the two branches of court and folk based on the criteria of where and who performed the music. When artistry is applied to traditional music, however, distinguishing this music by these categories becomes meaningless. Korean court and folk music possess unique styles that are not found in the neighboring countries of China and Japan.

In 1945 after independence, the National Center for Korean Traditional Performing Arts (Kungnip kugagwŏn) was established for the purpose of transmitting all branches of Korean music, both folk and court. Since the late 1950s, these two branches of Korean music have been taught in traditional music departments of universities throughout the nation. This teaching has been continued most recently (1998) at the School of Korean Traditional Arts (Chŏnt'ong yesulwŏn) of the Korean National University of Arts (Han'guk yesul chonghap hakkyo). This national institution's various departments of traditional art, music, dance, and theater were established in particular to train talented scholars to contribute to the development of the traditional performing arts, including the study of theory of both court and folk music. Korean traditional music, both court and folk music, will therefore be the root of the creation of new Korean music for the twenty-first century. And this new music will contribute to the development of world music as well.

TWO

The Traditional Opera of the Future? *Ch'anggŭk*'s First Century

ANDREW P. KILLICK

The incorporation of Korea into the modern world order, beginning in the late nineteenth century, has led not only to changes in its existing folk music traditions, but to the creation of new genres on the basis of the old. While it has not been easy for these new genres to attain the prestige and institutional support bestowed on art forms recognized as traditional, they have come to form a category of their own, basing their appeal on a relationship with the traditional while lacking its ethic of preservation and consciously adapting it to the needs of modern audiences—a category that I have called the "traditionesque" (Killick 2001, 1998a). Though unlikely to be referred to as *chŏnt'ong ŭmak* (traditional music), these genres might, if successful in their aims, be described as *chŏnt'ongjŏgin ŭmak*, perhaps best rendered as "music with an air of tradition about it," and it is this informal differentiation of usage that has suggested my more systematic dichotomy of "traditional" and "traditionesque."

Perhaps the first of these traditionesque genres was the musical theater form now known as *ch'anggŭk* (literally, "singing drama"). In *ch'anggŭk*, the musical and literary style of *p'ansori* (musical storytelling), and often its actual repertoire, is retained while the single singer-storyteller is replaced by a whole cast of singing actors, the fan and handkerchief held by the *p'ansori* singer become the increasingly elaborate props and scenery of the theatrical stage, and the instrumental accompaniment on a single drum

---

This study is derived from research conducted for my Ph.D. dissertation (Killick 1998a). This research was assisted by a grant from the Joint Committee on Korean Studies of the Social Science Research Council and the American Council of Learned Societies.

has been gradually expanded into a large orchestra of traditional instruments. *Ch'angguk* provides an instructive example of an art form that has steered a winding course through the twentieth century between the conflicting imperatives of tradition and modernity, and the dialectic of these two terms continues to inform the renegotiation of *ch'angguk*'s identity as the genre prepares to enter the third millennium and its own second century of existence. While *ch'angguk* has not yet won wide recognition as "traditional Korean opera," it retains the aspiration to become the traditional opera of the future, representing traditional Korean culture for domestic and international consumption, and it continues to base its appeal on a sense of tradition while striving to attract a contemporary audience that has in many ways moved away from traditional Korean expressive culture and lifestyles. It is this history of *ch'angguk*'s shifting relation to the traditional, with special emphasis on the activities of the National Ch'angguk Troupe since its foundation in 1962, that forms the subject of this study.

The findings presented herein draw on three years of fieldwork in Seoul beginning in January 1995, in the course of which I tracked down primary and secondary written and recorded sources on *ch'angguk*, observed a number of complete productions taking shape from the first rehearsals to the final night's performance, and interviewed directors, composers, writers, and members of the National Ch'angguk Troupe and of several other troupes performing *ch'angguk* and its all-female variant, *yŏsŏng kukkŭk*. Previous writings in English that have dealt with *ch'angguk* (e.g., Park-Miller 1995; Um Hae-kyung 1992; Pihl 1991; Kim Woo-ok 1980) have done so from the perspective of a primary interest in *p'ansori* and have generally been content to rely on the most accessible, rather than the most reliable, sources of information on *ch'angguk*'s history, some of which have been called into serious question—if not radically refuted—by more recent and painstaking Korean research (e.g., Paek Hyŏnmi 1997, 1996, 1995, 1989; Yu Minyŏng 1995). Where my account conflicts with earlier ones, it is through my interpretation of materials brought to light by research (both my own and that of my Korean colleagues) that takes *ch'angguk* as its main focus, and, in so doing, moves us closer to what I consider a proper understanding of the subject.

Ch'angguk Takes Shape

The history of *ch'angguk* to date can be conveniently divided into three "generations" beginning at roughly thirty-year intervals, each initiated by a stimulus from outside the world of traditional music and marked off by an intervening decline or hiatus in activity.[1] While it is primarily with the third of these generations that I will be concerned, the activities of that generation can only be understood in relation to its forebears, which established the art form we now know as *ch'angguk* but failed to sustain it as a commercially viable form of entertainment, thus creating both the possibility and the need for the government-sponsored revival that inaugurated what I call the third generation of *ch'angguk*. I begin, therefore, with a brief overview of the first and second generations, though I have treated each of these in more detail elsewhere (Killick 1998b, 1997a).

Ch'angguk's *Origin Myth*

Ch'angguk has acquired what I believe to be an "origin myth" that, however interesting as part of the cultural discourse around the genre, needs to be confronted before our view of the subject can be better squared with the surviving sources. Part of the myth is that, until the *p'ansori* singers created *ch'angguk*, Korea had no drama[2]—a view that is still frequently expressed despite the country's long history of theatrical art forms such as masked dance-dramas (*t'al ch'um*), puppet plays (*kkoktugakshi*), and court variety shows (*sandae nori* or *sandaehŭi*). In a narrower sense, it is true that before the twentieth century Korea had no "drama" if that term is taken to imply professional actors performing a previously composed script in an enclosed or indoor space before audiences who have paid fixed rates for admission. It is also true, according to the best available evidence, that *p'ansori* singers were the first to perform dramas matching this definition. The myth relates to how it happened.

---

[1] A tripartite periodization similar to mine was suggested by Song Hyejin (1987), though she drew the boundaries a little differently. Her title, "*Ch'angguk*: For a Leap Forward as Korea's Musical Drama of the Future," is also deliberately evoked by mine: its implication that, despite the venerable age of the genre, *ch'angguk*'s time has not yet come, is a paradox to which I hope to offer a solution.

[2] A representative statement of this view, by *ch'angguk* director Yi Chinsun, will be quoted and discussed later in this chapter.

As my "narrow" definition of drama might suggest, what is usually meant by the statement that Korea had no drama is that Korea lacked a distinctive, internationally recognized style of professional theater to compare with China's Peking opera or Japan's kabuki—and, as we shall see, it is precisely this that the National Ch'anggŭk Troupe is still struggling to establish. This being the case, it would make sense that the *p'ansori* singers, in seeking to create such a style, would look less to indigenous Korean theatrical traditions than to international sources of inspiration, and in particular their two powerful neighbor countries. And given Korea's historical tributary status and long recognition of its cultural debt to China, and its equally deep-rooted hostility and resentment toward Japan (especially in the twentieth century), a Chinese source of inspiration would be far more acceptable to most Koreans than a Japanese one. But in claiming such a source, the origin myth seems to spring more from wishful thinking and a desire to legitimize the genre than from an impartial evaluation of the evidence.

The myth itself appears to originate with the recollections of veteran *p'ansori* singer Yi Tongbaek when he was interviewed in the late 1930s, some three decades after the events he described. Yi Tongbaek stated that his colleague Kang Yonghwan conceived the first *ch'anggŭk* production on the model of the Peking opera he had enthusiastically watched in Seoul's Chinese theater around the turn of the century. This story was reproduced in the one published book on *ch'anggŭk*, Pak Hwang's *Ch'anggŭksa yŏn'gu* (A study of the history of *ch'anggŭk*; 1976:17), which was then taken as an authority by every scholar who wrote on *ch'anggŭk* in English until I began my research in 1995 (e.g., Pihl 1991:114). However, no primary evidence has been produced in support of this story, while Pak Hwang's book has been found to be so riddled with errors that Paek Hyŏnmi, in a recent dissertation on the early history of *ch'anggŭk*, chose not to use it at all except in illustrating points that could be confirmed from other sources (Paek Hyŏnmi 1996:5n20). The more rigorous research of Paek and others has found that Kang Yonghwan died well before the first *ch'anggŭk* performance of which we have any record (Paek Hyesuk 1992), that Peking opera may never have been performed in Seoul before *ch'anggŭk* was, and that the first productions were conceived not by a *p'ansori* singer, but by a writer and politician—one who, moreover, is regarded as anything but a hero in Korea today.

First Generation: Yi Injik and the Wŏn'gaksa

It now appears that although *ch'anggŭk* was indeed a product of international influence, that influence came not from China but from Japan, and the man who brought it was one of the most notorious of the political faction that has come to be known as "pro-Japanese," namely Yi Injik (1862–1916). A couple of years before the first *ch'anggŭk* productions, Yi Injik had introduced the modern novel to Korea, following Japanese models, with his *Hyŏl ŭi nu* (Tears of blood; 1906), and a couple of years later he would assist the Japanese government in its annexation of Korea. However unwelcome, the evidence for his leadership in the introduction of *ch'anggŭk* now seems overwhelming.[3]

While studying in Japan at the turn of the century, Yi Injik had seen the so-called new-school dramas (J. *shimpa geki*) that had developed there out of the political dramas (J. *sōshi geki*) of the previous decade,[4] and this may have led him to see the stage as a suitable platform for his political ideas. The resources to mount theatrical productions in Seoul were at last available, for the first indoor Korean theater, the Wŏn'gaksa, had been built there at royal expense in 1902;[5] and as performers, large numbers of *p'ansori* singers, most of them from the southwestern regions where the genre originated, had been attracted to the capital by increased sources of patronage as this folk art gained an audience among the upper strata of society. These *p'ansori* singers were perhaps the only available performers with skills in declamation and dramatic projection that were relevant to Yi Injik's objectives, while Yi was capable of writing in a style that would be familiar enough to them for performance in their accustomed mode of delivery, for he knew *p'ansori* well and had earlier translated one

---

[3] Some idea of how unwelcome this account of *ch'anggŭk*'s origins was can be gained from the fact that my own article, presenting this view for the first time in English (1997a), was followed by, and apparently prompted, what is in part a reply to it in the next issue of the same journal (Kim Jong-cheol 1997).

[4] On the new-school and political dramas of Japan, see Ernst 1974:249–52 and Bowers 1952:208–12. On new-school drama in Korea, the recollections of veteran actor Ko Sŏlbong include some vivid descriptions (1990:23). The most up-to-date general history of drama in Korea is probably Sŏ Yŏnho 1994.

[5] British traveler Isabella Bird Bishop had reported seeing a Japanese theater in Seoul as early as 1894 (Bishop 1970:43), but this would not have been open to Koreans, and she specifically states that there was no Korean theater (p. 60). She makes no mention of the Chinese theater that is supposed by some to have existed in Seoul in the 1890s (e.g., Pihl 1991:113). For a comprehensive history of theaters in Korea, see Yu Minyŏng 1980.

of the stories, "Pyŏljubu-jŏn" (another name for "Sugung-ga," or "Song of the Underwater Palace"), into Japanese (Paek Hyŏnmi 1996:39). He used this style in the first half of a story called "Ŭnsegye" (Silver world) in which he exposed the hopeless corruption (as he saw it) of Korea's traditional social order and thus, by implication, advocated the need for external intervention; and he arranged for this first part of the story to be performed in dramatic fashion by a group of *p'ansori* singers at the Wŏn'gaksa in November 1908.[6]

To defray the expenses involved in preparing the singers for this novel type of performance, the Wŏn'gaksa meanwhile offered performances of popular traditional arts. But these fund-raising performances already began to introduce the dramatic techniques that Yi Injik wanted the singers to learn, and in so doing, they appear to have become the first productions of what we would now call *ch'anggŭk*.[7] It was "Ŭnsegye," however, that would be recalled as the greatest "hit" of *ch'anggŭk* at the Wŏn'gaksa, for it appears that audiences appreciated this new work more than the familiar *p'ansori* stories and, in general, valued *ch'anggŭk* for its novelty rather than its appeal to tradition. Indeed, Yi Injik himself emphasized the novelty of the production by advertising it as "new drama" (*shinyŏn'gŭk*), a term that was derived from Japanese usage and suggested an analogy with the "new novel" (*shinsosŏl*) that Yi had already introduced to Korea. However, even before the production opened, Yi went back to Japan to observe the introduction of Western-style realist drama there, and new drama lost its only author capable of creating viable new repertoire. A few years later, when Korean companies began to perform actual new-school dramas based on the Japanese model, the *p'ansori* singers, left to their own devices, could produce

---

[6] The second half of "Ŭnsegye," which deals with events much later in time, was written in Yi Injik's usual "new novel" style. It is therefore assumed that only the first half was performed as *ch'anggŭk* and that Yi Injik hoped it would lead audience members to purchase and read his whole novel, which was published concurrently with the production (Killick 1997a:121). The text of "Ŭnsegye" is available in a modern edition (Yi Injik 1995).

[7] Sŏng Kyŏngnin (1980:338) was the first to suggest that these fund-raising performances were the earliest *ch'anggŭk* productions. I too came around to this position, revising my earlier view that "Ŭnsegye" itself was the first *ch'anggŭk* production (Killick 1997a), on discovering a narrative by one Major Herbert H. Austin who had visited Korea for a week in October 1908 and happened to see what appears to have been one of these performances (Austin 1910:196–97). The relevant passage is quoted in full in Killick 1998b:79.

nothing to compete with these for novelty value. Instead, they fell back on the familiar repertoire of episodes from the traditional *p'ansori* stories and changed the name of the new theatrical genre from new drama to old school (*kup'a*) or old drama (*kuyŏn'gŭk*) before it was in fact even five years old. Thus, in striving to sustain the success of the genre that Yi Injik had inaugurated while basing its appeal on tradition instead of novelty, *ch'anggŭk* became Korea's first traditionesque art form.

This early form of *ch'anggŭk* consisted largely of existing *p'ansori* material with the dialogue portions distributed among multiple singing actors who took the roles of characters and the remaining passages delivered from one side of the stage by a narrator who later became known as the *toch'ang* or "lead singer." At first all the performers were probably male, though female singers and even all-female troupes soon appeared.[8] Scenic effects were minimal or nonexistent, and tales of crude acting abound,[9] while the instrumental accompaniment was limited, as in *p'ansori*, to a single barrel drum (*puk*). Complete stories were rarely if ever presented. Instead, single scenes from the familiar stories would be given as part of a variety show of traditional performing arts, often constituting the finale of such a program. Accordingly, while moments of dramatic pathos were not excluded, the emphasis of these scenes was on lively music and dancing, and especially on comedy. The comic material was not always particularly appropriate to the characters appearing in the scene or to its position in the overall story, but was often developed from the punning tradition of *chaedam* or "witty talk," which had previously been performed independent of any narrative context. Despite the continued popularity of *p'ansori* singing, this early form of *ch'anggŭk* could hardly hold its own against the new theatrical entertainments and imported movies that poured into

---

[8] Despite the claims of Pak Hwang (1976) and of those who have followed him, to the effect that "the emergence of *ch'anggŭk* turned upon the availability of female performers" (Pihl 1991:113), there is no evidence that women participated in early *ch'anggŭk* performances except in the separate performances of *ch'anggŭk* scenes by groups of female entertainers (*kisaeng*) that began to appear in the mid-1910s (Paek Hyŏnmi 1996:62–63). On the contrary, cross-dressing in both directions appears to have been common, while mixed troupes were at first unknown.

[9] Thus, the first historical study of drama in Korea mentioned that in old drama (*kugŭk*, i.e., *ch'anggŭk*), the scenery was "laughable" and the painted backdrop "none-too-firmly fixed," while the same actor might play several roles without even changing makeup, and much of the action was conveyed by token gestures rather than realistic representation (Kim Chaech'ŏl 1933:129–30).

Korea during the colonial period, and its fortunes declined steadily over the next two decades. By the 1930s, it was all but extinct; but its social and cultural environment had begun to change in ways that would make a successful revival possible, and it was this revival that would establish the term *ch'anggŭk* and the genre we would now recognize by that name.

Second Generation: Pak Chin and the Chosŏn sŏngak yŏn'guhoe

The later 1920s and, even more so, the early 1930s, saw a growth of interest among both Korean and Japanese scholars in Korean indigenous folk culture, including *p'ansori*. In part this was an outgrowth of the "cultural nationalism" that began to be tolerated under the "cultural policy" introduced by the Japanese authorities after the March First Independence Movement of 1919 (Robinson 1988). Through the impetus of this "cultural movement" (*munhwa undong*), studies of Korean shamanism, Buddhism, and folk customs began to appear, and some of the increasingly rare masked dance-dramas (*t'al ch'um* or *kamyŏn'gŭk*) were revived and transcribed (Yang Jongsung 1994:24–44). Folk arts were particularly valued as authentic expressions of Korean national identity, in preference to the elite traditions, because Korea's elites had always been oriented toward external cultural sources—first China and now Japan and the West—and the arts they patronized were more cosmopolitan, while their reputation for exploiting the peasantry had cast them in the role of obstructors rather than promoters of indigenous cultural development (Sorensen 1995:334–36, 1999). The products of this interest in folk arts included the composition of a major text in *p'ansori* studies, Chŏng Noshik's *Chosŏn ch'anggŭksa* (History of Korean *p'ansori*;[10] 1940, reprinted 1994), and a revival of solo *p'ansori* singing, which was already under way in the 1920s, but which greatly accelerated under the auspices of the Chosŏn ŭmnyul hyŏphoe (Korean Music Association, 1930–33) and its successor, the Chosŏn sŏngak yŏn'guhoe (Korean Vocal Music Association, 1934–41).

A second factor promoting the emergence of a new generation of *ch'anggŭk* was the advent of a theater that was not (like other Korean theaters) used promiscuously for plays, movies, concerts,

---

[10] The word *ch'anggŭk* at this time referred to both the solo and the theatrical forms of *p'ansori* performance, but Chŏng Noshik's book deals almost exclusively with the solo form now known as *p'ansori*.

and lectures, but was devoted exclusively to presenting live drama: the Tongyang Theater, opened in November 1935 (Yi Tuhyŏn 1983:142; Yu Minyŏng 1980:144). The existence of such a theater indicates the extent to which drama (now influenced to varying degrees by Western realist models) had become a significant element among the performing arts in Korea, and the Tongyang Theater would take the lead in promoting popular drama in the late 1930s (Paek Hyŏnmi 1996:130; Sŏ Yŏnho 1994:224). In contrast to the variety-show format of many theatrical entertainments at the time, the Tongyang Theater presented complete plays unaccompanied by other acts, making this format available to the new incarnation of *ch'anggŭk*. It was especially fortunate for this reemergent genre that the Tongyang Theater proved able and willing to take *ch'anggŭk* under its wing and lend it theatrical expertise that represented the state of the art in Korea at the time. It should also be mentioned that the advent of an all-Korean-language radio station in 1933 stimulated interest in both traditional music and theater through live broadcasts of performances (Robinson 1999).

The Chosŏn sŏngak yŏn'guhoe (Korean Vocal Music Association) was founded with the objective of reviving *p'ansori* rather than *ch'anggŭk*, and it was initially concerned mainly with the training of successors to the senior *p'ansori* artists who were now approaching the ends of their careers.[11] That its endeavors in *p'ansori* would take a dramatic turn, both literally and figuratively, was unforeseen but perhaps inevitable in view of the growing popularity of theatrical performance in general—for, as was recognized at the time, "if this [*p'ansori*] is to appear before today's audience, it must step out on today's stage" (*Chosŏn ilbo*, October 10, 1939). In particular, it was apparently through the initiative of resident artists at the Tongyang Theater that the Yŏn'guhoe formed the close relationship with that theater that would enable it to develop a fully theatricalized form of *ch'anggŭk*.

This collaboration was recalled by veteran actor Ko Sŏlbong as follows:

At the Tongyang Theater, when we performed things like "Shim Ch'ŏng-jŏn" (Story of Shim Ch'ŏng) and "Ch'unhyang-jŏn" (Story of Ch'unhyang), we brought in [senior *p'ansori* singers from the

---

[11] The activities of the Chosŏn sŏngak yŏn'guhoe have been discussed and documented in Korean by Yu Minyŏng (1995) and Yi Sujŏng (1993), and in English by me (Killick 1998b).

Chosŏn sŏngak yŏn'guhoe] to sing *p'ansori* from behind the scenes.... The response of the audience was very positive. So people such as Pak Chin, Ch'oe Tokkyŏn, and Hong Haesŏng said, "Since it's been so well received, let's try putting on drama in the name of the Chosŏn sŏngak yŏn'guhoe," and they performed such pieces as "Ch'unhyang-jŏn," "Shim Ch'ŏng-jŏn," and "Paebijang-jŏn" (Story of Officer Pae), in the form of *ch'anggŭk* with the roles divided. The staff of the Tongyang Theater took responsibility for the costumes, makeup, props, and so on. (Ko Sŏlbong 1990:41)

The three figures credited by Ko Sŏlbong with initiating the collaboration were all associated with the Tongyang Theater rather than the Chosŏn sŏngak yŏn'guhoe. Hong Haesŏng and Pak Chin were resident directors of the theater schooled in Western-style drama, while Ch'oe Tokkyŏn, more commonly known by his pen name Sangdŏk, was a dramatist whose works were performed there. Thus, *ch'anggŭk* of this second generation, like that of the first, appears to have been developed at the instigation of intellectuals oriented toward Western-style drama, and not of the *p'ansori* singers themselves. By training the singers in a new method of acting, Pak Chin (perhaps in collaboration with his associates at the Tongyang Theater) may have become a kind of second Yi Injik for *ch'anggŭk*, providing the external impetus that was needed to assemble a troupe and supervise its first productions. Like Yi Injik, Pak Chin had studied in Japan and regarded the spoken drama that Korea learned from Japan as an appropriate model for *ch'anggŭk*, and it must have been this type of acting in which he instructed the singers.

Although the first efforts of the Chosŏn sŏngak yŏn'guhoe followed the example of Pak Chin's productions, in which new-school actors represented the dramatis personae while *p'ansori* was sung by different artists from behind the scenes, the group soon gained confidence and began to introduce innovations of its own that would help to shape *ch'anggŭk* as we know it today. These innovations began with "pursuing a new form of musical drama in which the actors who appear on the stage sing *ch'ang* themselves" (*Chosŏn ilbo*, September 12, 1936), although it appears that the offstage singers of earlier productions were also retained, eventually evolving into the *toch'ang* or narrator of today. The performance of entire stories at a sitting, unaccompanied by other acts, now replaced the earlier episodic or variety-show style of presentation as the standard practice in *ch'anggŭk*. Large amounts of spoken dialogue were added to the existing *p'ansori* material to provide both continuity and a dramatic convention acceptable to contemporary audiences. The scale of *ch'anggŭk* productions became larger in every respect: casts were swelled with extras, the lone *puk* drummer was supplanted by an orchestra of traditional instruments, and stage scenery developed to the point where sheer spectacle became a selling point for the genre.

As this new generation of *ch'anggŭk* came of age, the existing repertoire, limited to a handful of familiar *p'ansori* stories, was soon felt to be inadequate to sustain the newfound success of the genre, and efforts were made to create new works. Some of these were reconstructions of stories such as "Pae-bijang-jŏn" (Story of Officer Pae), which had once been part of the *p'ansori* repertoire but had been almost or completely lost; others were adaptations of old novels such as *Ongnumong* (Dream of the jade chamber). One production, "Yu Ch'ungnyŏl-jŏn" (Story of Yu Ch'ungnyŏl), even experimented with the combined use of film and live action in a genre known as "kino-drama" (*yŏnswaegŭk*), which had enjoyed a brief vogue in Korea around 1920 and in Japan a decade before that.

By the early 1940s, the retirement and death of several senior members, as well as difficulties with the Japanese colonial government, had brought an end to the activities of the Chosŏn sŏngak yŏn'guhoe, but the popularity of *ch'anggŭk* had led to the advent of several new troupes performing on tour throughout the peninsula. Inevitably, these new troupes consisted largely of younger and less experienced artists who lacked the older generation's rigorous training in *p'ansori* and were often more celebrated as glamorous actors than as masters of the *p'ansori* tradition. Accordingly, they developed a lighter, simplified style of *p'ansori* singing that came to be known by the pejorative term *yŏn'gŭk sori* (play singing), which the third generation of *ch'anggŭk* worked hard to outgrow. The new troupes also expanded the repertoire by introducing historical dramas (*yŏksagŭk*) based on legends and fanciful versions of history, usually from Korea's remote past. These historical dramas remained the mainstay of the repertoire after liberation in 1945, when *ch'anggŭk* came to be known as *kukkŭk* (national drama), and an all-female variant called *yŏsŏng kukkŭk* (women's national drama) began to steal the limelight.[12]

---

[12] The only published article in English on these all-female *ch'anggŭk* troupes is Killick 1997b. They are described in Korean in the memoirs of one of their leaders, Hong Sŏngdŏk (1996:135–55), and in an M.A. thesis by Kim Pyŏngch'ŏl (1997). On *ch'anggŭk* of this period, see Paek Hyŏnmi 1989:75–91.

The Traditional Opera of the Future?

Meanwhile, Korea's diverse collection of indigenous musical genres, which had in many cases been performed for quite different audiences and had little to do with each other, came to be brought together for the first time under the generic label of *kugak* (national music)[13] and was eventually supported together by government-sponsored institutions such as the Kungnip kugagwŏn (now known in English as the National Center for Korean Traditional Performing Arts, but more literally rendered as "National National Music Institute"). The new terminology is indicative of what has remained the modern criterion for admission to "traditional" status: the traditional tends to be equated with the national, that is, with art forms that are thought to have reached maturity in Korea before the colonial period and without significant influence from foreign sources other than Korea's acknowledged cultural fountainhead, China.

But the "nation" that was celebrated in these new terms and institutions was already divided and was about to be torn apart. The Korean War dealt a blow from which *ch'anggŭk* would never recover. The genre appears to have limped on for some years in North Korea, though too little is known about this to assert anything with certainty except that it no longer survives there. In South Korea, the growth of a thriving domestic film industry in the late 1950s was followed by the spread of television over the succeeding decades, and despite the lingering popularity of *yŏsŏng kukkŭk* and some last-ditch experiments such as all-female color kino-drama, it eventually became clear that *ch'anggŭk* could not compete with the modern entertainment media or even survive without government support. But, by that time, help was at hand.

The National Ch'anggŭk Troupe

By the early 1960s, even *p'ansori* was suffering from a lack of patronage, and *ch'anggŭk*, which was much more expensive to produce, had greater need but fewer sources of financial support. It was probably the turbulent political events of the early 1960s that provided a basis for the government support that would rescue

---

[13] On the introduction of this concept of *kugak*, see Song Bang-song 1984:577–78. The word *kugak*, derived from the posts of *kugaksa* (musician) and *kugaksajang* (head musician) during the brief reign of Korea's last monarch, Sunjong (r. 1907–10), had in fact been used for a few years early in the century, but only in reference to court music, not Korean traditional music in general (Song Bang-song 1984: 520–24).

this art form from extinction. The military junta that seized power in the coup of May 1961 was largely made up of men who, like its leader President Park Chung Hee, had been officers in the Japanese Imperial Army. This new and unelected government was faced with an urgent need to legitimize itself, as much because of its taint of collaboration with the Japanese as because of the strong-arm tactics by which it had imposed itself on the country. One way in which it sought this legitimacy was by becoming a generous patron of Korea's traditional culture, for which Park had shown nothing but contempt up to that time. In 1962, the Park regime passed the Cultural Assets Protection Act (Munhwajae pohobŏp), modeled (ironically enough) on the one Japan had introduced in 1950, which would provide subsidies to leading exponents of certain indigenous Korean art forms that were designated as important intangible cultural assets (*chungyo muhyŏng munhwajae*). These assets were conceived not so much in terms of techniques and practices as in terms of canonical repertoires to be maintained in a fixed (and often arbitrarily reconstructed) "original form" (*wŏnhyŏng*).[14] Recognition under the Cultural Assets scheme quickly became the most obvious mark of admission to the hallowed ranks of the traditional, and *p'ansori*, in its original solo form, was one of the first art forms to be so recognized.

In the same year, the government granted funds to the National Theater (Kungnip kŭkchang) enabling it to supplement its existing resident troupe, which performed only Western-style drama, with three additional troupes, including one devoted to *ch'anggŭk*. Thus, the National Ch'anggŭk Troupe was born, and a new generation of *ch'anggŭk* activity had once more been inaugurated by a stimulus from outside the world of the traditional arts themselves. But although the genre claimed the aura of the national (until 1973 the troupe was known as the Kungnip kukkŭktan, literally "National National Drama Troupe"), because of its short history and obvious foreign influences it failed to meet the criteria for traditional status and was therefore supported outside the cultural assets system.

The initial generous level of funding was not sustained, and the troupe in its early days was forced to concentrate on a more

---

[14] The doctoral dissertation of Yang Jongsung (1994) is devoted to this system and contains several examples illustrating just how arbitrary the process of establishing a *wŏnhyŏng* can be.

economical type of performance known as *yŏnch'ang* in which consecutive portions of a *p'ansori* story were delivered by a number of singers in succession. But within five years attention began to be given to the problem of attaining for *ch'anggŭk* the stability and coherent identity denoted by the much-used Korean word *chŏngnip*, which I will translate as "establishment."[15] Since then, the goal of the National Ch'anggŭk Troupe has been, quite explicitly, the establishment—we might say, the invention—of a "traditional" Korean opera form to rival those of other, more powerful nations. Such an invented tradition was felt to be necessary not only for bolstering Korea's domestic self-image, but for representing Korea to the world as a land with a vibrant and distinctive culture that was the equal of (but different from) those of its neighbors. This became an increasingly pressing concern as Korea prepared to host major international events like the Asian and Olympic games of the 1980s (see Dilling 2001), and has remained so in the "globalization" drive of the 1990s. But the goal was clearly formulated quite early on in a program note by director Yi Chinsun:

> The problem in establishing *ch'anggŭk* is how one can transform the abundant dramatic elements in *p'ansori* in order to establish a traditional drama (*chŏnt'ong yŏn'gŭk*). Our country originally had no theater and no stage. As a result, it could not have its own dramatic form. Taking the ancient drama of other countries for comparison, the Greek drama, Roman drama, and medieval drama of the West all had their own form [governing everything] from the design of the theater to the [style of] acting, while China's Peking opera and Japan's kabuki and noh bear their own excellent form transmitted through the ages. Our country, as mentioned above, had no theater and no stage, so it did not have its own form of musical drama (*ch'anggŭk*). It is this that we are now trying to create for the first time. (Yi Chinsun, director's note in program of National Ch'anggŭk Troupe production no. 16, "Ch'unhyang-jŏn," September–October 1971)

The quest for Korea's "own form of musical drama" has been inseparable from the attempt to incorporate in *ch'anggŭk* more elements that were traditional rather than modern, national rather than foreign, in the hope of making *ch'anggŭk*, paradoxically, more

---

[15] On the early history of the National Ch'anggŭk Troupe and the Ch'anggŭk chŏngnip wiwŏnhoe (Committee for the Establishment of Ch'anggŭk), see Sŏng Kyŏngnin 1980:344–66. For a survey of three decades of National Ch'anggŭk Troupe productions, see Paek Hyŏnmi 1993.

traditional than it had ever been in the past. This traditionalizing of *ch'anggŭk* has been pursued through three broad phases that we might summarize as, first, faithfulness to the "letter" of *p'ansori*; second, the attempt to recapture its "spirit"; and third, a dawning faith in the capability of *ch'anggŭk* to develop traditions of its own. Each of these phases will be considered in turn, followed by a final discussion of the countervailing tendency to accept and perpetuate the traditionesque nature of *ch'anggŭk*.

Phase 1: The Ch'anggŭk chŏngnip wiwŏnhoe

Faithfulness to the letter of *p'ansori* was the watchword of the Ch'anggŭk chŏngnip wiwŏnhoe (Committee for the Establishment of Ch'anggŭk), set up under the auspices of the National Ch'anggŭk Troupe in 1967. The committee, made up of senior performers and scholars, was given the task of arranging texts for *ch'anggŭk* productions and determining the manner of their performance in a way that would eliminate the earlier pandering to popular appeal and bring *ch'anggŭk* as close as possible to its *p'ansori* originals. This objective, and some of its consequences, were later recalled by the chairman of the committee, Sŏ Hangsŏk:

> The objective of this committee was to find the true form [of *ch'anggŭk*] within *p'ansori*, and to arrange it systematically.
>
> To mention some of the decisions of this committee that were put into practice: first, *ch'anggŭk* up to that time had treated the drummer and musicians like something equivalent to the "sound effects" in Western drama, and not exposed them on stage; but in the Wiwŏnhoe's opinion, the drummer and musicians were an organic part of *p'ansori*, so it was desirable to provide a space for them in one corner of the stage where they could give calls (*ch'uimsae*) properly. This was soon accepted by *ch'anggŭk*.
>
> Second, when *ch'anggŭk* was performed Western-style, the progress of the drama was conveyed through singing in dialogue, and the narrative singing (*sŏlmyŏngch'ang*) was performed offstage; but to show the true character of *p'ansori*, we proposed to provide a place for this too in one corner of the stage, calling it "lead singing" (*toch'ang*). This too was accepted by *ch'anggŭk*.
>
> Third, in the case of *p'ansori*-drama [i.e., *ch'anggŭk*], we suggested using the word "leader" (*toyŏn*) instead of "director" (*yŏnch'ul*). This was because we believed that, in establishing a proper form of *p'ansori*-drama, directing should not be a mode of creation but should be restricted to leading a production in keeping with that form, so as to transmit the form and protect it from corruption.

In this way, the Wiwŏnhoe strove to find the most appropriate method of performance for *p'ansori*-drama, and turned its hand to the task of gathering the variants of each *p'ansori* piece and establishing a standard text (*chŏngbon*). (Sŏ Hangsŏk 1979:29)

Just as the cultural assets system had conceptualized traditional performing arts in terms of repertoires rather than techniques or practices, the Wiwŏnhoe also approached the traditionalizing of *ch'anggŭk* primarily as the recasting of the repertoire (i.e., texts) closer to the "original" *p'ansori* ones (which themselves had to be newly arranged). It went without saying that this repertoire would shift away from the fanciful newly composed "historical" dramas, which had continued to appear in the early days of the National Ch'anggŭk Troupe, back to the familiar handful of stories derived from *p'ansori*. The Wiwŏnhoe began by seeking to establish "standard" versions of these texts, and its recommendations concerning performance practice arose from the desire to maintain these versions with their *p'ansori*-based characteristics as far as possible unchanged in *ch'anggŭk*. The narrative portions had to be presented by a narrator, fully visible on stage, unlike the offstage singers of second-generation *ch'anggŭk*; the instrumental musicians too had to be placed on stage in order to respond in the traditional way to the singers; and each production was to be prepared under the guidance of a "leader" whose job was to ensure the faithful maintenance of these and other "traditional" practices. The visual presentation would reflect the minimalism of *p'ansori*'s physical resources—probably a practical necessity when retaining the frequent changes of location that characterize *p'ansori* narratives. Although it resulted in some similarities to the earliest *ch'anggŭk* performances, this "traditionalizing" of *ch'anggŭk* was not at all conceived as a matter of restoring its own performance traditions, which had never been respected as "traditional" in themselves, but rather as the attempt to align *ch'anggŭk* more closely with its undisputedly traditional parent genre, *p'ansori*.

The objective of establishing *ch'anggŭk* as a traditional drama was constantly confronted by the fact that, as Sŏ Yŏnho has put it, *ch'anggŭk* had no "original form" (*wŏnhyŏng*; 1988:85)—a prerequisite for any cultural asset. Accordingly, *ch'anggŭk* sought its "original form" in *p'ansori*, and from this point on, the National Ch'anggŭk Troupe would struggle with the unenviable task of establishing a new genre whose success would be measured by its faithfulness to the content and aesthetics of another, already existing, genre.

Not the least of *ch'anggŭk*'s problems in using virtually unaltered *p'ansori* texts as a libretto was that most of these texts were far too long for the attention span of the average theater audience, and inevitably they had to be edited.[16] Another problem was that as drama, *ch'anggŭk* suffered from the constant intrusions of the narrator. It must have seemed at times as if the stage directions of the script were being recited by the *toch'ang*, and indeed, in the script of one 1970 production, *toch'ang* texts were actually used as stage directions:

> (Hyangdan enters carrying a lighted lantern and a soup bowl.)
> *Hyangdan:* The curfew has sounded, so I'll go before my lady.
> (They act as the *toch'ang* indicates below.)
> *Toch'ang:* Hyangdan goes in front holding the lantern, and Ch'unhyang's mother opens the door and goes out [after her]. The Royal Inspector, as if unable to resist, goes down behind Ch'unhyang's mother to the prison. (Kang Hanyŏng, unpublished libretto of National Ch'anggŭk Troupe production no. 15, "Ch'unhyang-jŏn," 1970:143)

In practice, however, while the Wiwŏnhoe was the dominant influence in *ch'anggŭk* during the decade following its foundation, not all of its recommendations were consistently applied even during that period. The use of the onstage *toch'ang* did become standard at least until the 1990s, but the orchestra soon returned to the pit, and the influence of directors schooled in Western theater, though often decried (e.g., Lee Bo-hyung 1997), was never shaken off, evidently because *ch'anggŭk* did not succeed in establishing a "proper form" that could be maintained under the guidance of a "leader" conceptualized as a guardian of tradition rather than as a creative artist. Moreover, it eventually became clear that *p'ansori* by itself did not contain all of the resources that were needed to create a satisfying theatrical art form. Ultimately, the committee failed to establish fixed texts and performance practices for *ch'anggŭk*, and its influence declined.

Phase 2: Hŏ Kyu and Madanghwa

A second phase in the traditionalization of *ch'anggŭk* came in 1977 with the advent of writer and director Hŏ Kyu, who would dominate productions of the National Ch'anggŭk Troupe for the

---

[16] *Wanp'an* (complete text) *ch'anggŭk* productions lasting five hours or more were, however, given in the early 1980s and again in the late 1990s.

next dozen years and reshape them in accordance with a new vision of the genre. Other directors and librettists who worked with the National Ch'angguk Troupe did so more or less as a sideline, whether their main interest was in Western-style drama, opera, ballet, or traditional performing arts, and this had also been true of earlier influential figures like Yi Injik in the first generation of *ch'angguk* and Pak Chin in the second. But in Hŏ Kyu, the genre came as close as it ever did to having a distinguished director and dramatist who was a specialist in the genre, though he also remained active in other forms of drama and served from 1981 to 1989 as head of the National Theater.

In the program note for his first *ch'angguk* production, "Shim Ch'ŏng-jŏn" (reprinted in Hŏ Kyu 1991:305–9), Hŏ Kyu shows some degree of sympathy with the aims of the Ch'angguk chŏngnip wiwŏnhoe: for instance, he expresses the desire to use traditional *p'ansori* singing as far as possible, rather than the simpler, more easily intelligible *yŏn'guk sori* that had become standard in second-generation *ch'angguk*. He shows himself willing to go even further than the Wiwŏnhoe in using minimal stage scenery, an approach that would enable the production to follow the twists and turns of the original plot through some twenty scenes that could follow each other without pauses for moving scenery. But he also shows a more acute critical awareness than had hitherto been apparent in *ch'angguk* and a willingness to depart from tradition and experiment with conventions where dramatic expediency seems to dictate this. For instance, he comments on the difficulty of relying exclusively on existing *p'ansori* music where a mixed cast is used, in view of the difference in register between the male and female voices.[17] He also criticizes the story of "Shim Ch'ŏng-jŏn" itself, pointing out the disparity between its two halves, since the first is dominated by the noble sentiment of filial self-sacrifice and the second by lewd antics in which Blindman Shim appears stupid and lecherous. Hŏ's solution, however, would have pleased the Wiwŏnhoe: he found a more respectful portrayal of Blindman Shim in the version of "Shim Ch'ŏng-ga" recorded by nineteenth-century *p'ansori* patron Shin Chaehyo, which he therefore used as the main source in preparing his own libretto.

---

[17] This issue was still being discussed when I conducted my fieldwork in 1995–97.

Finally, Hŏ Kyu announced his intention to break with both sentimentalism and with the Western-style realism that had been introduced by another director of the 1970s, Yi Wŏn'gyŏng, by using deliberately stylized acting and lighting and radically simplified scenery with a projecting forestage that would bring the actors closer to the audience. This stylization and minimization of visual resources was closely associated with Hŏ Kyu's attempt to negotiate a new "contract" (*yaksok*) with the audience, which would be called the *madanghwa* of the *ch'anggŭk* stage, a return to the free-and-easy interaction of performers and audiences that is supposed to have characterized the *madang* or open-air performance space of the traditional village (Song Hyejin 1987:239). The assumption was that a more active audience would be a more imaginative one, willing to accept whatever codes of representation were shown to apply, without demanding a naturalistic depiction of the events they were supposed to be witnessing (or, ideally, participating in). This *madanghwa* would remain a consistent feature of Hŏ Kyu's style, often marked by direct audience address and even audience sing-alongs of familiar tunes. It led him to prefer the small hall of the National Theater to its better equipped but less intimate main hall (Hŏ Kyu, personal interview, February 16, 1996).

Hŏ Kyu's notion of the tradition to which *ch'anggŭk* should be faithful was not so much a repertoire of stories with fixed words and music as a particular kind of relationship between performer and audience, namely, that of the open *madang* in which *p'ansori* would traditionally have been performed. In pursuit of that relationship, he was prepared to go far beyond the existing resources of *p'ansori* in both repertoire and musical style, for he recognized that *ch'anggŭk* was a separate genre from *p'ansori* with aesthetic needs of its own. Thus, Hŏ Kyu went further than any previous *ch'anggŭk* director in the extensive use of Korean musical styles other than *p'ansori* where appropriate for particular scenes, a practice that remains standard today. Nevertheless, he shared the Wiwŏnhoe's broad philosophical goal of making *ch'anggŭk* more traditional, though he conceived this in terms of the spirit, rather than the letter, of the *p'ansori* tradition.

According to drama scholar Sŏ Yŏnho, however, in a review of Hŏ Kyu's later production "Karojigi" (another name for "Pyŏn Kangsoe t'aryŏng," or "Song of Pyŏn Kangsoe"), this *madanghwa* could be no more than partially successful because the theater itself was designed for a frame stage with a proscenium arch (review reprinted in Sŏ Yŏnho 1988:338–41), and Hŏ Kyu's attempts to break down the separation between performers and audience would be in constant conflict with the use of performance spaces (almost exclusively those of the National Theater) designed to ensure precisely that separation. Frustration with these performance spaces would lead Hŏ to write of the need for a specialized theater devoted to *ch'anggŭk* (1991:98), an idea that was also taken up in an M.A. thesis in interior design by Ku Hyesŏn (1988), who proposed a detailed plan for such a theater incorporating Hŏ Kyu's idea of the projecting apron stage. No such theater, however, seems likely to be built in the foreseeable future.

Phase 3: Kim Ilgu and the Revival of Ch'anggŭk's *Own Traditions*

Since Hŏ Kyu's retirement from regular involvement with *ch'anggŭk* in 1989, the National Ch'anggŭk Troupe has lacked a comparable figure to provide sustained and consistent leadership, and in the absence of a clear new direction the genre seems to have reverted to an unabashedly traditionesque approach, relying largely on the format of Western opera and musicals as a mold into which *p'ansori* material might be poured, though without compromising (as the second generation did) on the quality of the *p'ansori* singing itself. But one question that has emerged is whether *ch'anggŭk*, as it nears its centennial, might have traditions of its own that qualify it for a higher degree of recognition and respect than it has hitherto received in the world of traditional Korean performing arts, and the beginnings of this recognition constitute what I consider the third phase in the traditionalization of *ch'anggŭk*.

A hint of this recognition appeared at the beginning of the 1990s in a publication of the National Theater that declared the National Ch'anggŭk Troupe's intention to continue performing "traditional works based on the surviving *p'ansori* scripts" annually in rotation, alternating with new works, to "preserve the most orthodox works while giving the audiences an opportunity to see how the form is developing" (National Theater of Korea 1991:15; original in English). The twin functions of preservation and innovation were, however, defined in terms of repertoire rather than performance practices, and even in its productions of the *p'ansori* classics, the troupe continued to prepare new scripts and to bring in new directors with new ideas. Thus, the only tradition within *ch'anggŭk* that is thought to be worth preserving turns out to be (as before) that of performing dramatizations of the *p'ansori* stories with *p'ansori*-style singing, and there is as yet no recognition of any claims *ch'anggŭk* itself might make to having traditions different from those of *p'ansori*.

It was outside the National Ch'anggŭk Troupe that these claims were taken more seriously, chiefly at the National Center for Korean Traditional Performing Arts (NCKTPA). Soon after that body moved from its humble premises in the National Theater to its present facilities in the Seoul Arts Center (Yesul ŭi chŏngdan) in 1988,[18] the idea of its forming a resident *ch'anggŭk* troupe was mooted—an idea that may have been an outgrowth of the organization's fifteen-year residence at the National Theater, but one that could hardly be implemented without seeming unduly competitive as long as that residence continued. This idea was discussed in detail at a seminar hosted by the NCKTPA in October 1990. Eventually, the proposal was dropped for want of funds, but the discussion is worth examining for the possibilities it reveals of an alternative version of *ch'anggŭk* to that offered by the National Ch'anggŭk Troupe and for the light it sheds on the values associated with "tradition" that lie behind the debate.

The main presenter was musicologist Lee Bo-hyung (Yi Pohyŏng), who argued that a *ch'anggŭk* troupe at the NCKTPA would be worthwhile only if its approach to the genre was significantly different from that of the National Ch'anggŭk Troupe. Specifically, and in keeping with the brief of the NCKTPA, it should emphasize preservation rather than innovation, cultivate a traditional Korean quality in every aspect of the performance, and eschew the influence of overpowerful directors schooled only in Western-style drama.[19] Lee especially emphasized that *ch'anggŭk* needed a traditional quality (*chŏnt'ong sŏng*) rather than just a legitimate or orthodox quality (*chŏngt'ong sŏng*), which the productions of the National Ch'anggŭk Troupe already possessed in that they resembled the legitimate drama (*chŏngt'ong yŏn'gŭk*) of the West. To that end, he advocated a revival not merely of specific performance techniques, but of the whole composite art of the versatile singing troupes (*ch'angu chiptan*) that had

---

[18] It was, however, eight years before these sumptuous facilities were completed, and it is surely a reflection of the traditional arts' position in contemporary Korea that the NCKTPA buildings are at the far end of the Seoul Arts Center complex, beyond the opera house and other buildings devoted to Western arts; the latter were built first and are closer to public transport.

[19] Lee Bo-hyung would publicly express this view again in a later article (1997:68).

toured Korea performing a variety of traditional entertainments before *ch'anggŭk* was first developed (National Center for Korean Traditional Performing Arts 1990:27–32). Although Lee Bo-hyung, like the leaders of the National Ch'anggŭk Troupe, was advocating the creation of a new (and newly "traditional") form of *ch'anggŭk* rather than the revival of one that had existed in the past, the performers of the first *ch'anggŭk* productions undoubtedly included men with experience in these "singing troupes," so that in practical terms, Lee's recommendation would probably represent a return to something resembling first-generation *ch'anggŭk*. This was, so far as I am aware, the first time it had ever been suggested that *ch'anggŭk* already possessed, or had once possessed, a tradition of performance practices (other than those deriving from *p'ansori*) that was worth reviving and preserving.

Although the NCKTPA was unable to establish a permanent *ch'anggŭk* troupe, it did eventually present performances aiming to restore some of the earlier practices of *ch'anggŭk*. Two of these performances took place in the autumn of 1995, and though neither was a complete *ch'anggŭk* production, this incompleteness in itself carries an air of authenticity since *ch'anggŭk* of the first generation was rarely if ever performed complete. The first, a modest production performed as one item in a varied program of traditional music, was an excerpt from "Shim Ch'ŏng-ga," the scene in which Shim Ch'ŏng is reunited with her blind father and his eyes are miraculously opened. It was performed in the format known as *ipch'ech'ang* (concrete singing) or *punch'ang* (divided singing), in which existing *p'ansori* material was distributed among several singers who took the roles of characters and used a degree of dramatic projection comparable to that of a solo *p'ansori* singer, while there was no attempt at stage scenery or differentiation of costumes by character. In this case, the narrative material was assigned partly to a male *toch'ang* who stood at one side and partly to a small chorus of women who stood in a line in front of the rear curtain and behind the principals, Shim Ch'ŏng and her father.

The latter role was taken by Kim Ilgu, a senior *p'ansori* singer and teacher employed by the NCKTPA, who also directed the performance and taught his version of the *p'ansori* material to the other performers. The participation of so many female *p'ansori* singers, and the accompanying orchestra of seven instruments, would have been unlikely in first-generation *ch'anggŭk*, but the performance may have resembled those given by touring variety troupes of the second generation.

A more ambitious production was mounted the following month, again under Kim Ilgu's supervision, when a temporary troupe was assembled for a fully theatrical *ch'anggŭk* performance of the second half of "T'o-saengwŏn-kwa Pyŏljubu." By using only the second half of the story, from the point at which the rabbit and turtle descend together to the Underwater Palace, Kim was able to use his *p'ansori* text without much abridgement and even to interpolate some new material of his own, such as a scene in which the rabbit, caught in a trap set by some woodcutters, is visited by a swarm of flies (Kim Ilgu, unpublished libretto of NCKTPA production, "T'o-saengwŏn-kwa Pyŏljubu (hup'yŏn)," 1995:24–26). The story was, of course, well enough known to avoid any confusion arising from its incomplete presentation.

The National Ch'anggŭk Troupe had performed the same story in the main hall of the National Theater earlier the same year (production no. 86, March 1995), and the comparison with this production in the small hall of the NCKTPA makes for a sharp contrast. The former troupe had presented a visual spectacle with which the NCKTPA could not hope to compete, but in its relatively small scale and its symbolic rather than naturalistic scenery and costumes, it achieved an intimacy that represented a real alternative to the earlier grand opera–like treatment. The costumes of the animal characters in the NCKTPA production were mostly based on traditional Korean dress in colors appropriate to the animal and supplemented by only token identifying features such as the turtle's shell or the rabbit's ears and tail. There was no attempt at extravagant effects like the giant squid of the National Ch'anggŭk Troupe's production, nor at hiding the orchestra below the level of the stage: the ten accompanying musicians were divided into two fully visible groups, one at each side of the stage. No musical notation was used, the musicians relying instead on known melodies and on the extemporaneous accompanying technique known as *susŏng karak*.[20]

Certain aspects of the production would clearly belie any claim to represent an early form of *ch'anggŭk*: all the cast used wireless microphones, and only two of the cast were male. Nevertheless, the NCKTPA's *ch'anggŭk* productions have offered a form of the

---

[20] A more complete description of this production, with photographs, is included in Killick 1996.

genre with certain subtle differences evoking the *ch'angguk* of the past. One of these is the interpolated scene (*sabimmak*) of the flies in "T'o-saengwŏn-kwa Pyŏljubu," for while the addition of a certain amount of new material to the existing *p'ansori* texts is a normal part of a *ch'angguk* production, the interpolation of entire new episodes has been almost unknown at least since the foundation of the National Ch'angguk Troupe. That it was practiced in earlier times is evidenced by the insertion of the humorous episode "Ŏsa-wa ch'odong" (The royal inspector and the woodcutter) into the Ch'unhyang story during the colonial period, and Kim Ilgu would practice it again in his next production, "Ch'unhyang," prepared for the opening of the NCKTPA's new main hall in May 1997, in which the early scene between Yi Mongnyong and his servant at the Kwanghan Pavilion was fleshed out with a substantial new comic episode involving a second, drunken servant.

Kim Ilgu's productions have shown that at least some of Lee Bo-hyung's desiderata can be achieved—in particular, that *ch'angguk* can be successfully produced without reliance on directors trained in Western theater.[21] These productions have perhaps been too infrequent as yet to offer a serious alternative to the National Ch'angguk Troupe, but if such an alternative does emerge, it will probably be through the reconstruction and refinement of *ch'angguk*'s own earlier performance practices. If this is successful, *ch'angguk* may yet be "established" as a traditional performing art without unduly distorting its history.

Traditionesque Ch'angguk: *Kang Hanyŏng and the Abolition of the Narrator*

At the National Ch'angguk Troupe, on the other hand, the prevailing trend of the 1990s has been an implicit resignation to the traditionesque nature of the genre, in response to the inconclusive outcome of the earlier attempts to make *ch'angguk* more traditional through faithfulness to either the letter or the spirit of *p'ansori*. This was perhaps nowhere more clearly seen than in the policies of Kang Hanyŏng when he served as head of the troupe and writer of its libretti for the standard *p'ansori*-based works from

---

[21] *P'ansori* singer Cho Sanghyŏn has also amply demonstrated this point in his productions with the Kwangju shirip kukkŭktan (Kwangju Municipal Ch'angguk Troupe), which he founded in 1989. Since both Cho and Kim Ilgu are former members of the National Ch'angguk Troupe, however, it might be observed that they have at least a secondhand experience of the techniques of Western theater.

1991 to 1995. Kang Hanyŏng was a literary scholar specializing in *p'ansori* who had earlier edited Shin Chaehyo's *p'ansori* texts for publication, and his attitude toward *ch'anggŭk* had been not atypical of the *p'ansori* aficionado: "As the authentic *p'ansori* was transformed into a new theatrical *ch'anggŭk*, the singing of traditional *p'ansori* came to lose its importance. The rise of *ch'anggŭk*, therefore, was an error in the history of *p'ansori*" (Kang Hanyŏng 1977:38; translation from Um Hae-kyung 1992:52).

On my first meeting with Kang, he seemed almost equally disparaging about the genre for which he now held a paramount responsibility, comparing it to a dish popular in Korea's Chinese restaurants and known as *tchamppong*, a stew in which miscellaneous ingredients are thrown together with little apparent regard for the harmonization of flavors (Kang Hanyŏng, personal interview, August 17, 1995). Kang had, however, been a founding member of the Ch'anggŭk chŏngnip wiwŏnhoe and, in that capacity, had prepared the libretti for two successive productions of "Ch'unhyang-jŏn" in 1970 and 1971, the second revised in the light of public response to the first. These had been among the most literal-minded of the products of the Wiwŏnhoe's guidelines, retaining extensive passages of narration for their value as *p'ansori* material, regardless of their effect in a theatrical context. As head of the troupe, however, Kang performed a volte-face, and abolished the narrator altogether.[22]

The role of narrator was perhaps the nearest thing *ch'anggŭk* had to a venerable tradition of its own, with an indigenous origin and a precedent of some eighty years behind it, as well as a history of performance by some of the most senior and distinguished *p'ansori* singers of those years. Although the term *toch'ang* was introduced in the late 1960s by the Ch'anggŭk chŏngnip wiwŏnhoe when they brought the offstage narrative singers of second-generation *ch'anggŭk* back on stage, the early use of a narrator on stage is confirmed by the very first surviving description of a *ch'anggŭk* performance: "At the end of each scene a red-and-white curtain, running along a wire, was pulled across the stage from one side, and a member of the company would come before the footlights and hold forth to the audience, whom he was

---

[22] There had been previous productions in which the role of the *toch'ang* was greatly diminished, or even dispensed with altogether; but these had been newly composed works based on sources outside the *p'ansori* repertoire, while Kang extended the practice to *ch'anggŭk* adaptations of the traditional *p'ansori* stories too.

apparently informing what might be expected in the scene about to follow" (Austin 1910:197). But since *ch'angguk* itself was not recognized as traditional, its own traditions have been accorded no guarantee of preservation, and they have been readily sacrificed in the pursuit of either entertainment value or traditional elements derived from recognized "national treasures" such as *p'ansori*.

At a seminar held by the National Ch'angguk Troupe in July 1995, Kang Hanyŏng explained this decision as follows:

> On the whole, the rationale for the *toch'ang* lies in the falling of the curtain. Until now, each time the curtain descended, the spotlight would fall on the *toch'ang* standing by the microphone at one side of the stage.
>
> But certain foreigners studying musical drama advised me, "Why do you bring down the curtain and use the *toch'ang* like that in the middle of the drama? Doesn't it break or interrupt the mood that's been built up? Of course there has to be a rise and fall, but isn't it a mistake to cut [the action] by constantly stopping and starting?" And I thought the same.
>
> We had no option [but to use the *toch'ang*] in the past when our technology was less advanced. Before the state of stage scenery and scene changes reached their current level, we had to bring down the curtain and arrange the scenery behind it. We made the best of this by having someone who sang well act as *toch'ang*. I believe this was a good solution as long as there was a need for it, but this is no longer the case, and with the progress that has been made, whether it be in stage scenery, lighting, or sound effects, everything has been developed to the highest level, and the need no longer exists. (National Ch'angguk Troupe 1995:14)

In prioritizing the needs of a contemporary audience over the faithful preservation of material from the past, as indeed in accepting an influence from abroad, Kang Hanyŏng was relinquishing the long-cherished hope of making *ch'angguk* more traditional through the use of the *toch'ang*, and instead shifting the genre back in the direction of the traditionesque.

That shift has outlasted Kang Hanyŏng's tenure as head of the National Ch'angguk Troupe, for although the *toch'ang* has begun to appear again since his retirement,[23] it has come to be seen as

---

[23] Kang Hanyŏng was replaced as head of the National Ch'angguk Troupe by dancer and choreographer Chŏn Hwang, who served for two years from January 1996, until *p'ansori* singer An Suksŏn took over, to be replaced by Choi Jong Min (Ch'oe Chongmin) in 2000. Of the six productions given under Chŏn Hwang during the period of my research, two reinstated the narrator, while one was planned with a narrator who was later eliminated by the director. The Kwangju Municipal

one optional resource among many, on which directors may draw at their discretion. Thus, it remains difficult to identify in *ch'anggŭk* any sustained tradition that is not a direct borrowing from *p'ansori*.

Conclusion

One of the archetypes of postcolonial consciousness is represented by the protagonist of Salman Rushdie's novel *Midnight's Children,* Saleem Sinai, who is born at the very instant that India achieves independence and who clearly comes to symbolize the nation itself, but whose parentage turns out to be half Indian and half British, his father being the descendant and heir of a prominent East India Company colonist. But Saleem remarks, "My inheritance includes this gift, the gift of inventing new parents for myself whenever necessary" (Rushdie 1980:125).

In the same way, *ch'anggŭk*, like so many aspects of postcolonial Korean life, owes its parentage only half to indigenous Korean sources, and half to the colonial encounter and its lingering aftereffects. All three generations of *ch'anggŭk* have been affected by this encounter. The first generation would perhaps never have come into existence at all without the influence of Japanese new-school drama and Yi Injik's pro-Japanese political agenda. The second generation was affected both positively, by the creative input of Japanese-trained directors such as Pak Chin, and negatively, by the oppressive policies of the late colonial government, which included the stipulation that at least part of every public performance be in Japanese. The third generation, which arose after the colonial period, was perhaps less directly affected, though the foundation of the National Ch'anggŭk Troupe may have owed something to President Park Chung Hee's desire to erase the taint of his earlier collaboration with the Japanese. On a more general level, that troupe's self-conscious project of establishing a distinctive national tradition follows a widespread pattern of postcolonial cultural politics. And part of this colonial inheritance, as in Saleem Sinai's case, has been *ch'anggŭk*'s "gift of inventing new parents" in the form of an origin myth that denies the colonial parentage itself.[24]

Ch'anggŭk Troupe (Kwangju shirip kukkŭktan), since its formation in 1989, has continued to use a narrator regardless of Kang Hanyŏng's policy.

[24] In Rushdie's novel, Saleem Sinai is not raised by his biological parents but by an Indian couple who believe him to be their natural son and whose adoptive

Nevertheless, because of its theatrical format, so different from anything in the recognized "traditional" arts of Korea, *ch'anggŭk*'s mixed parentage is plainly visible in its features. While the Japanese part of that parentage tends to be played down in favor of the Western and (supposed) Chinese, the palpable foreignness of the genre has excluded it from recognition as a traditional art form on a par with Korea's intangible cultural properties. Eric Hobsbawm suggests that most "invented traditions" are in place within a few years (1983:1), but the sustained and systematic attempt to invent a tradition of Korean opera remains inconclusive after three decades, perhaps in large part because a persistent lack of respect for the genre's own history makes *ch'anggŭk*, at most, the traditional opera of a not immediately foreseeable future.

References

Austin, Herbert H. 1910. "A Scamper through Korea." In *Korea: Its History, Its People, and Its Commerce*, by Angus Hamilton, Herbert H. Austin, and Masatake Terauchi, 151–214. Boston and Tokyo: J. B. Millet.

Bishop, Isabella Bird. 1970. *Korea and Her Neighbours*. Seoul: Yonsei University Press. First published London: John Murray, 1898.

Bowers, Faubion. 1952. *Japanese Theater*. New York: Hill and Wang.

Chŏng Noshik. 1994. *Chosŏn ch'anggŭksa* [A history of Korean singing-drama]. Seoul: Tongmunsŏn. First published Seoul: Chosŏn ilbo ch'ulp'ansa, 1940.

Dilling, Margaret. 2001. "The Script, Sound, and Sense of the Seoul Olympic Ceremonies." In *Contemporary Directions: Korean Folk Music Engages the Twentieth Century and Beyond*, ed. Nathan Hesselink, 173–234. Berkeley: Institute of East Asian Studies, University of California.

Ernst, Earle. 1974. *The Kabuki Theater*. Honolulu: University of Hawai'i Press. First published Oxford: Oxford University Press, 1956.

Hŏ Kyu. 1991. *Minjok kŭk-kwa chŏnt'ong yesul: Yŏn'gŭk 30 nyŏn yŏnch'ul chagŏp* [Folk drama and traditional arts: Thirty years of directing]. Seoul: Munhak segyesa.

---

status he does not reveal until quite far into the story.

Hobsbawm, Eric, and Terence Ranger. 1983. *The Invention of Tradition.* Cambridge: Cambridge University Press.
Hong Sŏngdŏk. 1996. *Nae ttŭs-ŭn ch'ŏngsaniyo: Hong Sŏngdŏk chajŏn esei* [My heart is the green hills: Autobiographical essays by Hong Sŏngdŏk]. Seoul: Hanttŭt.
Kang Hanyŏng. 1977. *P'ansori.* Seoul: Sejong taewang kinyŏm saŏphoe.
Killick, Andrew P. 1996. "A Night at the Korean Opera." *Morning Calm* 20.6:38–44.
――――. 1997a. "Putting *P'ansori* on the Stage: A Re-study in Honor of Marshall R. Pihl." *Korea Journal* 37.1:108–30.
――――. 1997b. "The Secret of Korean Women's Opera." *Morning Calm* 21.7:32–38.
――――. 1998a. "The Invention of Traditional Korean Opera and the Problem of the Traditionesque: *Ch'anggŭk* and Its Relation to *P'ansori* Narratives." Ph.D. dissertation, University of Washington.
――――. 1998b. "The Chosŏn Sŏngak Yŏn'guhoe and the Advent of Mature *Ch'anggŭk* Opera." *Review of Korean Studies* 1:76–100.
――――. 2001. "*Ch'anggŭk* Opera and the Category of the 'Traditionesque.'" *Korean Studies* 25.1:51–71.
Kim Chaech'ŏl. 1933. *Chosŏn yŏn'gŭksa* [A history of Korean drama]. Seoul: Chosŏn munhakhoe.
Kim, Jong-cheol [Kim Chŏngch'ŏl]. 1997. "Some Views of the Evolution of *Ch'anggŭk*." *Korea Journal* 37.2:84–99.
Kim Pyŏngch'ŏl. 1997. "Han'guk yŏsŏng kukkŭksa yŏn'gu" [A study of the history of Korean women's drama]. M.A. thesis, Dongguk University.
Kim, Woo-ok [Kim Uok]. 1980. "P'ansori: An Indigenous Theater of Korea." Ph.D. dissertation, New York University.
Ko Sŏlbong. 1990. *Chŭngŏn yŏn'gŭksa* [Eyewitness history of drama], ed. Chang Wŏnjae. Seoul: Tosŏ ch'ulp'an chinyang.
Ku Hyesŏn. 1988. "Ch'anggŭk chŏnyong sogŭkchang shillae tijain-e kwanhan yŏn'gu" [A study of the interior design for a small theater devoted to *ch'anggŭk*]. M.A. thesis, Hongik University.
Lee, Bo-hyung [Yi Pohyŏng]. 1997. "From *P'ansori* to *Ch'anggŭk*." In *Korean Cultural Heritage.* Vol. 3: *Performing Arts*, ed. Joungwon Kim, 64–69. Seoul: Korea Foundation.
National Center for Korean Traditional Performing Arts [Kungnip kugagwŏn]. 1990. "P'ansori ŭi chinhŭng-kwa palchŏn" [The

promotion and development of *p'ansori*]. Unpublished papers presented at a seminar, October 19.

National Ch'anggŭk Troupe [Kungnip ch'anggŭktan]. 1995. "'Sugung-ga' mit 'Pak-ssi-jŏn'-e taehan haksul yŏnch'an" [Seminar on "Sugung-ga" and "Pak-ssi-jŏn"]. Unpublished papers presented and discussion recorded at a seminar, National Theater of Korea, July 15.

National Theater of Korea [Kungnip kŭkchang]. 1991. *The National Theater of Korea*. Seoul: National Theater of Korea.

Paek Hyesuk. 1992. "Han'guk kŭnhyŏndaesa ŭi ŭmakka yŏlchŏn V: Hyosan Kang T'aehong ŭi saengae-wa ŭmak" [Biographies of Korean musicians of the modern and contemporary periods, 5: The life and music of Kang T'aehong (stage name Hyosan)]. *Han'guk ŭmaksa hakpo* 8:75–93.

Paek Hyŏnmi. 1989. "Ch'anggŭk ŭi pyŏnmo kwajŏng-kwa kŭ sŏnggyŏk" [The nature of the transformation process of *ch'anggŭk*]. M.A. thesis, Ehwa Woman's University.

———. 1993. "Kungnip ch'anggŭktan kongyŏn-ŭl t'onghae pon ch'anggŭk kongyŏn taebon ŭi yangsang" [The development of *ch'anggŭk* libretti as seen through productions of the National Ch'anggŭk Troupe]. In *Han'guk kŭk yesul yŏn'gu* 7.3:171–95. T'aedong: Han'guk kŭk yesul hakhoep'yŏn.

———. 1995. "Wŏn'gaksa ŭi sŏllip kwajŏng-kwa yŏn'gŭksajŏk sŏnggyŏk" [The foundation process of the Wŏn'gaksa and its position in theater history]. *P'ansori yŏn'gu* 6:253–87.

———. 1996. "Ch'anggŭk ŭi yŏksajŏk chŏn'gae kwajŏng yŏn'gu" [A study of the historical development process of *ch'anggŭk*]. Ph.D. dissertation, Ewha Woman's University.

———. 1997. *Han'guk ch'anggŭksa yŏn'gu* [A study of the history of Korean *ch'anggŭk*]. Seoul: T'aehaksa.

Pak Hwang. 1976. *Ch'anggŭksa yŏn'gu* [A study of the history of *ch'anggŭk*]. Seoul: Paengnok ch'ulp'ansa.

Park-Miller, Chan Eung. 1995. "P'ansori Performed: From Strawmat to Proscenium and Back." Ph.D. dissertation, University of Hawai'i.

Pihl, Marshall R. 1991. "Putting *P'ansori* on the Stage." *Korea Journal* 31.1:110–19.

Robinson, Michael. 1988. *Cultural Nationalism in Colonial Korea, 1920–1925*. Seattle: University of Washington Press.

———. 1999. "Broadcasting, Cultural Hegemony, and Colonial Modernity in Korea, 1924–1945." In *Colonial Modernity in Korea*,

ed. Shin Gi-Wook (Shin Kiuk) and Michael Robinson, 52–69. Cambridge: Harvard University Press.
Rushdie, Salman. 1991. *Midnight's Children*. London: Penguin Books. First published London: Jonathan Cape, 1980.
Sŏ Hangsŏk. 1979. "Na-wa kungnip kŭkchang" [The National Theater and me]. *Kŭkchang yesul*, November.
Sŏ Yŏnho. 1988. "Ch'anggŭk ŭi palchŏn-kwa kwaje" [The development and tasks of *ch'anggŭk*]. In *Tongshidaejŏk salm-kwa yŏn'gŭk* [Contemporary life and drama], 81–86. Seoul: Yŏrumsa.
———. 1994. *Han'guk kŭndae hŭigoksa* [A history of modern Korean drama]. Seoul: Koryŏ University Press.
Song Bang-song [Song Pangsong]. 1984. *Han'guk ŭmak t'ongsa* [Complete history of Korean music]. Seoul: Irhogak.
Song Hyejin. 1987. "Ch'anggŭk, mirae Han'guk ŭmakkŭk-ŭrosŏ ŭi toyak-ŭl wihayŏ" [*Ch'anggŭk*: For a leap forward as Korea's musical drama of the future]. *Ŭmak tong'a*, February, 236–43.
Sŏng Kyŏngnin. 1980. "Hyŏndae ch'anggŭksa" [A history of modern *ch'anggŭk*]. In *Kungnip kŭkchang samshimnyŏn* [Thirty years of the National Theater], 335–66. Seoul: National Theater of Korea.
Sorensen, Clark. 1995. "Folk Religion and Political Commitment in South Korea in the 1980s." In *Render unto Caesar: The Religious Sphere in World Politics*, ed. Sabrina Petra Ramet and Donald W. Treadgold, 325–53. Washington, D.C.: American University Press.
———. 1999. "National Identity and the Constitution of the Category 'Peasant' in Colonial Korea." In *Colonial Modernity in Korea*, ed. Shin Gi-Wook (Shin Kiuk) and Michael Robinson, 288–310. Cambridge: Harvard University Press.
Um, Hae-kyung [Ŏm Hyegyŏng]. 1992. "Making P'ansori: Korean Musical Drama." Ph.D. dissertation, Queen's University, Belfast.
Yang, Jongsung [Yang Chongsŭng]. 1994. "Folklore and Cultural Politics in Korea: Intangible Cultural Properties and Living National Treasures." Ph.D. dissertation, Indiana University.
Yi Injik. 1995. *Ŭnsegye* [Silver world]. In *Shinsosŏl* [Early modern novels], ed. Kim Yunshik and Pak Wŏnsŏ, 255–344. Seoul: Tonga ch'ulp'ansa. First published Seoul: Tongmunsa, 1908.
Yi Sujŏng. 1993. "Ilche shidae ch'anggŭk hwaltong ŭi yŏn'gu" [A study of *ch'anggŭk* activity during the colonial period]. M.A. thesis, Chungang University.

Yi, Tu-hyŏn. 1983. "History of Korean Theater, 1908–1945." In *Korean Dance, Theater, and Cinema*, ed. the Korean National Commission for UNESCO, 134–44. Seoul: Si-sa-yong-o-sa.

Yu Minyŏng. 1980. "Han'guk kŭkchangsa" [A history of Korean theaters]. In *Kungnip kŭkchang samshimnyŏn* [Thirty years of the National Theater], 115–255. Seoul: National Theater of Korea.

———. 1995. "Chosŏn sŏngak yŏn'guhoe-wa pon'gyŏk ch'anggŭk undong" [The Chosŏn sŏngak yŏn'guhoe and the full-fledged *ch'anggŭk* movement]. *Kugagwŏn nonmunjip* 7:209–36.

THREE

On the Road with "Och'ae Chilgut": Stages in the Development of Korean Percussion Band Music and Dance

NATHAN HESSELINK

The idea that music is never "just music"—merely a sonic arrangement of events—has increasingly become acceptable on both sides of the musicological and ethnomusicological divide (DeNora 1995; Leppert and McClary 1987; Wolff 1987). So-called extramusical factors, such as space, dress, gender, historical period, and other symbolically encoded devices, very much determine the way (or ways) in which a particular piece or event is understood and appreciated. Music, or whatever term or related set of concepts an individual or group chooses to use in its stead, is a total activity, and its performance stands as a metaphor for ideal relationships. These relationships are not limited to human participants, but rather encompass mediations between the individual and society as well as humanity and the natural or supernatural world (Small 1998:13).

Ethnomusicologists in particular have focused on musical change as part of this overarching totality, examining the roles played by urbanization, Westernization, industrialization, and the related emergence of technology (Lysloff 1997; Keil 1984; Kartomi 1981; Nettl 1978). I have chosen in this chapter, however, to isolate one element common to all of these various approaches—the performance space—as the focal point for discussion that will follow. What better way to explore relationships than to document and analyze the *place* in which the participants meet and engage in musical activity? My focus is further narrowed by examining a single piece, "Och'ae chilgut" (literally, "five-stroke road ritual"), in all of its various guises as it travels to different stages—and here I mean both a literal stage (a space where it is performed) as well as a conceptual stage in terms of development by genre.

Concentrating our attention in such a manner simplifies the theoretical playing ground, at the same time revealing the flexibility of music as a sound system or gestural language. In the context of this chapter, a core rhythm or succession of rhythmic patterns will remain recognizable even as the context for the performance and its attendant set of relationships change.

An established set of questions (based largely on Small 1998:194–96) will provide the framework for discussing these various stages, which in turn will stimulate further related inquiry. These questions include the following broad categories:

- Location—Is the performance indoors or outdoors? Is it marked off in some way from other activities (such as by a building or special boundary)? Is the event predominantly urban or rural?
- Performers—How do they interact with each other (such as movement, placement, or eye or body contact)? Do they play with a score or by memory? Is the membership set? Who is the leader of the ensemble?
- Audience—Are they on the same level as performers (either physically or philosophically)? Is money exchanged for admission to the performance? Do they talk or move or remain silent or still during the performance? Is there any interaction before, during, or after the performance with each other or the performers?[1]

The order of my presentation is roughly chronological, tracing the arc of Korean percussion band music and dance as it traveled through the latter half of the twentieth century. Conclusions will be offered after a discussion of four individual cases.

Country Roads

I first saw Iri Nongak perform in Seoul during the summer of 1994. Its leader, Kim Hyŏngsun, had founded the group in the early 1960s in a place by the name of Iri, then a little village in the southwest province of North Chŏlla. While his group was and continues to be composed mainly of provincial players, they nonetheless have from their very modest beginnings set their sights on touring and national exposure. Years of hard work and

---

[1] Many of these parameters informed an earlier study of mine on traditional Japanese performance behavior in the late twentieth century (Hesselink 1994).

consistent lobbying in the capital Seoul have paid off; today Iri Nongak is designated Important Intangible Cultural Asset (*chungyo muhyŏng munhwajae*) No. 11 by the South Korean government, one of only five regional bands to receive such recognition.[2]

The group hails from a long tradition of percussion band music and dance, known in the Korean language as either *nongak* or *p'ungmul(gut)*.[3] Predominantly a rural phenomenon until only the past couple of decades, *nongak/p'ungmul* served at least within more traditional village society as musical accompaniment to religious, work, and entertainment activities. Many of the older contexts for intensive manual labor and shamanistic ritual events have disappeared, however, and Iri Nongak has over the past fifteen years or so abandoned these types of performances in favor of entertainment, gatherings known generically as *p'an kut* (*p'an*, communal meeting space in a village; *kut*, ritual or performance or both). The *p'an kut* traditionally came after a long day of communal labor or fund-raising and would last three or four hours into the middle of the night. The performance I saw that summer in 1994—and most since—was in contrast roughly an hour and a half in length, performed during the day, and divorced from any direct work or ritualistic context, trends that define almost all active *nongak/p'ungmul* bands today.

Iri Nongak's *p'an kut* consists of four movements (*madang*), each a self-contained unit made up of a set series of rhythmic patterns (*karak/changdan*) and ground formations (*chinbŏp*) that are performed without fail. The title of the opening movement, "Och'ae chilgut," refers both to the entire movement and to the rhythmic pattern that begins it (see appendix A). This pattern is found in various forms throughout the majority of band repertoires of the western counties of North and South Chŏlla provinces—the so-called right-side school or way (*Honam udo*)—yet the following opening phrase is played almost verbatim by all:

---

[2] These bands are (in order of recognition) Chinju Samch'ŏnp'o Nongak (1966), P'yŏngt'aek Nongak (1985), Iri Nongak (1985), Kangnŭng Nongak (1985), and Imshil P'ilbong Nongak (1988). See Hesselink 1998a:292–96, Munhwajae kwalliguk 1993:21–25 (in Korean), and Office of Cultural Properties 1990:328–29 (in English) for more detailed information regarding band specifics.

[3] Aware of the debate surrounding competing usage of percussion band terminology (e.g., Hesselink 1998b:59–60; Chu Kanghyŏn 1996; Kim Inu 1993:113; Howard 1990:28–33; Yang Chinsŏng 198?:11), I nonetheless choose to use both *nongak* and *p'ungmul* (*gut*) throughout this chapter for matters of convenience and familiarity.

I kaen I — I kaen I - ji I gen I kaen I - ji I gen I kaen I — I[4]
Instrumentation includes a small hand-held gong (*soe* or *kkwaenggwari*), a larger hand-held gong (*ching*), an hourglass-shaped drum (*changgo* or *changgu*), a barrel drum (*puk*), and a smaller hand-held drum (*sogo*), which is used more as a dance prop. Most semiprofessional to professional groups include a player of the double-reed instrument called the *hojŏk* (or *t'aep'yŏngso*), as well as a battery of actors (*chapsaek*) whose role today is largely one of stirring up audience enthusiasm and creating some lively commotion during the ongoing event.

A performance of the first movement of the *p'an kut* by Iri Nongak in 1996 will serve as the first stage for the present discussion (notated in Hesselink 1998b:365–84). Like the first outing of theirs that I saw back in 1994, this one took place at the Seoul Norimadang, an outdoor venue sponsored by the Seoul city government and the Ministry of Culture and Sports that features free live performances of Korean traditional music during the spring and summer months. While the Norimadang was constructed specifically as a performance space for music and dance, it is meant to resemble the (*nori*) *p'an*, or communal village meeting ground, which is generally a multipurpose location for various often unrelated functions (see Chŏng Pyŏngho 1988). Performances by Iri Nongak at home and throughout the countryside tend to coincide with significant lunar calendar holidays—determined by agricultural and religious cycles—yet their cultural asset status requires them to travel to Seoul for nearly half of their yearly season, generally regardless of other considerations.

Nearly forty or so musicians, dancers, actors, and flag bearers stand in close proximity to each other in a circular formation, with most members at any particular time looking inward (plate 1). The entire movement is danced—instruments or props are held in the hand or strapped to the body—and is played from memory, creating increased eye contact and a sense of intimacy. Ranking is recognized within individual instrument families, such as lead small-gong player (*sangsoe*), second small-gong player (*pusoe*), and so on, but group members on the whole retain a fair amount of autonomy. Although leadership is maintained by the first small-gong player, who signals beginnings and endings of rhythmic

---

[4] This figure, roughly equivalent in Western musical terms to 10/8, is written with Korean oral mnemonics (*kuŭm*): *kaen* and *gen* represent stronger strokes on the small gong; *ji*, weaker ones; horizontal dashes indicate silences or "rests."

Plate 1: A *nongak/p'ungmul* performance.

patterns and leads the group through the elaborate ground formations, that player does not monopolize the creative act; performers are allowed a certain amount of freedom in regard to the type and placement of footsteps as well as rhythmic variations. Membership in Iri Nongak is set and must be checked regularly with members of the Office of Cultural Assets, who approve or reject new recruits.

Rural or semirural performances by Iri Nongak are predominantly attended by community members made up of personal friends and relatives, creating a homey, tight-knit atmosphere. While productions in Seoul introduce anonymous elements into the audience makeup, a number of friends, family, and former students often make it to these urban performances, inducing a warm response by all present. The audience is seated at ground level or slightly above with no partitions or barriers between them and the ongoing performance. The vast majority of the band is either semi- or full-time employed in other professions with only a few leadership positions receiving pay, a situation that under normal conditions would create little division between professional and onlooker. In the case of Iri Nongak, however, their cultural asset status bestows on them a certain air of specialist. Admission is never charged, either in the countryside or in metropolitan centers, though outings at the Seoul Norimadang are subsidized by local and national governmental agencies. The audience move about as they please, some talking and even eating, events not usually noticeable in outdoor locales where sounds and attention tend to spread out and dissipate. Interaction occurs among the audience at all stages of the performance, with musicians and dancers being visible and accessible before the commencement of the day's event. At the end of the entire performance the audience even joins in by dancing or playing with band members in the performance space.

We can briefly characterize this first stage of percussion band music and dance by its overall closeness, and here I mean both physically—the intimate space between musicians, audience, and musicians and audience—as well as cyclically, for life cycles connect these performances (at least in the countryside) to larger agricultural and spiritual happenings. Related to this proximity is a high density of social relations, defined by the number of different people that you have relationships with who also have relationships with each other. These relations have been associated with a strong sense of solidarity and community, in contrast to the large metropolis with correspondingly low-density social relations (see Boissevain 1974 and Mitchell 1969).[5]

We can additionally think in terms of openness. Interaction before, during, and after the performance is not only allowed but encouraged through the lack of formal barriers, the placement of seats, and the accessibility of the performers. Audience members may talk, eat, move about, or even dance along as they wish, with little or no threat of negative repercussions from the musical participants or concert organizers. The performers, on the other hand, must abide by certain conventions, which include playing the rhythmic patterns and dancing the various ground formations in order; yet they may improvise both musically and choreographically (within prescribed limits), gestures that will similarly not elicit boos or entice observers to throw rotten foodstuffs. It has even been argued that certain events, such as the actor playing the village lady feigning defecation on the open ground (or similar type of lewd behavior), are allowed only in such a performance falling under the conditions stated above (Kim Sunam and Kim Misuk 1986:98–99).

Fo(u)rward Marching

In the late 1970s *nongak/p'ungmul* underwent a metamorphosis that changed the face of the tradition forever. In early 1978, under the leadership of drumming virtuosos Kim Duk Soo (Kim Tŏksu) and Kim Yongbae, a concert was held at the Space Theater in downtown Seoul featuring a new form of performance art.[6] The group was composed of four percussionists, one each on the core drums and gongs representative of a *nongak/p'ungmul* band, and the rhythmic patterns they used borrowed heavily from regional band repertoires as well as that from the now extinct itinerant troupes known as the *namsadang* (both founders claimed ties to each of these older traditions; Yi Kyuwŏn and Chŏng Pŏmt'ae 1997:567–70 and Howard 1991:540–41). The quartet called itself "SamulNori" (*samul*, the four core percussion instruments; *nori*, "to play"),[7] and the parallel development of this new ensemble

---

[5] Korean scholars have been and continue to be fascinated with village life and its effect on communal consciousness (Kim Hŭngju 1993; Kim Inu 1993; Kim Chaeŭn 1987; Yun T'aerim 1964).

[6] This event is well documented in both English and Korean (Kim Hŏnsŏn 1994:90; Ku Hee-seo 1994:24–25; Howard 1991:539).

[7] Romanization of this term is a headache for any researcher or translator, as

alongside rapid urbanization in South Korea during the 1970s was not lost on Kim Duk Soo, here speaking in retrospect:

> More recently I have seen the birth of something that perhaps can be best described as mass culture. Yet in the same way that the culture which arose from our agrarian lifestyle gave structure to that society, so too, does this newer, urban mass culture define our now almost exclusively urban society. This relationship has interesting ramifications for a person like myself engaged in "traditional" music, but very much living in the 20th century. (1992:7)

SamulNori soon established a canon of secular and religious pieces, each averaging ten to twenty minutes in length, which were either mimicked or copied directly by other such quartets in the years that followed as the term *samul nori* increasingly came to denote a genre. Of particular interest here, however, is the entertainment-based composition known by the alternate titles of "Honam karak" (Rhythmic patterns of Chŏlla province) or "Honam udo kut" (Chŏlla province "right-side" ritual or performance), direct references to the rhythmic patterns and style of playing characteristic of *nongak/p'ungmul* bands of the western counties of Chŏlla province (the area, interestingly enough, represented officially by Iri Nongak). The piece does not, however, pick and choose from the entire *p'an kut* performance as one might guess—remember that ninety minutes must be condensed to fifteen to twenty minutes—but rather faithfully reproduces the first movement "Och'ae chilgut" in nearly every musical detail (see appendix A). Certain asymmetries in the *nongak/p'ungmul* rhythmic patterns are regularized in the *samul nori* version, and overall tempos are taken at a faster clip, but anyone familiar with the older style has little problem instantly recognizing the newer variant form. The rhythmic pattern in the opening phrase of "Och'ae chilgut" is identical to that played by Iri Nongak:

| kaen | — | kaen | -ji | gen | kaen | -ji | gen | kaen | — |

A 1992 performance transcription by a *samul nori* team from the National Center for Korean Traditional Performing Arts (Kungnip kugagwŏn), a rival team started by Kim Yongbae of the original 1978 quartet,[8] will serve as a model from which to work (Ch'oe

---

scholars and the artists themselves are inconsistent in their usage. To maintain some semblance of order throughout this chapter, I have chosen the following spellings to aid the most likely befuddled reader: *samul nori* (general designation for the genre), Samulnori (title of a professional team), and SamulNori (romanization favored by Kim Duk Soo for his group only).

[8] A beautifully detailed account of Kim's life and work has recently been pub-

Pyŏngsam et al. 1992:168–204). This second stage in Korean percussion band music and dance is very much an urban phenomenon, at least among the more professionally established groups. Performances are generally indoors in concert halls or arenas and are held on dates or at times that have no particular seasonal or religious significance (which often means the weekend, in conformance with more urban cycles).[9] For this composition the performers are seated in close proximity in a semicircular formation angled toward each other, with the dance movement now being transferred from the legs to exaggerated motions by the head and upper body.[10] It is played by memory, and because transitions are signaled by the small-gong player who is also the leader, a fair amount of eye contact is required, creating a certain sense of intimacy (plate 2). Membership is set among professional *samul nori* groups.

In addition to changes that have occurred on the performance end of this piece are changes in the composition of and manner in which the audience listens and participates. Audience members are separated physically by a stage that situates them apart from the performers and on a different level. They are further removed philosophically as relative amateurs or connoisseurs, in contrast to the artists on stage who are seen as specialists, virtuosos, or even idols commanding rock-star levels of followers (this is particularly true of Kim Duk Soo). The more famous *samul nori* groups charge admission to their performances, and members are themselves frequently employed full-time in the music business. Audiences, on the whole, are more anonymous in makeup (not forgetting, of course, that friends and family members do come) and sit quietly and somewhat passively during the performance. They do not, as a rule, interact with each other or the musicians during the concert; and because of the intrinsic setup of the halls, contact with the musicians before or afterward must be specifically arranged.

The first and most important change that takes place in this new performance aesthetic is the introduction of the concert hall in a large, urban setting. Percussion band music and dance as a

---

lished (Kim Hŏnsŏn 1998).

[9] The effect of indoor venues and the larger issue of urban consumption in the realm of Korean folk performing arts has been documented and analyzed by one of Korea's leading musicologists (Hahn Man-young 1991:219–31).

[10] *Samul nori* is played in two ways, depending on the composition: *anjŭnban* (seated form) and *sŏnban* (standing form). The seated form is more commonly practiced at the amateur to semiprofessional level.

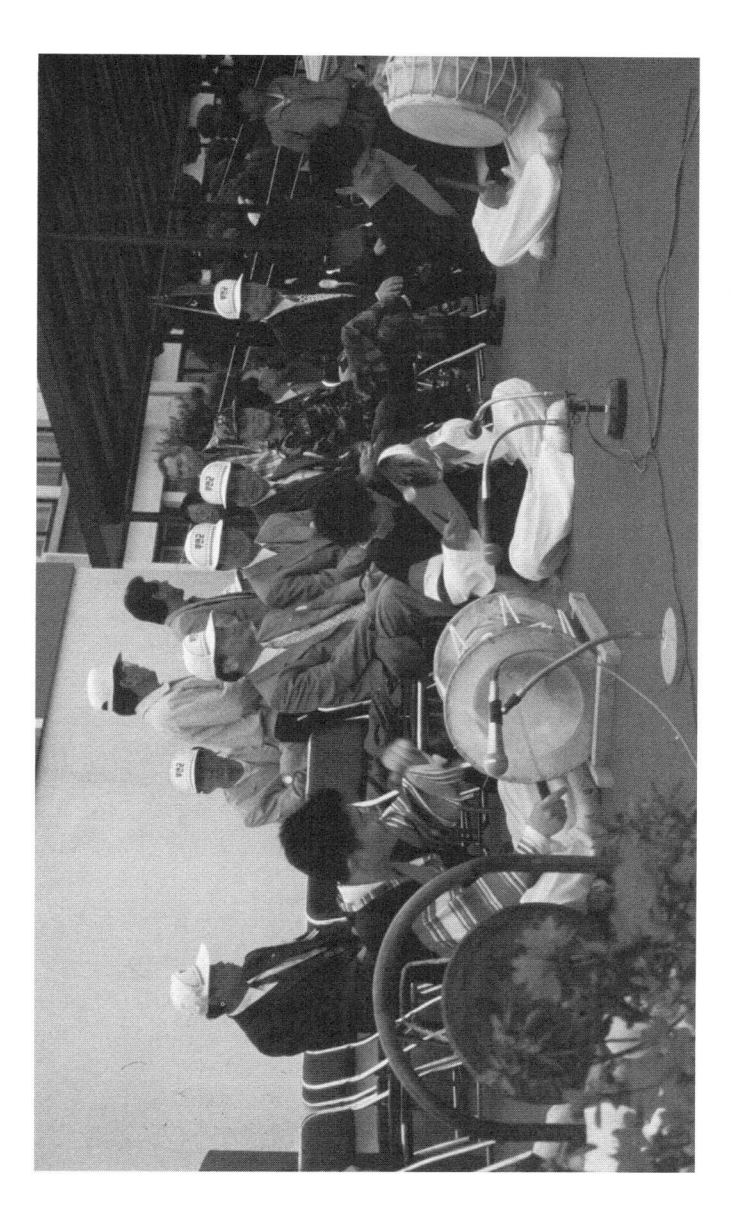

Plate 2: A *samul nori* performance.

multifaceted artistic act linked to specific village functions is now removed from its original social context(s). Dancing (or movement in general), eating, and socializing are no longer seen as beneficial or important to the total event. Performances are mostly clock-governed and are held at times that are both convenient to city dwellers and profitable to concert organizers, cycles following the flow of money rather than the flow of seasons (see especially Simmel 1950). Paid admission to a concert, not membership in any particular community group, determines the right to attend, so audiences become more and more strangers to each other. This impersonal atmosphere is further strengthened by the hall's layout and construction, which distance the performers while discouraging any communication among audience members.

Attending such a concert reinforces the notions that public music making must belong to the sphere of professionals, that music for most of us is for listening to rather than performing, and that it is appropriate and even desirable to have a formal and independent setting where people can come for the sole purpose of performing and listening to music (Small 1998:71). The structure of most auditoriums is built for one-way communication—stage to audience—with an indoor venue making for greater concentration of sounds as well as general attention. This setup alters the nature of the listening as well, promoting and valorizing distinctively Western concert-hall values "characterised by a seriousness and an indwelling in the work of art as an integral 'event-world'" (Witkin 1998:185–86). We often assume that composers or performers make technical and structural changes in musical traditions independent of outside influences, yet equal evidence suggests that when the needs and wants of the audience change, so too must the music (Copland 1952:107).

The "Right" Way

In the spring of 1996 when I was well into the second half of my fieldwork period, I encountered a third stage of the piece "Och'ae chilgut." I had driven with one of my principal mentors from the North Chŏlla provincial capital of Chŏnju—my home base for research—to the city of Kunsan to attend a *samul nori* concert by Kim Duk Soo and his group. The concert itself did not present anything I wasn't already familiar with, but a stand set up outside after the performance selling various SamulNori paraphernalia offered, among other things, a newly released, double-CD set with the enticing title of *Kim Duk Soo SamulNori: The Definitive Edition, Volumes I and II* (the original Korean title is *Kim Tŏksu samulnori: Kyŏlchŏng p'an, I & II* [King SYNCD-114, 1996]; plate 3). My mentor grabbed up a set on the spot, and we spent the drive back to Chŏnju listening to it, engaged in lively debate over the relative merits and drawbacks of the new purchase.

The CDs and program notes contained a number of interesting new developments as well as ambiguities. In addition to most of the core repertoire was added, for the first time, a composition made up of rhythmic patterns from the eastern counties of North and South Chŏlla provinces, the so-called left-side school or way (*Honam chwado*). The standard right-side piece based on the *nongak/p'ungmul* movement "Och'ae chilgut" was still present, but it had undergone a name change to "Honam udo p'ungmulgut karak" (*P'ungmul(gut)* rhythmic patterns of the right [western] counties of Chŏlla province). Did the inclusion of "p'ungmul(gut)" in the title now mean that the piece no longer belonged to the *samul nori* repertoire but was in fact the older tradition of percussion band music and dance? (Program notes did not separate this track as being based on or rooted in the Honam *p'ungmul* tradition, but rather sidestepped the issue completely; see appendix B.) A quartet still performed the piece, but noticeable and significant augmentations included a double-reed *hojŏk* player and condensed renditions of the middle two movements, sets of rhythmic patterns absent in every other recording or performance up to that time.[11] This blurring of lines must be ignored for the time being, as well as contemplation of the full meaning of the choice of the word "definitive" printed on the CD case.

A listening to this recording, however, reveals an essentially *samul nori* version of the "Och'ae chilgut" movement with the subsequent two movements of the *p'an kut* given only 7 minutes out of a total 21 minutes and 15 seconds (the "Och'ae chilgut" movement is listed in appendix A). The piece is performed by Samulnori Chŏnsoe, a quartet ostensibly from the right-side school, which is employed under Kim Duk Soo's umbrella SamulNori organization. The performers were in the same room and seated in

---

[11] Check, for example, the compact disks *Samullori* (Ensemble for four percussion instruments; Jigu JCDS-0050, 1986, track 1); *After ten years... SamulNori: Master Drummers/Dancers of Korea* (SKC SKCD-K-0236, 1988, track 3); and *Korean Folk Music* (Jigu JCDS-0077, 1989, track 1).

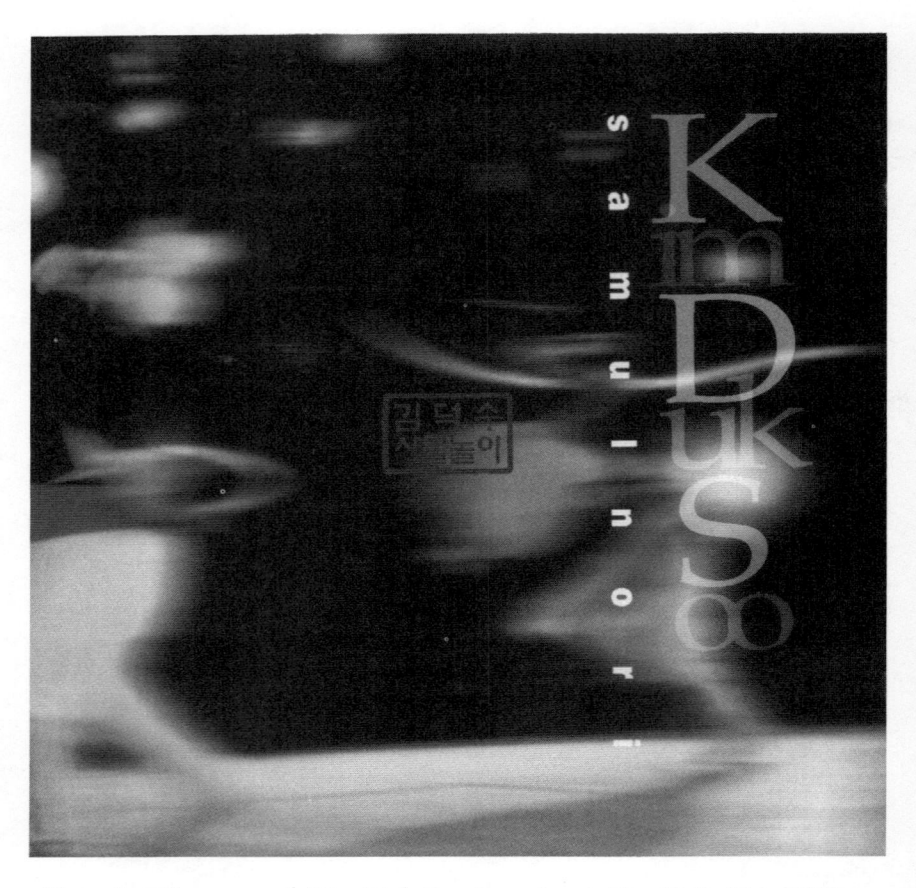

Plate 3: CD cover of *Kim Duk Soo Samulnori: The Definitive Edition, Volumes I and II*

typical *samul nori* style for the recording, but these particulars are rendered practically meaningless in terms of live audience reception as the work in this version exists only on CD (you cannot, to my knowledge, go and see a performance of it). The audience of this digitized presentation is obviously consumers, though the liner notes and packaging are almost exclusively in Korean, suggesting a local target group. Because of the narrow scope of the selections, we may also assume that most purchasers are themselves amateur *samul nori* players or enthusiasts and that they will view the performers on the CD as specialists, especially with the title "definitive edition." Money is paid for the right to listen, or at least for the opportunity of sharing it with others, yet we can only surmise where and under what conditions the CD is heard. There is no interaction with the performers whatsoever; individual musicians' names are not even listed in the liner notes.

CDs and other such forms of recorded, commodified art define distinctively (though not exclusively) urban forms of listening and reception. The piece is now freed from performing human agents, which means it can be heard at any time, in any place where there is a CD player, and in any manner. As its original social functions are forgotten or obscured, there is the trend toward "isolated, self-contained works intended as the objects of disinterested contemplation" (Small 1998:107). Physicality in the form of dance or visual motion is erased, signaling perhaps a change in values toward a more Western classical music aesthetic (McClary 1991:136), and as the recording disperses through predominantly urban spaces it heightens the sense of atomized and estranged masses, versus a more coherent and connected community (Witkin 1998:75). The composition is not, however, completely disconnected from its older performance contexts; its title and liner notes still hearken back to the *nongak/p'ungmul* repertoire, albeit in modified *samul nori* form.

The Road Ahead

In 1997 I returned to Korea to participate in the Seventh World SamulNori Competition, sponsored by Kim Duk Soo's organization. These events are always a great way to meet other foreign performers and enthusiasts, check out who is hot among the up-and-coming local talent, and observe what new trends and developments have resulted as an outgrowth of Kim Duk Soo's imagination. There seems to be an unspoken, almost karmic connection between the various *samul nori* groups that compete each year in regard to the piece chosen for presentation before the judges; in the sixth competition it was overwhelmingly "Yŏngnam karak," or the rhythmic patterns of Kyŏngsang province, and this particular year it was "Honam karak," the piece based on "Och'ae chilgut" that has been examined numerous times throughout this chapter. More important, however, was that a new CD had just been released.

The recording, titled *From the Earth, to the Sky: Kim Duk Soo Samulnori and Red Sun Group* (Samsung/ak SCO-123NAN, 1997; plate 4), was a collaborative effort with the West German

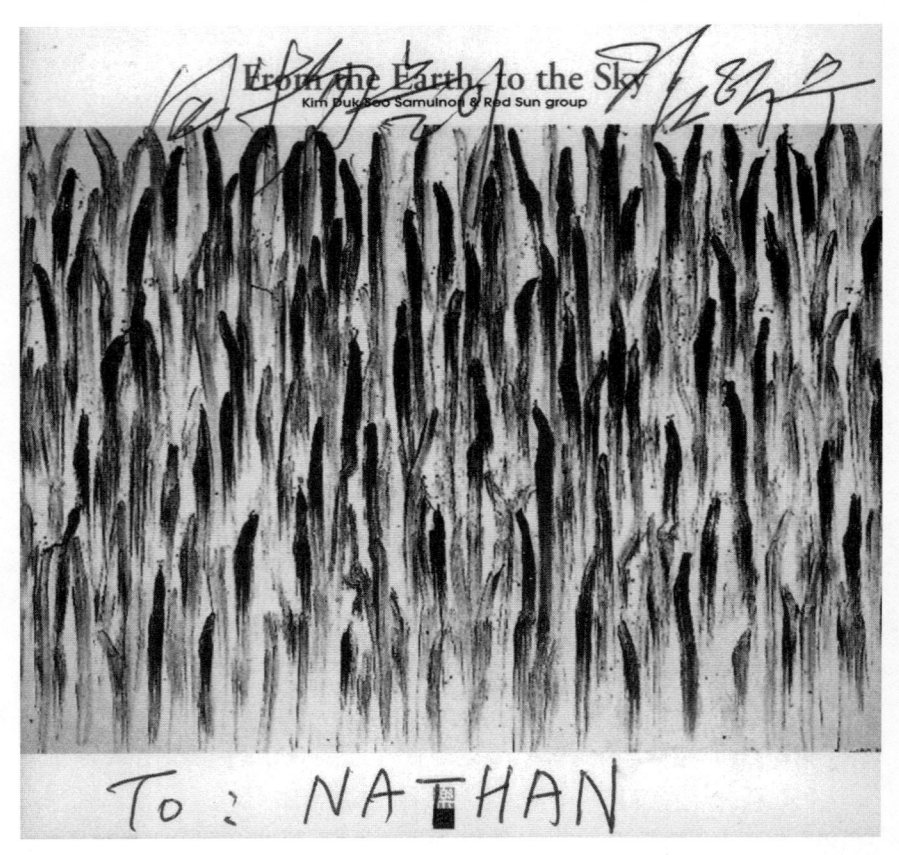

Plate 4: CD cover of *From the Earth, to the Sky: Kim Duk Soo Samulnori and Red Sun Group*

jazz/avant-garde ensemble Red Sun Group, the fourth of such joint projects dating back to 1989.[12] The goal of the collaboration, according to the liner notes written by the co-producer and composer Wolfgang Puschnig (also the leader of Red Sun Group), was to combine "Ying and Yang, East and West, Rhythm and Melody, [and] Harmony and Modality," with special attention paid to improvisations. The recording claims to have achieved a new unity, covering a "vast field of musical possibilities and expressions by giving and taking from each other." Complementing the

---

[12] The other three include in chronological order *Red Sun—SamulNori* (Polygram DZ 2433, 1989), *Then Comes the White Tiger* (ECM 1499, 1994), and *Nanjang—A New Horizon* (King KSC-4150A, 1995).

core Korean percussion quartet are an alto saxophone, electric guitar, bass guitar, and a number of supporting vocalists.

The titles of the various tracks are atmospheric (e.g., "Burdens of Life," "Going Places," "Another Step to the Sky"), and do not really suggest what type of compositions these might be. As I began listening to the CD upon my arrival back in the United States, however, I discovered to my delight that the second track, titled "The Road Ahead," was in fact melody and harmony layered over the first three rhythmic patterns of the "Och'ae chilgut" movement! It was cleverly disguised and took some radical reorientation on my part to hear these patterns with Western voices and instruments, but the overall impression now seems quite agreeable and does not, in my opinion, jar the listener with any awkward juxtapositions (refer to appendix A).

Most surface details of this recording parallel those of the previous collection discussed earlier. The musical work exists only in digital format as a commodity, so that its reception is very open-ended in terms of time, place, and the conditions under which it is heard. The audience is again consumers, yet with a broader and perhaps more international target group in mind as can be inferred from the CD's instrumentation and sound and from the fact that case and liner notes are in both Korean and English. Unlike the previous three manifestations of "Och'ae chilgut," however, this new context is nearly completely divorced from a traditional Korean folk percussion aesthetic. Most listeners, especially foreigners, will miss the *nongak/p'ungmul* connection altogether; more significantly, the rhythmic patterns have for the first time been reduced to the role of accompaniment. Is this the direction Korean percussion band music (no longer including "dance") will continue to take in the future? Kim Duk Soo may well be the only one qualified to respond.

Conclusion

By examining the various parameters of location, performer, and audience and their contributions to the construction of a performance space, I hope to have revealed the multifaceted nature of the larger activity we call music. The constant throughout this chapter was a fairly consistent, recognizably related succession of rhythmic patterns known as "Och'ae chilgut," yet as it traveled among the various stages of percussion band music and dance in the late twentieth century it came to mean very different things to an increasingly diverse set of musical participants. "Och'ae chilgut" began in the countryside as entertainment for villagers after a hard day of labor or for ritual fund-raising, and even as the older contexts began to disappear, contemporary groups continued to honor these events by holding performances on dates of particular agricultural or religious significance. As urbanization on a large scale took place in the 1970s, bringing with it a characteristic set of constraints on time, place, and appropriate behavior, so too did the context for this piece change toward more urban cycles and modes of presentation and reception. Commodification of the tradition was soon to follow, with variously packaged CDs creating new frameworks for listening and understanding both domestically and abroad.

Musical performance as a complex design formed by various angles and perspectives dictates a set of idealized relationships. As "Och'ae chilgut" made its journey from the village to the city and beyond, its nature rapidly transformed from one of closeness to one of distance. In social terms this change reflected the move from a tight-knit, communal society characterized by high-density relationships to a more scattered, largely anonymous global crowd made up of low-density relationships. This is obviously only one reading or interpretation of these trends, yet I believe these insights can contribute to the further understanding of other forms of predominantly abstract, performative art. What is certain is that as "music" continues both to shape and adapt to new social structures and technologies of the twenty-first century, so too will Korean percussion band music and dance and its practitioners, whoever they might be.

Appendix A: Comparison of Rhythmic Patterns by Stage

NAME OF GROUP	Iri Nongak	Kungnip Kugawŏn Samulnori	Samulnori Chŏnsoe	Kim Duk Soo SamulNori & Red Sun Group
MOVEMENT/ COMPOSITION	Och'ae chilgut	Honam udo kut	Honam udo p'ungmulgut karak	The road ahead
RHYTHMIC PATTERNS	och'ae chilgut ujilgut chwajilgut chilgut yangsando samch'ae maedoji	och'ae chilgut ujilgut chwajilgut p'ungnyugut (chilgut) kukkŏri yangsando samch'ae maedoji	och'ae chilgut ujilgut chwajilgut p'ungnyŏn'gut (chilgut) kukkŏri p'ungnyŏn'gut (chilgut) yangsando samch'ae maedoji	och'ae chilgut ujilgut chwajilgut

Titles have been regularized and rhythmic variations/transitions omitted to provide visual clarity at the deep structural level.

Appendix B: Compact Disc Program Notes

Kim Tŏksu samulnori (1996), track 2, "Honam udo p'ungmulgut karak" ["Right-side" *p'ungmulgut* rhythmic patterns of the Chŏlla provinces].

> Today the Honam region is divided into upper and lower and is called North Chŏlla province and South Chŏlla province, but in the past it was divided into left and right, or Honam "left side/way" and Honam "right side/way." In those days, however, "left" or "right" was not literally left or right, but rather referred to when residents of Seoul looked down toward Honam. The "right" or western region, then, included the areas of Kunsan, Puan, Chŏngŭp, Koch'ang, Naju, Muan, Mokp'o, and Haenam; the "left" or eastern region included Chŏnju, Imshil, Chinan, Namwŏn, Kurye, Sunch'ŏn, and Yŏsu. To these ancestors, the "left" had many mountainous regions, the "right" many plains, and these geographical characteristics were reflected in the features of the rhythmic patterns as well. Compared to the "right-side" patterns, "left-side" patterns were strong, fast, masculine, and possessed a coarse nature like unglazed earthenware; "right-side" patterns, in contrast, possessed a splendid yet reserved character. Musically speaking, in the "right-side" *p'ungmulgut* tradition there are many comparatively slow patterns, as well as many rhythmic variations, and the technique and method of tension and release can be considered [highly] developed. [translated from the Korean]

From the Earth, to the Sky (1997), track 2, "*Kil*—The Road Ahead."

> The road is always a metaphor for life. Though it is long, it is one we must travel. The rhythmic pattern used in this piece is rightly *kil kunak* [literally, "road military music"]. It is a characteristic military march of Korea. Red Sun, understanding this meaning exactly, performed a new road music of their own. [translated from the Korean]

References

Boissevain, Jeremy. 1974. *Friends of Friends: Networks, Manipulators and Coalitions.* London: Basil Blackwell.
Ch'oe Pyŏngsam, Ch'oe Hŏn, Yi Pohyŏng, and Kang Yewŏn. 1992. *Han'guk ŭmak che 27 chip: Samul nori (Anthology of Korean Traditional Music Volume 27: Samullori Percussion Ensemble).* Seoul: Kungnip kugagwŏn.
Chŏng Pyŏngho. 1988. "Norip'an ŭi kusŏng-kwa kinŭng" [The composition and functions of the *norip'an*]. In *Nori munhwa-wa ch'ukche* [Play culture and festivals], ed. Yi Sangil, 9–23. Seoul: Sŏnggyun kwandae hakkyo ch'ulp'anbu.
Chu, Kanghyŏn. 1996. "Categories and Classifications of National Culture." Lecture presented at the Korea Foundation, Seoul, April 16.
Copland, Aaron. 1952. *Music and Imagination.* Cambridge: Harvard University Press.
DeNora, Tia. 1995. *Beethoven and the Construction of Genius: Musical Politics in Vienna, 1792–1803.* Berkeley and Los Angeles: University of California Press.
Hahn, Man-young [Han Manyŏng]. 1991. *Kugak: Studies in Korean Traditional Music,* trans. and ed. Inok Paek and Keith Howard. Seoul: Tamgu Dang.
Hesselink, Nathan. 1994. "Kouta and Karaoke in Modern Japan: A Blurring of the Distinction between *Umgangsmusik* and *Darbietungsmusik.*" *British Journal of Ethnomusicology* 3:49–61.
———. 1998a. "Of Drums and Men in Chŏllabuk-do Province: Glimpses into the Making of a Human Cultural Asset." *Korea Journal* 38.3:292–326.
———. 1998b. "A Tale of Two Drummers: Percussion Band Music in North Chŏlla Province, Korea." Ph.D. thesis, University of London.
Howard, Keith D. 1990 [1989]. *Bands, Songs, and Shamanistic Rituals: Folk Music in Korean Society.* Seoul: Royal Asiatic Society, Korea Branch.
———. 1991. "Samul Nori: A Re-Interpretation of a Korean Folk Tradition for Urban and International Audiences." In *Tradition and Its Future in Music: Report of SIMS 1990 Osaka,* ed. Yoshijiko Tokumaru et al., 539–46. Osaka: Mita Press.
Kartomi, Margaret J. 1981. "The Process and Results of Musical Culture Contact: A Discussion of Terminology and Concepts." *Ethnomusicology* 25:227–50.

Keil, Charles. 1984. "Music Mediated and Live in Japan." *Ethnomusicology* 27.1:91–96.
Kim Chaeŭn. 1987. *Han'gugin ŭi ŭishik-kwa haengdong yangshik* [Consciousness and behavioral patterns of Koreans]. Seoul: Ihwa yŏja taehakkyo ch'ulp'anbu.
Kim Duk Soo [Kim Tŏksu]. 1992. "Author's Introduction." In *Korean Traditional Percussion: Samulnori Rhythm Workbook I, Basic Changgo*. Korean Conservatorium of Performing Arts, Samul-Nori Academy of Music (Kim Duk Soo [Kim Tŏksu], Lee Kwang Soo [Yi Kwangsu], Kang Min Seok [Kang Minsŏk]), 7–11. Seoul: Sam-Ho Music Publishing.
Kim Hŏnsŏn. 1994 [1991]. *P'ungmulgut-esŏ samulnori-kkaji* [From *p'ungmulgut* to *samul nori*]. Seoul: Kwiinsa.
―――. 1998. *Kim Yongbae ŭi salm-kwa yesul: Kŭ widaehan samul nori ŭi sŏsashi* [The life and art of Kim Yongbae: The epic of that grand *samul nori*]. Seoul: Pulbit.
Kim Hŭngju. 1993. "Nongmin ŭi kajok-kwa kongdongch'e saenghwal" [Family and communal life of the farmer]. In *Han'guk nongmin ŭi puran-kwa hŭimang: 1992 nyŏn Han'guk nongmin ŭishik chosa* [The anxieties and aspirations of the Korean farmer: An examination of the Korean farmer's consciousness in 1992], Kim Ilch'ŏl, Kim T'aehŏn, and Kim Hŭngju, 9–47. Seoul: Sŏul taehakkyo ch'ulp'anbu.
Kim Inu. 1993. "Pungmulgut-kwa kongdongch'ejŏk shinmyŏng" [*P'ungmulgut* and communal spirit]. In *Minjok-kwa kut: Minjok kut ŭi saeroun yŏllim-ŭl wihayŏ* [Folk and ritual: Toward a new understanding of folk ritual], 102–44. Seoul: Hangminsa.
Kim Sunam and Kim Misuk. 1986. *Homi ssishi: Han'gugin ŭi nori-wa cheŭi* [*Homi ssishi*: Play and ritual of the Korean people]. Seoul: P'yŏngminsa.
Ku Hee-seo [Ku Hŭisŏ]. 1994. "*SamulNori*: Taking Korean Rhythms to the World." *Koreana* 8.3:24–27.
Leppert, Richard, and Susan McClary, eds. 1987. *Music and Society: The Politics of Composition, Performance and Reception*. Cambridge: Cambridge University Press.
Lysloff, René, T. A. 1997. "Mozart in Mirrorshades: Ethnomusicology, Technology, and the Politics of Representation." *Ethnomusicology* 41.2:206–19.
McClary, Susan. 1991. *Feminine Endings: Music, Gender, and Sexuality*. Minneapolis and London: University of Minnesota Press.
Mitchell, J. Clyde, ed. 1969. *Social Networks in Urban Situations:*

Analyses of Personal Relationships in Central African Towns. Manchester: Manchester University Press.

Munhwajae kwalliguk [Office for Cultural Asset Management]. 1993. *Chungyo muhyŏng munhwajae hyŏnhwang* [The present condition of Important Intangible Cultural Assets]. Seoul: Munhwajae kwalliguk.

Nettl, Bruno, ed. 1978. *Eight Urban Musical Cultures: Tradition and Change*. Urbana: University of Illinois Press.

Office of Cultural Properties. 1990. *Cultural Properties of the Republic of Korea: An Inventory of State-Designated Cultural Properties*. Seoul: Office of Cultural Properties, Ministry of Culture.

Simmel, Georg. 1950. "The Metropolis and Mental Life." In *The Sociology of Georg Simmel*, ed. with an introduction by Kurt H. Wolff, 409–24. Glencoe, Ill.: Free Press.

Small, Christopher. 1998. *Musicking: The Meanings of Performing and Listening*. Hanover and London: Wesleyan University Press.

Witkin, Robert W. 1998. *Adorno on Music*. New York: Routledge.

Wolff, Janet. 1987. "Foreword: The Ideology of Autonomous Art." In *Music and Society: The Politics of Composition, Performance and Reception*, ed. Richard Leppert and Susan McClary, 1–12. Cambridge: Cambridge University Press.

Yang Chinsŏng. 198?. *Honam chwado: P'ilbong maŭl p'ungmulgut* [Chŏlla province left-side style: P'ungmulgut of P'ilbong village]. Namwŏn: Honam chwado p'ungmul p'an'gut palp'yohoe shilmut'im.

Yi Kyuwŏn and Chŏng Pŏmt'ae. 1997 [1995]. *Uri-ka chŏngmal araya hal uri chŏnt'ong yein paek saram* [One hundred of our traditional artists we should know]. Seoul: Hyŏnamsa.

Yun T'aerim. 1964. *Han'gugin ŭi sŏnggyŏk* [The character of Korean people]. Seoul: Hyŏndae kyoyuk ch'ongsŏ ch'ulp'ansa.

FOUR

Some Westernized Aspects in Korean Folk Songs

SHEEN DAE-CHEOL

Korea entered an age of rapid change under the influence of Western culture after the opening up of its borders to the outside world at the end of the nineteenth century. This change is still in progress and will continue to be so into the unforeseeable future of Korea as well. Western culture influenced all aspects of Korean society, more powerfully than any other culture had in such a short period since the beginning of its history. It may be fairly said that this influence would thoroughly change the frame of Korean culture. For this reason, it is very difficult these days to trace the phenomenon of traditional culture in modern Korea.

The realm of Korean music was not an exception to this change. A long time has passed since the musical environment of Korea shifted to Western music, music that today is understood by most Koreans as the basis of all music. Music education at every level, from elementary school to university, focuses mainly on Western music. It is not an exaggeration to say that Korean music withers daily for this reason. Today the musical master of Korea hails not from the homeland but from the West.

"Music" as a term is representative of all Western music in Korea. There is no need to use the adjective "Western," except for some special occasions, because most Koreans naturally understand "music" as Western music. These days we have to say *kugak* (short form of *Han'guk ŭmak*, or "Korean music") or "Korean traditional music" if we want to refer to Korean music, or most people will not understand. This is the extent of the influence of Western music in Korea.

It was inevitable under these circumstances that Korean music would change. An obvious example of this change is seen in the creative act of composition. In 1939, the native composer Kim

Kisu (1917–86) wrote "Hwanghwa mannyŏnjigok" (Ode to his majesty the emperor), a new piece of Korean music based on Western-style models. This piece led to the composition of many new works of Korean music, works written specifically for orchestra (including concertos), chamber ensemble, choir and orchestra, solo voice, and the various individual instruments. After the 1960s, many avant-garde pieces were composed. Today the music of *samul nori* (an urbanized "traditional" percussion genre) is played with a jazz ensemble or symphony orchestra, and many pieces of traditional music are often used as material for Korean popular music (Song Hyejin 1998:100–3; Howard 1996:246–49). In addition, the Seoul City Korean Music Orchestra—modeled on the Western symphony orchestra—was founded in 1965, after which many similar such groups including the Korean Music Orchestra of the Korean Broadcasting System (KBS) were established throughout Korea.

Korea in the past was greatly influenced by the music of China. Musical instruments, music theory books, and scores were imported from China until the early nineteenth century. These Chinese imports, however, influenced the music of the court only, and almost all were later "Koreanized" during the course of Korean music history (Sheen Dae-Cheol 1997:119–20; Chang Sahun 1975:51–52). Korea was under the influence of Japanese culture and music as well during the first half of this century as a result of Japanese imperialism. Korea had no choice but to accept the circumstances of that time, regardless of the people's will—but in the end, Japan's music made an impression only on Korean popular songs. That is to say, the influence these two countries had on the music of Korea cannot compare with that of the West.

The purpose of this study, then, is to examine the degree to which aspects of Western music have influenced the performance and perception of Korean folk songs, in an attempt to help improve our understanding of the present-day situation. While there is little doubt that these songs were influenced by Western music after its importation into Korea, no essay to my knowledge has specifically focused on this topic. Some Korean folk songs have been arranged by native composers and are sung by local singers to the accompaniment of a piano or an orchestra, like the *lied* and chorus of Western music. Many of these composers use Korean folk songs directly in their compositions; they write classical or popular music in a mixed Western and Korean style using this material as motifs and subjects. These new pieces are so popular that some Koreans even think of them as original Korean folk songs. Although these two examples could be interpreted as Westernized aspects in folk song, I don't deal with these styles of arranged or composed music because to me they represent the products of a Western-style creative act. This study examines only the Westernized aspects found in more "traditional" Korean folk songs.

The Origins of *Shin Minyo* and Its Incorporation into Korean Folk Songs

The end of the nineteenth century marks Korea's opening up to the world. Western culture made major inroads into Korea, and local folk songs soon began to change as a result of this encounter. The appearance of a new style of folk song was one of the most pronounced changes in Korean music. This new style was created artificially as a result of contact from the outside. The Korean people called this *shin minyo* (new-[style] folk song) to differentiate it from the older tradition of *minyo* (folk song).

Generally speaking, composers of folk songs are unknown regardless of the East/West dichotomy. In Korea, melodies and texts of folk songs have been changed continuously by many hands as they passed through the country's long history. All folk songs have naturally changeable properties, yet almost all composers and songwriters of *shin minyo* are known to people, and their compositions do not allow this degree of flexibility. Without adaptation, *shin minyo* would become fixed.

We do not know exactly when *shin minyo* first appeared. The titles "Shinje nongbuga" (New-style farmers' song), "Shinje ip'al ch'ŏngch'un'ga" (New-style song for the blooming of youth at sixteen years), and "Shinje sanyŏmbul" (New-style Buddhist song) appeared in Korean music circles in 1915 (Chŏng Chaeho 1984:31, 51, 85). According to this information, we are certain that these kinds of songs were already being sung around this time. "Shinshik yangsando" (New-style *yangsando*) and other new forms of songs were recorded on standard-play records (SPs) in the 1920s, but the term *shin minyo* was not yet used. These new styles of folk song appeared on stage full-scale in the 1930s (Yi Chinwŏn 1997:372–73), at the same time that the term *shin minyo* appeared (Pak Ch'anho 1992:229). This music was immediately called *shin minyo*, after which the terminology then circulated broadly.

After its initial appearance, *shin minyo* soon spread throughout the country by means of radio broadcasts and the phonograph. It became tremendously popular among the fashionable songs of the day, with almost 220 pieces of *shin minyo* being composed and recorded on SPs from 1927 to 1943 (Yi Chinwŏn 1997:380–88; Kim Chŏmdo 1995). The *shin minyo* of that period was that of Westernized Korean folk songs (more on this below), yet many Koreans today regard them as "original." Some *shin minyo* were even incorporated back into more traditional songs, meaning that some Westernized *shin minyo* were "Koreanized" again sometime after their genesis.

How, then, can the origins of *shin minyo* be explained? Various opinions exist. Some believe that *shin minyo* began under the influence of Japanese *shin minyo* of the same period (Pak Ch'anho 1992:229). The Japanese *shin minyo* movement in literature reached its peak in the 1920s, so it could, therefore, have certainly influenced Korea, which was then under Japanese rule. This movement, however, was literary in nature, not musical. There is also the view that *shin minyo* were written by some conscientious Korean composers to inspire patriotism in the hearts of the Korean people under Japanese imperialism (Ŏm Hajin 1992:23–29). But many *shin minyo* texts contained love stories, leading others to believe that they were composed and recorded not for patriotism but rather for business reasons (Yi Chinwŏn 1997:373).

The phonograph industry in Korea was very prosperous in the 1920s and 1930s. *Shin minyo* and popular songs that were transmitted through radio broadcasts and SPs became immensely popular among the general public at that time, firmly establishing their marketability. Composers and singers, then, had great interest in *shin minyo*, and this interest led to a number of new compositions and recordings. In light of these observations, we cannot deny the possibility of the business origins of *shin minyo*. The *shin minyo* movement in Japan, however, was realized under the influence of imported Western culture and capitalism, specifically radio broadcasting, phonographs, and the commercial means for the distribution of recordings. I believe, therefore, that Korean *shin minyo* should be interpreted as a product of imported Western culture as well, a view that seems to me to be more reasonable than the others provided. Besides, almost all *shin minyo* were written by composers who had studied Western-style compositional techniques in Japan (Yi Chinwŏn 1997:373), stylistic influences that appear in nearly every musical detail. This repertoire can, accordingly, be considered to be made up of Korean folk songs influenced by the West, albeit indirectly through Japan.

Korean notational systems and traditional methods of music making were seldom employed in *shin minyo*. Composers tended to use Western staff notation, and while at times they tried to express the flavor of Korean folk song through the use of more traditional modes and rhythms, the compositions were tuned to equal temperament and sung in a Western-style singing voice. Occasionally Korean folk songs were arranged for *shin minyo*, a technique obviously inspired by Western-style music making. *Shin minyo* were also sung to the accompaniment of Western instruments (Yi Chinwŏn 1997:375, 397), Korean instruments, or a mixture of the two. All these methods of music making are not of Korean origin but rather of a Western or Westernized style.

The popularity of *shin minyo* has since declined in South Korea, in contrast to North Korea, where it continues to thrive even today. Although *shin minyo* is considerably less popular now in South Korea than it was in the first half of the twentieth century, some *shin minyo*, both in the South and the North, have nevertheless secured a new position in Korean music. The general public has come to regard them as traditional Korean folk songs. Professional folksingers like to include these *shin minyo* as part of their repertoire, singing them in concerts of Korean folk songs.

In fact, the most famous Korean folk song, "Arirang," originated as a *shin minyo* during the opening decades of the twentieth century; this is the extent to which Western culture influenced the genre. The five songs below are perhaps the most well known of such origins.

"*Arirang*": This song is considered the most representative folk song of Korea. Each local area has its own unique version; some have said that there are more than thirty versions of "Arirang" throughout the peninsula (Yi Pohyŏng 1987:3). Although each region boasts of the special musical characteristics of its particular version, all variants share a common feature, namely, the text of the refrain. The most famous and representative "Arirang" is that of Kyŏnggi province, called "Ponjo [original] arirang" (figures 1 and 2), though the prefix *ponjo* is usually omitted.

Some Westernized Aspects in Korean Folk Songs 81

Figure 1: "Arirang"

Figure 2: "Arirang"

Because "Arirang" plays a central role in the uniting of the Korean people, it has received special affection, and many have put forth their best efforts to find out its true origin. Currently there are hundreds of theories (Pak Ch'anho 1992:15), though none is yet considered definitive.

As I stated previously, the "Arirang" of figures 1 and 2, which is now considered the most representative of all existing versions, originated as *shin minyo*. In 1926, this piece was used as background music in a movie of the same title directed by the famous movie director and actor Na Un'gyu (1902–37). Na composed this version of "Arirang" (Yi Pohyŏng 1987:4, 12), sung to the accompaniment of a Western orchestra. This version was then recorded on an SP label, and soon it spread throughout the country, causing many Koreans who were under the control of Japanese imperialism to weep. The true origin of our most famous and representative folk song has finally become known to the world. I cannot stress enough the extent to which this *shin minyo* version of "Arirang" has influenced more-traditional folk songs in Korea.

"Nodŭl kangbyŏn": This famous folk song of Kyŏnggi province was also a *shin minyo* (Yi Ch'angbae 1976:784). Composed in 1934, it refers to the beautiful riverside of the Han River in Noryang-jin, Seoul (figure 3).

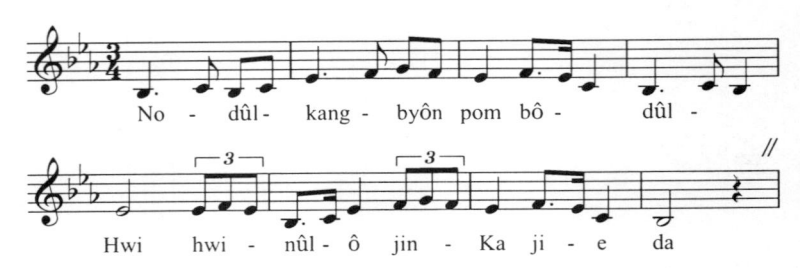

Figure 3: "Nodŭl kangbyŏn"

"T'aep'yŏngga": This piece was previously believed to have been composed after 1945 (Chang Sahun 1961:170), though now we are certain of its composition as a *shin minyo* in 1935 (Yi Chinwŏn 1997:395). It means "Song of great peace." It is also regarded as a folk song of Kyŏnggi province (figure 4).

Figure 4: "T'aep'yŏngga"

"Nilli riya": This song was composed in the 1920s (Chang Sahun 1961:119–20, 159–60) and is also regarded as a Kyŏnggi folk song (figure 5). "Nilli riya" represents a series of nonsense syllables that express a joyful mood.

Figure 5: "Nilli riya"

"Ulsan agassi": This piece has traditionally been considered a variation of "Miryang arirang" of Kyŏngsang province (Yi Ch'angbae 1976:865; Chang Sahun and Han Manyŏng 1975:235; Chang Sahun 1961:156). Its musical structure, however, differs from others of that region, and today we know that it too was composed as a *shin minyo* in the early 1930s (Ŏm Hajin 1992:213). The title means "young lady of Ulsan" (figure 6).

Figure 6: "Ulsan agassi"

It is interesting to note that most *shin minyo* are regarded as belonging to Kyŏnggi province. This provenance can be attributed to a couple of related factors. First, most composers of *shin minyo* resided in that area and naturally liked to borrow local musical material when composing, though the manner in which they composed was that of the West. Second, the three most important means of diffusion of *shin minyo* throughout the country—the phonograph industry, its distribution system, and the broadcasting industry—were all centralized in Seoul (which falls under the folk song area of Kyŏnggi). Composers of *shin minyo* became easily acquainted with the folk songs and professional folksingers of the Kyŏnggi area as a result.

Most Koreans think of these five pieces not as *shin minyo* but as traditional folk songs. A number of professional traditional folksingers view these five songs as belonging to Kyŏnggi or Kyŏngsang province as well.[1] So while *shin minyo* began as Westernized Korean music, either as arranged Korean folk songs or as pieces composed in a Western style under the influence of Western culture and music, some of its repertoire ended up being recognized as traditional folk song, a process that can be interpreted as a kind of acculturation (though some pieces of *shin minyo* have, interestingly enough, undergone a process of "re-Koreanization"). *Shin minyo* should, accordingly, be evaluated as music that played a very important role in the history of Korean folk songs.

Changes in the Accompaniment

Korean folk songs are generally sung to the accompaniment of a *changgo* (hourglass-shaped drum) and a small instrumental ensemble composed of a *taegŭm* (large transverse flute), *p'iri* (double-reed wind instrument), *kŏmun'go* (6-stringed plucked zither), *haegŭm* (2-stringed bowed fiddle), and *kayagŭm* (12-stringed plucked zither) in some combination. The instrumentalists do not play along in strict unison, but rather extemporize melodies using *shigimsae*, a particular Korean style of embellishments and figurations that creates the musically beautiful effect known as heterophony. This style of accompaniment displays the peculiar beauty of Korean folk songs. Although it is unknown exactly when this style began, it is (or was) recognized as the proper method of accompaniment by native musicians. Change began to occur, however, after the full-scale introduction of Western music.

At the height of its popularity, *shin minyo* (as well as more traditional folk songs) were sung to the accompaniment of Korean instruments, Western instruments, or a mixture of the two (Yi

---

[1] See, as examples, *Muk Kyewŏl Kyŏnggi sori '95* (Folk songs of Kyŏnggi '95, sung by Muk Kyewŏl; Oasis ORC-1498, 1995), *Im Chŏngnan Han'guk minyo* (Korean folk songs sung by Im Chŏngnan; Jigu JCDC-0426, 1994), *Chŏn Yŏnghŭi Han'guk minyo* (Korean folk songs sung by Chŏn Yŏnghŭi; Jigu JCDC-0496, 1994), and *Kugak taejŏnjip* (A comprehensive collection of Korean music; Oasis OSKC-1051 and 1052, 1994).

Chinwŏn 1997:375).[2] These last two styles were created under the influence of Western music in conjunction with the beginnings of *shin minyo* and are still in use today. One such example of their continued use is seen in Kim Yŏngim, one of the most famous and popular professional Korean folksingers in Korea at the present time. She sings to the accompaniment of Western instruments such as the guitar, violin, saxophone, and drums, as well as to a mixed ensemble of Korean and Western instruments. The musical accompaniments of her folk songs are, needless to say, arranged by a composer in a Western style. Examples of both styles are found on a CD recording made by Kim in the early 1990s.[3]

Sŏng Ch'angsun is one of the most famous virtuosos of *p'ansori* (long narrative song), for which she has been recognized as a human cultural asset (*in'gan munhwajae*) by the Korean government. Like most female singers of *p'ansori*, she includes folk songs as part of her overall repertoire (in addition to *p'ansori* she has recorded many Korean folk songs). In 1994, she released a CD of sixteen folk songs sung to the accompaniment of a small Korean ensemble made up of a *changgo, haegŭm, p'iri, taegŭm, kayagŭm,* and *ajaeng* (8-stringed bowed zither).[4] On the surface this seems traditional, yet the arranger for the recording, Kim Hŭijo (b. 1920), is a famous composer who studied Western-style composition. During the 1960s and 1970s, he directed the Seoul City Korean Music Orchestra (Seoul shirip kugak kwanhyŏn aktan), composing and arranging many pieces of Korean music. So while the instruments that were used in Sŏng Ch'angsun's recording are Korean, the pieces, folk songs that were arranged and orchestrated by a composer, can only be interpreted as an example of a Westernized aspect—here in the form of the compositional process— found in Korean folk songs.

The National Center for Korean Traditional Performing Arts (NCKTPA) and KBS jointly produced two CDs in 1998 for the purpose of education.[5] Twenty-seven short Korean folk songs were

---

[2] The compact disc *Kyŏngsŏdo myŏngch'ang Kim Nanhong* (Folk songs of Kyŏnggi, Hwanghae, and P'yŏngan provinces, sung by virtuoso Kim Nanhong; Seoul ŭmban SRCD-1108, 1993), remastered from SP sound recordings of the 1930s, includes all three styles of accompaniment.

[3] See *Kim Yŏngim Han'guk minyojip* (A collection of Korean folk songs sung by Kim Yŏngim; Jigu JCDS-0187 and 0188, 1991).

[4] See *In'gan munhwajae p'ansori myŏngch'ang Sŏng Ch'angsun Han'guk minyo moŭm* (Selected Korean folk songs sung by the *p'ansori* human cultural asset Sŏng Ch'angsun; Sŏngŭm DS0053, 1994).

[5] See *Aidŭl-kwa hamkke ttŏnanŭn hyangt'o minyo chŏn'guk yŏhaeng* (Korean folk

recorded on volume 1, thirty-two on volume 2. Five pieces on volume 1 and ten on volume 2, however, were sung and recorded to an arranged and orchestrated small Korean ensemble like that of Sŏng Ch'angsun. More interesting, though, is that twelve of the overall songs were work songs—eleven farming and one fishing. Traditional work songs of Korea were not originally sung to the accompaniment of an instrumental ensemble. Some of the work songs on these two CDs, however, were accompanied by the above ensemble, a further example of Westernized elements finding their way into Korean folk songs.

The NCKTPA is a national institute built to preserve, develop, and promote Korean traditional music. That this institute played a leading role in the production and dissemination of these CDs shows the degree to which Western influences have penetrated the traditional Korean music world.

Korean Folk Songs Sung in Western Chorus Style

Originally there was no polyphonic or harmonic music like that of the West in Korea. Even ensemble pieces were played in a monophonic or heterophonic style. The two CDs by the NCKTPA and KBS, however, contain some pieces that were sung in the manner of a Western-style chorus. One such example is the famous Korean folk song "Kanggangsulle," recorded on volume 1. It is composed of nine short pieces sung in call and response style—soloist call and response in unison. Many Korean folk songs are realized in this way, yet all the response sections of "Kanggangsulle" were sung in two-part chorus similar to Western music. The same was true of seven work songs in volume 2.[6]

A number of Korean folk songs have been arranged in Western four-part chorus with piano accompaniment. These arrangements are frequently sung by professional or amateur choirs, a trend to which the Korean general public has become accustomed; many pieces of Korean music have actually been composed or arranged in a Western chorus style. This trend can, therefore, be said to represent another Westernized aspect of Korean folk songs.

A similar example is seen in the playing of *sanjo*. *Sanjo* of Korea is a unique artistic genre of solo instrumental music that

---

song travels throughout the country with school children; NCKTPA and KBS SRCD-717, 1998).

[6] Ibid.

originated in *p'ansori* and shaman's music. Recent performance practice in *taegŭm* (large transverse flute) *sanjo*, however, reveals the occasional use of two-part ensemble playing at the fifth and the octave. Western canon style has also been introduced.[7]

The chorus style for folk songs is not the norm in South Korea. The situation in North Korea is quite different, though. Since the founding of the DPRK in the 1940s, folk songs in the North have often been sung by duets, trios, quartets, a male or female chorus, a mixed chorus, and so forth. The DPRK not only adopted Western equal temperament but the use of Western major and minor scales in all of its music, traditional or imported (Yi Ch'anggu 1990:2–4, 174). Many such examples are found in an anthology of North Korean folk songs published out of P'yŏngyang (Ŏm Hajin 1992:6–223).

Changes in Farming Songs

Korea was a nation of primary industries in the first half of the twentieth century, before transforming into a modern industrial one. Koreans in particular regarded agriculture as the most important of these industries; the saying "agriculture is the foundation of a nation" (*nongja ch'ŏnhaji taebon*) was, therefore, indisputable common sense. Until about the 1960s, farming songs could be heard in fields throughout the countryside, as most Korean farmers still tilled the soil by traditional methods. Because of changes in farming technology, however, farmers today scarcely sing these songs.

Farming songs (*nongyo*) were generally sung in conjunction with the tilling of the soil, the high points being spring planting and fall harvesting. There were many kinds of farming songs in Korea, each matching a particular season of the year. The function of these songs was to soothe the weariness caused by intensive labor and to improve the workers' efficiency. Entertainment played an important role as well.

With the discontinuation of traditional farming methods and the employment of modernized or Westernized agricultural techniques (including the use of machinery), the music has largely disappeared. The few farming songs that have survived exist only

---

[7] This was true of a concert commemorating the forty-fourth anniversary of the opening of the National High School of Korean Traditional Music on May 21, 1999, at the Yeaktang (Hall of Decorums and Music) of the NCKTPA.

in the memories of a few old farmers. As a result of the cultural policies of the central and local governments, most of these songs are no longer sung in the fields but on the stage. This means that the nature and performance context of these songs have, for the most part, changed. Happily, not all Korean farming songs are protected by such policies, though their rate of disappearance is disturbing.

Korean farming songs that have been preserved are sung on stage in a form similar to a vocal suite. That is to say, a number of songs are selected according to the needs of a public performance, generally regardless of any farming concerns, with the result that the original function of these songs no longer remains. Though examples of this process can be found everywhere in Korea, I will focus on the farming songs of Kangnŭng, a city on the central eastern coastal area of Korea in Kangwŏn province.

The repertoire of farming songs of Haksan village in Kangnŭng consists of thirteen pieces: (1) a song for plowing rice fields, (2) a song for pulling rice seedlings out for transplanting, (3) "Chajin arari" (a song for transplanting rice), (4) "Odokttegi," (5) "Kkŏgŭm odokttegi," (6) "Chapka," (7) "Sarirang" (pieces 4–7 are songs for weeding), (8) "Tamsŏngga" (a song for when farmers form a ring during weeding), (9) "Ssadae sori" (a song for when farmers form a ring at the end of weeding), (10) "Pullim" (a song for mowing the rice plant), (11) "Tŭngjim sori" (a song for carrying the mowed rice plant on the back), (12) "Madengi" (a song for threshing rice), and (13) "Yŏngsanhong" (a song that refers to a kind of azalea).[8] Originally, each song was sung according to its place in the overall work cycle, starting from the plowing of the fields to the harvest season in the fall. Changes in agricultural techniques resulting from Westernized technology have eliminated the traditional purpose of singing these songs—encouraging the farmers and soothing the pains of intensive labor—while cultural policies have altered the nature of their performance. As vocal suites, these songs became music for the stage, as well as festivals including Tano (May 5 according to the lunar calendar) and Taeborŭm (January 15 according to the lunar calendar). These days these songs are only sung occasionally by a few old farmers or schoolchildren for the purpose of preservation (Sheen Dae-Cheol 1999:4, 8).

---

[8] This last piece is not a farming song, but it is usually included with the other twelve as one set.

Thoughts and Attitudes about Korean Folk Songs

Music education in Korea—from primary school all the way through to university—has focused on Western music since nearly the time of its importation. In 1993, Korean traditional music (including folk songs) occupied only a small portion of textbooks on music: 12.58 percent at the primary school level, 11.5 percent at the middle school level, and 12.85 percent at the high school level (Council of Korean Music Education 1993:43). Though the contents of these various textbooks have steadily improved in quality and quantity, there is still room for improvement, especially when compared to the overall treatment of Western music. Moreover, inasmuch as most music teachers know very little about Korean music, even this small portion is not taught well. Because the teachers themselves didn't learn this music properly at college or university, they are unable to teach Korean music and folk songs to their students. As a result, the Korean population has not been given the chance to learn traditional music through their school education. With the exception of Korean traditional musicians and musicologists, most Koreans' thoughts and attitudes about their folk songs have changed to a Western perspective. Let us examine that changed perspective.

Pitch and Equal Temperament

Most Korean traditional musicians and professional folksingers look at Korean folk songs from a traditional point of view. In general, however, Koreans perceive the melodies, intervals, modes, and scales of these songs through Western equal temperament. Because they don't recognize Korean musical style, those who sing folk songs do so in a manner that is distinctively Western in tuning. Some are actually bothered by the traditional way of vocalizing, rejecting as a consequence not only Korean folk songs but Korean music in general. This trend has only increased.

Why do most Koreans either not recognize or outright reject the traditional style of singing Korean folk songs? I think that such attitudes stem from the way music is taught. Music education in Korea from the earliest stages is based on equal-tempered Western music. Most music teachers and professors at every level of school—excluding, of course, departments of Korean music in universities—teach Korean folk songs in the equal-tempered Western method. All Korean folk songs in music textbooks are notated in Western staff notation, and most are taught to the accompaniment of piano or organ. It does not help the cause that Korean folk songs make up only a small proportion of these textbooks: six among fifty-six at the third-grade level, seven among fifty at the fourth-grade level, six among forty-six at the fifth-grade level, and five among forty-seven at the sixth-grade level (Chang Ch'anghwan et al. 1999:4–64).[9] The situation in secondary schooling is nearly the same, with six among sixty-eight in one high school text (four of these are for Western-style chorus) and twelve among sixty-four in another being notated in Western notation and taught in equal temperament as well (Shin Kwibok and Kang Tŏgwŏn 1997:6–166; Cho Ch'angje 1995:6–174).[10]

Nevertheless, the overall situation in music textbooks has improved over the past five years, and I hope it will continue to do so. Primary and secondary school textbooks were revised after 1994, one of the most noticeable changes including the recommendation that Korean folk songs should occasionally be taught to the accompaniment of the *changgo*. While this teaching method will help students get out of the Western equal-temperament style of singing, there are still few music teachers at the primary and secondary school level who majored in Korean music. The teaching of Korean folk songs in the proper style would seem, therefore, to be impossible, at least for the time being. A radical change in perception will not occur if the situation does not improve.

In February 1993, the Council of Korean Music Education was inaugurated under the support of the Korean central government to strengthen the presence of Korean music in music education. Proposals were published by the council including "An Anthology of Standard Korean Folk Songs" for this purpose. Authors of music textbooks were to select Korean folk songs from this document and include them in their own publications. All twenty-two folk songs in this proposal, however, were notated not in traditional notation but in Western staff notation (Council of Korean Music Education 1996:41–68). It meant that Korean folk songs had not yet escaped equal temperament. This proposal, therefore, can be seen as a symbolic indication of the above-mentioned Westernized thought patterns in regard to traditional music. This is one of the greatest obstacles to overcome in the teaching of Korean folk song at the primary and secondary school levels. The

---

[9] All textbooks for elementary school in Korea are state-designated.
[10] All textbooks for secondary school in Korea are authorized.

finding of a prompt and wise solution bears heavily on the minds of Korean musicologists and musicians.

Changes in Meter and Singing Method

With the exception of work songs, most Korean folk songs are sung to the *changdan* (rhythmic patterns) of the *changgo*. The majority of these songs are composed in triple subdivision, so that the accompanying *changdan* too are in compound meter. Examples of these patterns include *semach'i, kukkŏri, chungmori,* and *chungjungmori,* which can be regarded respectively as 9/8, 12/8, 12/4 (12/8), and 12/8 in Western musical terms for convenience' sake. Use of Western time signatures are, in fact, recommended in the council's "Anthology," so while admittedly this can be seen as another borrowing from the West, it will at least contribute to a more Korean way of feeling if the folk songs are played and sung in these meters.

The famous folk song "Arirang" is sung to *semach'i changdan*, which, according to Western meter, should be notated in 9/8. Most Koreans, however, were taught to sing it in 3/4 before the publication of the council's proposal (see figure 1), and many still do. Other Korean folk songs in *semach'i* tend to be sung in 3/4 as well. These are not isolated examples—"P'ungnyŏn'ga" is a song in slow *chungmori* (12/8 or 12/4; figure 7), though it is usually sung in 3/4 (figure 8). Generally speaking, most Koreans sing folk songs in *chungmori* in 3/4, giving the feeling of a slow waltz. Because of the current nature of music education in Korea, singers follow the meter of Western music. If we sing Korean folk songs these ways, we will not feel their unique musical characteristics.

A more extreme example is the folk song "Saeya saeya," which should be notated in 5/4. Folk music in quintuple rhythm is not uncommon in Korea, yet most Koreans sing and play "Saeya saeya" in 3/4 (figure 9), or slow 6/4 and 12/4 (Yang Chaemu 1997:21; Chŏng Yŏngt'aek 1996:26; Cho Sŏngnae 1993:57)—because they were taught it this way in school. They have become unaccustomed to 5/4 measures. This piece has, consequently, changed into completely different music in terms of meter and rhythm.

As Koreans have become used to Western equal temperament and meter, they cannot help but sing their folk songs in a Western style. The influence of school music education has, however, spread even to the *manner* in which these songs are sung. Briefly stated, traditional vocal techniques are completely disregarded in

Figure 7: *chungmori*

Figure 8: "P'ungnyŏn'ga"

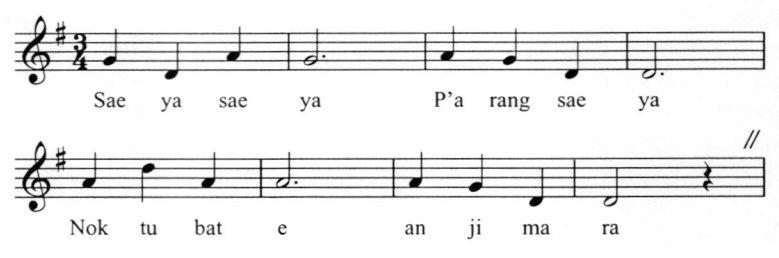

Figure 9: "Saeya saeya"

favor of Western classical ones, so that vocal lines tend to be realized more like soprano melodies in bel canto style. As a result, the Korean way of singing folk songs is becoming uncommon or even strange to Korean ears.

These thoughts and attitudes about Korean folk songs by the Korean people under the influence of Western culture and music can be considered internal changes. Internal changes are a major factor in the damaging or hindering of Korean folk song identity, a problem I see as much more serious to its future than external changes such as surface-level musical elements discussed above. Although external changes might be more easily overcome than internal ones, addressing the root of Koreans' Westernized perceptions of folk songs is more beneficial in the long run.

Conclusion

Shin minyo was one end result of the Westernization of Korean folk songs. The concept of "new" was already present in the 1910s and 1920s under the influence of Western culture and music imported indirectly through the phonograph industry and radio broadcasting. These new-style folk songs were very popular in Korea until the early 1940s, a phenomenon that can be traced to these new developments in technology. They were created as arranged or composed folk songs in a Western style, many borrowing their musical materials from Seoul and the surrounding Kyŏnggi province. Some *shin minyo*, however, that were created as Westernized folk songs, including "Arirang," were changed or Koreanized again and reincorporated into the body of traditional folk songs through a peculiar process of acculturation.

An additional Westernized aspect of the genre is the accompaniment of Korean folk songs by either Western instruments or a mixture of Western and traditional instruments, practices that have been in use since the genesis of *shin minyo*. Purely Korean ensembles arranged or orchestrated in a Western fashion can likewise be considered in the same way. The addition of Korean ensemble accompaniment to farming and fishing songs is yet another.

Chorus-style singing was not a part of Korean vocal music, particularly not of traditional folk songs. Folk songs released on CD by the National Center for Korean Traditional Performing Arts and the Korean Broadcasting System, in contrast, were sung in two-part chorus. With the adoption of modernized or Westernized agricultural technology, farming songs today are disappearing from "the field," the few remaining ones having been changed into a kind of vocal suite sung only by old farmers and school children on stages or during festivals for the purpose of preservation.

The thoughts and attitudes of the Korean people that come from the Westernized music education they received in school, however, have the most serious ramifications. Training rooted in Western equal temperament, rhythmic construct, and manner of singing has caused most Koreans to view the various musical elements of interval, melody, scale, mode, meter, and singing method from a distinctively Western point of view. These internal changes will hinder or damage the identity of Korean folk songs if not checked.

References

Chang Ch'anghwan et al. 1999. *Ŭmak 3–6* [Music 3–6]. Seoul: Ministry of Education.
Chang Sahun. 1961. *Kugak kaeyo* [An outline of Korean music]. Seoul: Chŏngyŏnsa.
———. 1975. "Pohŏja nonsokko 2" [A study of *Pohŏja* (2)]. In *Han'guk chŏnt'ong ŭmak ŭi yŏn'gu* [A study of Korean traditional music], 13–63. Seoul: Pojinjae.
Chang Sahun and Han Manyŏng. 1975. *Kugak kaeron* [An introduction to Korean music]. Seoul: Korean Musicological Society.
Cho Ch'angje. 1995. *Kodŭng hakkyo ŭmak 1* [Music for high school 1]. Seoul: T'aesŏng Publishing.
Cho Sŏngnae. 1993. *Tanso kyobon* [A manual for the *tanso*]. Vol. 1: *Kich'o p'yŏn* [For beginners]. Seoul: Hansori Publishing.
Chŏng Chaeho. 1984. *Han'guk chapka chŏnjip 2* [A complete collection of Korean *chapka*, volume 2]. Seoul: Kyemyŏng Publishing.
Chŏng Yŏngt'aek. 1996. *Chunghakkyo ŭmak 1* [Music for middle school 1]. Seoul: Chihaksa.
Council of Korean Music Education. 1993, 1996. *Ch'o, chung, kodŭng hakkyo kugak kyoyuk naeyong t'ongiran 1, 2* [Discussion on the contents of Korean music education for primary, middle, and high school 1 and 2]. Seoul: Council of Korean Music Education.
Howard, Keith. 1996. "The Development of Korean Traditional Music in the Twentieth Century and Prospects for the Future." In *A Hundred Years of Modernization in Korea: Towards the Twenty-first Century*, 229–52. Sŏngnam: Academy of Korean Studies.
Kim Chŏmdo. 1995. *Han'guk shin minyo taejŏn, sang* [A large collection of Korean *shin minyo*, volume 1]. Seoul: Samho Publishing.
Ŏm Hajin. 1992. *Chosŏn ŭi minyo* [Folk song of Korea]. P'yŏngyang: Yesul Kyoyuk Publishing.
Pak Ch'anho. 1992. *Han'guk kayosa* [A history of Korean song]. Seoul: Hyŏnamsa.
Sheen Dae-Cheol [Shin Taech'ŏl]. 1997. "Some Koreanized Aspects of Chinese Music in the History of Korean Music." *Journal of the Asian Music Research Institute* 19:97–121.
———. 1999. "The Musical Structures of the Farming Songs of Kangnŭng in Korea." Paper presented at the Fifth International

Conference of the Asia Pacific Society for Ethnomusicology, Fuzou, China, April 3.

Shin Kwibok and Kang Tŏgwŏn. 1997. *Kodŭng hakkyo ŭmak 1* [Music for high school 1]. Seoul: Hyŏndae Ŭmak Publishing.

Song Hyejin. 1998. "Sejongjo ŭmak munhwa-rŭl t'onghae pon hyŏndae kugak ŭi mirae" [The future of modern Korean music viewed through the musical culture during the reign of King Sejong]. In *Sejong shidae munwha ŭi hyŏndaejŏk ŭimi* [The contemporary meaning of culture during the reign of King Sejong], 97–109. Sŏngnam: Academy of Korean Studies.

Yang Chaemu. 1997. *Chunghakkyo ŭmak 1* [Music for middle school 1]. Seoul: Ŭmak ch'unch'usa.

Yi Ch'angbae. 1976. *Han'guk kach'ang taegye* [An outline of Korean vocal music]. Seoul: Hongin Publishing.

Yi Ch'anggu. 1990. *Chosŏn minyo ŭi choshik ch'egye* [The scale system of Korean folk songs]. P'yŏngyang: Yesul Kyoyuk Publishing.

Yi Chinwŏn. 1997. "Shin minyo yŏn'gu 1" [A study of newly composed folk song, 1]. *Han'guk ŭmbanhak* 7:367–419.

Yi Pohyŏng. 1987. "Arirang-e kwanhan ŭmakchŏk koch'al" [A musical study of *Arirang*]. *Minhak hoebo* 15:3–12.

FIVE

The Development of the Construction and Performance Techniques of the *Kayagŭm*

LEE CHAESUK

The *kayagŭm*, a musical instrument indigenous to Korea, has been with Koreans for the past two thousand years and has served as a tool to express their emotions. Characteristics of the *kayagŭm* are consistent with that of the long zither family in that its strings are stretched along the length of the soundboard, the pitch of each string is tuned by adjusting a goose-foot-shaped bridge, and it is played laid down on the floor by plucking with the fingers of the right hand. Although the *kayagŭm* has maintained all of these characteristics, its construction and its tuning system, as well as performance techniques, have changed significantly through various time periods, especially since the mid-twentieth century. Variations of the *kayagŭm* have been created, and new *kayagŭm* pieces composed and performed on them. The purpose of this chapter is to examine the origin of the *kayagŭm* and the changes in its construction, tuning system, and performance techniques over time.

The Origin of the *Kayagŭm*

A written record of the *kayagŭm* first appears in the *Samguk sagi* (History of the three kingdoms), specifically, in the twelfth and thirteenth years (551–52) of the chronicles of King Chinhŭng of the Shilla kingdom (57–676):

Translated by Kim Jin-Woo. Trans. note: Lee's chapter has been edited and translated into English with comments; the translator is grateful to Susie Lim for her time and efforts in copyediting the translation.

King Kashil of Kaya[1] made the *kayagŭm*, imitating a zither of the nation of T'ang. Kashil said: "Different nations have different languages. How, then, could their music be the same?" He ordered Urŭk, a musician, to compose twelve musical pieces for the *kayagŭm*. Afterward, while Kaya was in turmoil, Urŭk requested asylum in Shilla during the reign of King Chinhŭng. The king had him live in Kugwŏn and sent *taenama* Kyego and Pŏpchi and *taesa*[2] Mandŏk as Urŭk's disciples. (vol. [*kwŏn*] 32.8a2–b2)

However, historical and recent archaeological evidence shows that zithers similar to the *kŭm, sŭl*, and *ch'uk* of China existed in Korea long before the *kayagŭm*. According to the music volume of the *Sanguo zhi* (C.: History of the three kingdoms) written by the Chinese author Chen Shou (233–97), the Pyŏnjin kingdom[3] had "an instrument similar to the *ch'uk* played by plucking its strings. Musical pieces for the instrument also existed" (vol. 30.42b5).[4] The *Samguk sagi* also shows that the musician Mulgyeja played the *kŭm* and composed pieces for it during the reign of King Naehae (196–230) of the Shilla period. Paekkyŏl, a musician who lived during the reign of King Chabi (458–79), played the *kŭm* producing a rice-pounding sound and titled it "Tae-ak." Thus, the instrument *kŭm* that appears in the *Samguk sagi* seems to be the predecessor of the *kayagŭm* (Song Bangsong 1984:39–40; Chang Sahun 1976:37).

Vestiges of an antique wooden zither were discovered in Shinch'ang-dong, Kwangju city, and the Imdang housing development area of Kyŏngsan city in 1997 and 1998 respectively (plate 1). They are 77–79 centimeters long and 27–28 centimeters wide and are dated between 1 B.C.E. and 1 C.E. The vestiges are thought to be the prototype of the *kayagŭm* (*Chosŏn ilbo*, July 19, 1997, and

---

[1] Kaya was an ancient confederacy of tribal states in the southern part of the peninsula; the demise of Kŭmgwan Kaya occurred in 532 C.E., that of Tae Kaya in 562 C.E.

[2] *Taenama* is the official title for the tenth degree of the Shilla seventeen ranks; *taesa* refers to the twelfth degree.

[3] The term "Pyŏnjin" is a combination of the Pyŏn (?–42 C.E.) and Chin (?–57? C.E.) Kingdoms that existed in the southern part of the peninsula.

[4] Kaya was later established in the land of Pyŏnjin. Because instruments similar to the *ch'uk* were called *ko* in the indigenous Korean language (according to the old textbook the *Hunmongjahoe*) and the Chinese characters for the zithers *kŭm* and *chaeng* are pronounced as *koto* in Japanese, the term *kayago* (*kaya+ko/-go*) can be understood as a "stringed instrument of Kaya." The epistemology of the musical instrument the *kŏmun'go* (6-stringed half-tube zither) is also similar to the *kayago*.

Plate 1: The antique wooden zither discovered in Shinch'ang-dong, Kwangju city.

June 10, 1998). If this assumption proves to be correct, this zither with its essential and characteristic features can be said to have existed in the southern area of the peninsula approximately two thousand years ago.

After the *kayagŭm* was introduced to the Shilla kingdom upon Kaya's demise, it became popular as one of the *samhyŏn samjuk* (three stringed and three wind instruments), which included the *kŏmun'go, hyang pip'a* (5-stringed long-necked lute), *taegŭm* (large transverse flute), *chunggŭm* (medium transverse flute), and *sogŭm* (small transverse flute). The performance tradition of *samhyŏn samjuk* continued through the Koryŏ period (918–1392; *Samguk sagi,* vol. 32.5b6–9; *Koryŏsa* [History of Koryŏ] vol. 71.30b8, 31a2). The *kayagŭm* was also introduced to Japan at this early time. The *kŭm* (*koto*) that appears in ninth-century Japanese literature such as the *Nihon kōki* (Postscript of Japan) and the *Koji ruian* (Ancient garden) refers to the *shiragi koto* (the Japanese pronunciation for the *shillagŭm*) or the *kayagŭm* (see Song Bangsong 1984:83).

Traditional *Kayagŭm*

The P'ungnyu Kayagŭm

Two *shillagŭm* (*shiragi koto*) in almost perfect shape and known to be from the early ninth century are preserved at the Shōsōin repository in Japan.[5] These are the oldest extant *kayagŭm,* and they maintain the structure and size of the current *p'ungnyu* (literally, "elegant music") *kayagŭm* (also known as the *pŏpkŭm,* literally, "law zither"). The *p'ungnyu kayagŭm* has twelve twisted silk strings that stretch along the length of the body from the *hyŏnch'im* (literally, "the strings' pillow") on the performer's right side of the body, down to the *yangidu* to the performer's left side. The body of the *kayagŭm* is hollowed out from paulownia wood. The front of the soundboard is rounded; the back is flat (plate 2).

The *yangidu* in particular is one of the main characteristics that differentiates the *kayagŭm* from other types of zithers. The structure of the *yangidu* is clearly shown in a couple of *t'ou* (terra cotta figure) carvings. The first carving, dated sometime during the

---

[5] The two *kayagŭm* are named *kŭmbagap shillagŭm* and *kŭmni shillagŭm*. There are also a badly damaged *shillagŭm,* a *yangidu* (literally, "sheep's horn"; the head of the instrument), and a vestige of a *yangidu* at the repository (Hayashi Kenzō 1964:38–40).

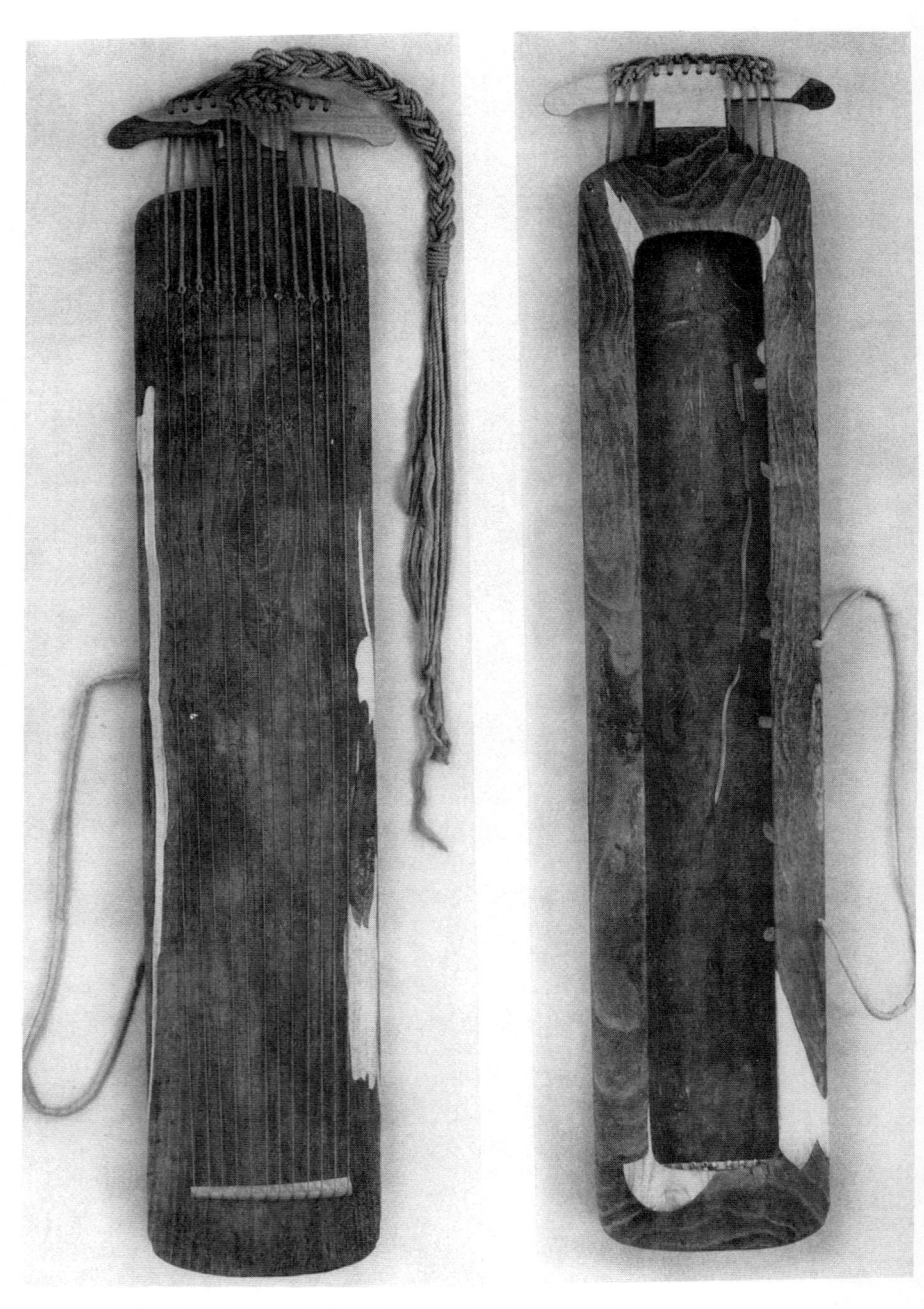

Plate 2: A *shillagŭm* at the Shōsōin repository in Japan.

reign of King Mich'u (261–84), shows a *t'ou* carrying the *kayago* (plate 3); the second *t'ou*, performing on the *kayago* (plate 4), was molded on a long-necked vase discovered in Hwangnam-dong, Kyŏngju city, in 1974 (currently owned by the National Museum of Korea; Howard 1994:6–7; Chang Sahun 1976:72). The structure of the contemporary *kayagŭm* is very much like that of the *kayago* of the *t'ou*, with the exception that on the *t'ou kayago*, a cord that can be hooked onto the side of the instrument is shown. This cord, however, is no longer seen in the illustrations of instruments in the *Chinch'an ŭigwe* (Court writings on Chinch'an banquets) of 1848 (Hayashi Kenzō 1984:136). Thus, one may say that the thousand-year gap between the ancient *kayago* and the contemporary *kayagŭm* explains the difference in what is otherwise the same instrument.

The prototype of the *kayagŭm* was transmitted down through to the Chosŏn period (1392–1910). In volume seven of the 1493 *Akhak kwebŏm* (Treatise on music), the structure of the *kayagŭm* is recorded in detail, including its precise measurements. What is different in this particular source is that the *yangidu* of the *kayagŭm* is curved outward like an ox's horns, rather than those of a sheep as is customary today. However, the basic shape of the *kayagŭm* is consistent with various treatises of different time periods, as well as with the contemporary *p'ungnyu kayagŭm* (Kim Ujin 1989:92; figures 1 and 2).

The Sanjo Kayagŭm

The design of the *sanjo kayagŭm*,[6] a smaller version of the *p'ungnyu kayagŭm*, facilitates the performance of rapid techniques necessary for *sanjo*. The body is both shorter and narrower than that of the *p'ungnyu kayagŭm*, and there is less distance between the strings. The soundboard, made of paulownia, is curved, and the back of the body, made of chestnut, is flat and rectangular in shape. In contrast, the entire body of the *p'ungnyu kayagŭm* is chiseled out from a paulownia log. There is no *yangidu* on the *sanjo kayagŭm*, and the twelve twisted silk strings stretch from the *hyŏnch'im* at the top end of the instrument along the length of the soundboard to the *pongmi* (literally, "phoenix's tail") at the lower

---

[6] *Sanjo* (literally, "scattered melodies") is a solo instrumental genre that originated in the southern region of the Korean peninsula. Kim Ch'angjo, a *kayagŭm* performer, supposedly first formed the structure of *sanjo*.

Plate 3: A *t'ou* carrying the *kayago*.

end. Inasmuch as Kim Ch'angjo (1865–1919) first formed the structure of *sanjo* in the late nineteenth century, the *sanjo kayagŭm* is assumed to have appeared around this period (see figure 3 for its tuning system).

Table 1 shows the different measurements of the various *kayagŭm*, such as those at the Shōsōin repository, the *kayagŭm* described in the *Akhak kwebŏm*, and the current *p'ungnyu* and *sanjo kayagŭm* (see Hwang Pyŏngju 1990:39–40 and Hayashi Kenzō 1964:39–40).[7]

---

[7] The measurements of the *kayagŭm* in the *Akhak kwebŏm* provided in table 1 are a result of converting one *ch'ŏk* (an older standard of measurement) to 31.2 cm (see

Plate 4: A *t'ou* performing on the *kayago*.

Contemporary *Kayagŭm*

As noted above, the *p'ungnyu kayagŭm* that has maintained its earlier structure is used in *chŏngak* (elegant music) pieces. The *sanjo kayagŭm*, on the other hand, is used in *sanjo*, in other folk music genres, and in newly composed pieces, often with a modified tuning system.

Since the 1960s, efforts to develop the structure, material, and acoustics of the *kayagŭm* have continued under the heading "the modification of Korean instruments."[8] These experiments were executed or supported by the Kungnip kugagwŏn (National Center for Korean Traditional Performing Arts, or NCKTPA), and exhibitions of the modified instruments were held a number of

---

Pak Hŭngsu 1980:190).

[8] I consider the frequently used term *kaeryang* (to be improved) to be inappropriate, as it can have derogatory connotations in relation to more traditional instruments. I will, as a result, use the words *pyŏn'gyŏng* or *kaejo* (to be modified).

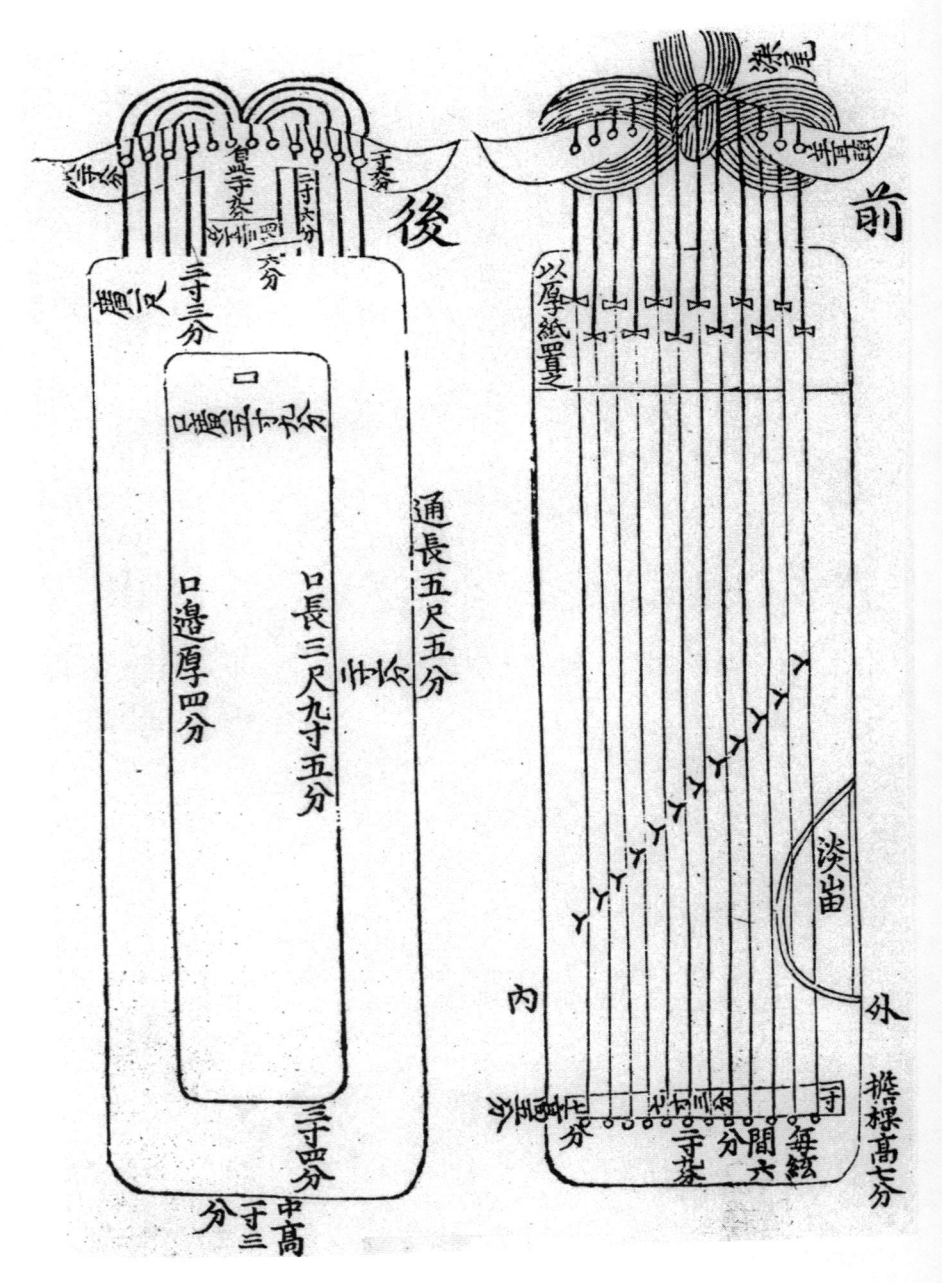

Figure 1: The *kayagŭm* in the *Akhak kwebŏm*.

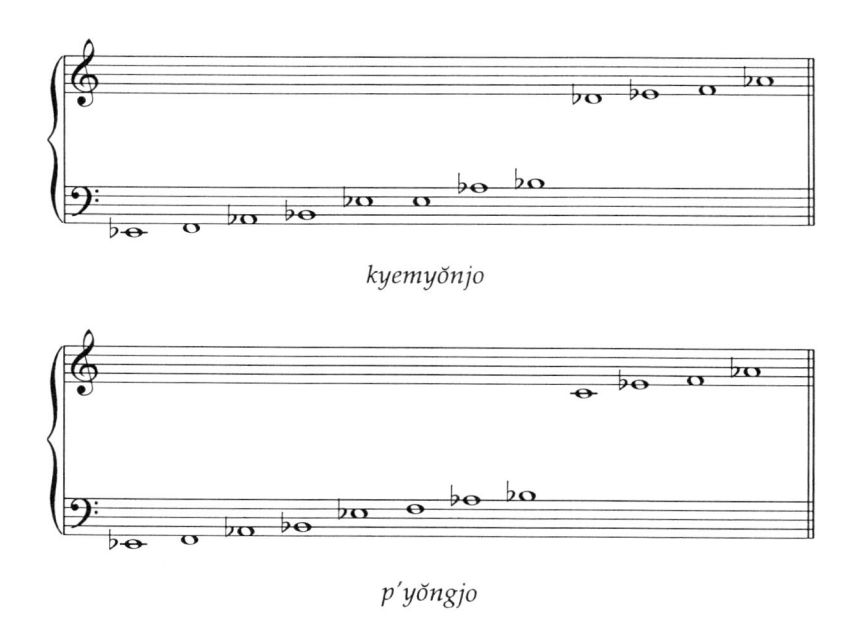

Construction and Performance Techniques of the *Kayagŭm* 105

kyemyŏnjo

p'yŏngjo

Figure 2: The tuning system of the *p'ungnyu kayagŭm*.

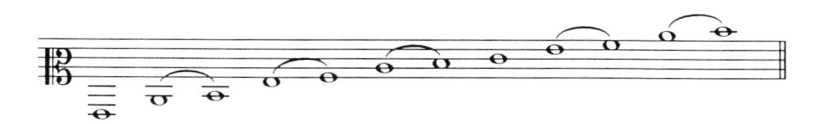

Figure 3: The tuning system of the *sanjo kayagŭm*.
The interval of ∩ is narrower than a major second and larger than a minor second.

times.[9] All of the thirteen *kayagŭm* that have been shown to this day have maintained the number of strings and the range of the *kayagŭm* (see plate 5 for examples of these modified instruments).

---

[9] For the processes and results of these projects carried out four times since 1964, refer to Kungnip kugagwŏn 1996 and Kugakki kaeryang wiwŏnhoe 1989.

Table 1. A Comparison of Various *Kayagŭm*

	Length (cm)	Width (cm)	Miscellany (cm)
Shōsōin I	158.1	30.9	length of *yangidu*: 37.7
Shōsōin II	153.3	30.5	length of *yangidu*: 37.3
Akhak kwebŏm	157.6	31.52	distance between strings: 1.8
Current *p'ungnyu kayagŭm*	166.7	28.5	distance between strings: 1.8
Current *sanjo kayagŭm*	145.4	20.6	distance between strings: 1.52

Since the focus of these experiments was on enhancing the volume, the material of the strings, the body, and the bridges was altered. In addition, pegs instead of *pudŭl* (cords for stretching the strings) were used for tuning, and an amplifying hole and semitone controlling device were employed.

In 1966 and 1969, Chang Sahun presented the processes and the results of the modification of the *kayagŭm* and other Korean instruments, such as the *kŏmun'go* and the *wŏlgŭm* (4-stringed lute; 1993). His experiments were also geared toward modifying the material of the strings, *hyŏnch'im*, resonator, bridges, and *tolgwae* (wooden peg for hooking the string) for acoustical purposes while maintaining the original structure of the *p'ungnyu kayagŭm*.

Although Chang's new models of the *kayagŭm* have not been distributed widely, the accumulated know-how and the basic ideas have greatly influenced the construction of other new *kayagŭm*, especially those with an increased number of strings. Today, there are metal-stringed *kayagŭm*; smaller *kayagŭm* for children; low-, middle-, and high-registered *kayagŭm*; and a variety of *kayagŭm* with more than twelve strings to enrich musical expressions in newly composed pieces.

The Metal-stringed Kayagŭm

The metal-stringed *kayagŭm* was created by Pak Sŏngok during the late 1960s and early 1970s for dance accompaniment.[10] Metal strings are used instead of twisted silk strings; the tuning system is maintained.

The 15-stringed Kayagŭm

Sŏng Kŭmyŏn created and used the 15-stringed *kayagŭm* in the 1960s. A string is added between the first and second, between the third and fourth, and after the twelfth string (the strings are numbered counting from the side facing the audience to the performer; see figure 4 for its tuning system). It is almost the same size as the *sanjo kayagŭm*. Because it has three more strings, it is feasible to modulate without changing the tuning system in the middle of the piece in folk songs, *p'ungnyu* (elegant music), and dance and music accompaniments. In addition, octave melodies are adopted more frequently. Chi Sunja, Sŏng Kŭmyŏn's daughter, says

---

[10] See Pak Pŏmhun 1994:152–57 for a brief introduction to *kayagŭm* invented before the 1980s.

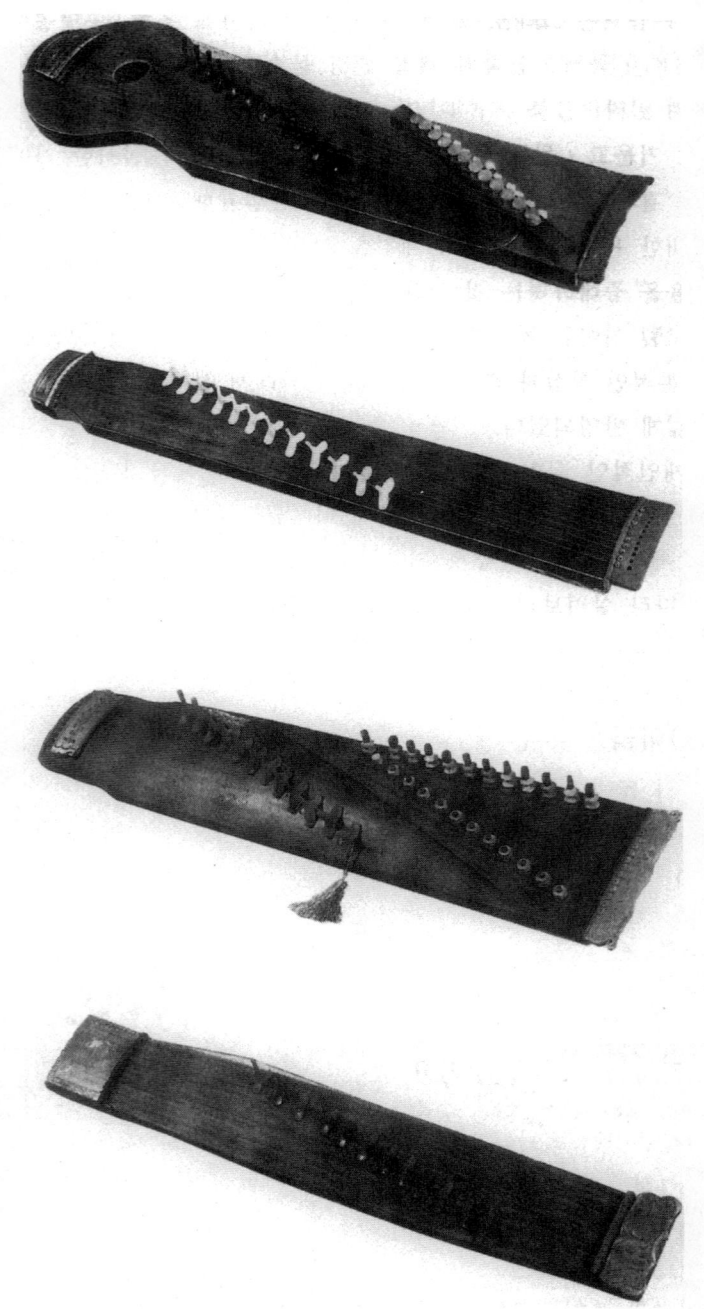

Plate 5: Examples of modified *kayagŭm*.

that Sŏng had also possessed a 13-stringed *kayagŭm* before the Korean War, a design popular in North Korea until the 1950s.[11]

In 1985, the composer Yi Sŏngch'ŏn commissioned a 21-stringed *kayagŭm* from the instrument maker Ko Hŭnggon. It was first used on October 23 the following year at the Munye Center in downtown Seoul. Compared to the *sanjo kayagŭm*, it has three more strings in the lower register and six more strings in the higher register (see figure 5 for its tuning system). Yi Sŏngch'ŏn has composed pieces such as "Matpoegi" (A taste), Solo Op. 32, "Pada" (The sea), Solo Op. 33, and "Duo" Op. 13 (a *sanjo* duet) for this *kayagŭm*. When it was first used, the strings were of twisted silk, the same as those of the *sanjo kayagŭm*. Later, however, the silk strings were replaced by polyester, the *pudŭl* and *yangidu* were eliminated, and pegs were adopted for tuning.

Low-, Middle-, and High-registered Kayagŭm

Low-, middle-, and high-registered *kayagŭm* were commissioned by Pak Pŏmhun for Ko Hŭnggon in 1987, and they were performed on the following year. The high-registered *kayagŭm* is both narrower and shorter (by a third) than the *sanjo kayagŭm*. The middle-registered *kayagŭm* is the same as the *sanjo kayagŭm*, and the low-registered *kayagŭm* can be substituted for the *p'ungnyu kayagŭm* (figure 6). There are ensemble pieces written for these three *kayagŭm* of different tuning systems, such as "Three Variations on 'Sangju moshimgi norae' [Sangju rice-planting song] for Three Kayagŭm," written by Paek Taeung, and "Mori [literally, "a rushing for or driving toward"] for Three Kayagŭm," written by Pak Pŏmhun.

The 18-stringed Kayagŭm

The 18-stringed *kayagŭm* was made by Ko Hŭnggon for Pak Ilhun in 1988, and was first performed on in October of 1989 at the Munye Center (see figure 7 for its tuning system). It has retained the material and the tone color of the *sanjo* and *p'ungnyu kayagŭm*. Pieces for this instrument include "Chulp'uri [String exorcism] No. 2" written by Yi Haeshik and "Kŭmbing" (Ice strings) by Pak Ilhun.

---

[11] Pak Hyŏngsŏp (1994:156) implies that the 13-stringed *kayagŭm* was frequently used: "Originally, the *kayagŭm* has been made by hollowing out a paulownia log using it as a soundboard. Twelve strings are hung along the length of the soundboard.... Later, the *kayagŭm* was developed into a 13-stringed *kayagŭm*."

Figure 4: The tuning system of the 15-stringed *kayagŭm*.

Figure 5: The tuning system of the 21-stringed *kayagŭm*.

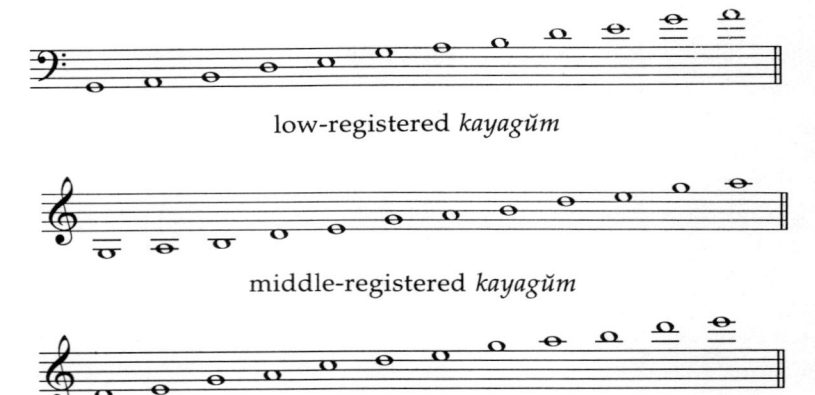

low-registered *kayagŭm*

middle-registered *kayagŭm*

high-registered *kayagŭm*

Figure 6: The tuning system of the low-, middle-, and high-registered *kayagŭm*.

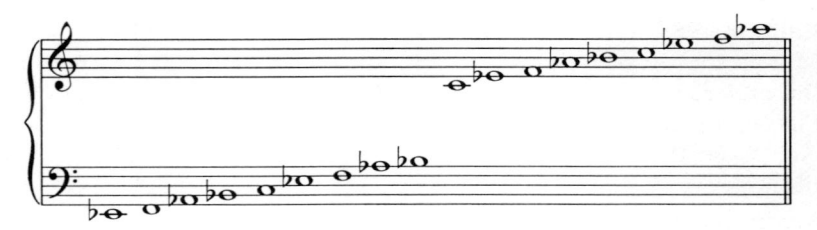

Figure 7: The tuning system of the 18-stringed *kayagŭm*.

The Children's Kayagŭm

The children's *kayagŭm* was made by Ko Hŭnggon for Yi Sŏngch'ŏn in 1989. The general shape imitates that of the *kŭmbagap shillagŭm* at the Shōsōin repository in Japan, and there are no coiled reserved strings. The tuning system is the same as that of the traditional *kayagŭm*, even though it is smaller.

The 17-stringed Kayagŭm

The 17-stringed *kayagŭm* was commissioned by Hwang Pyŏnggi for Pak Sŏnggi in 1986 and was first performed on in November 1991 at KBS (Korean Broadcasting System) Hall. Because its tuning system combines that of the *p'ungnyu* and the *sanjo kayagŭm*, the 17-stringed *kayagŭm* can be used in various genres including *chŏngak*, folk music, and newly composed music (figure 8). The strings are made of polyester, the *pudŭl* and the *yangidu* are eliminated, and tuning is achieved by controlling the pegs. Moreover, because of the material of the strings, it generates bright tones and longer resonance (see Hwang Pyŏngju 1990 for more detailed information).

The 22-stringed Kayagŭm

The 22-stringed *kayagŭm* was made by Ko Hŭnggon for Pak Pŏmhun and was performed on in the National Theater (Kungnip kŭkchang) in October 1995. Its volume was increased by enlarging the resonator of the traditional *kayagŭm* and by using synthetic strings. "Sae sanjo" (New *sanjo*) by Pak Pŏmhun is written for this *kayagŭm* (see figure 9 for its tuning system).

The Development of *Kayagŭm* Performance Techniques

The *kayagŭm* is traditionally performed by pushing, plucking, and flicking the string with the right hand and vibrating, pushing, and pulling the string with the left hand. These simple performance techniques have varied in recent years. I will now give an account of the development of performance techniques, distinguishing those that are traditional from those that are modern.

Traditional Kayagŭm *Performance Techniques*

The performance techniques of the *chŏngak kayagŭm* (also known as the *p'ungnyu kayagŭm*) have developed since the Chosŏn period (1392–1910). This development is traced through various

Figure 8: The tuning system of the 17-stringed *kayagŭm*.

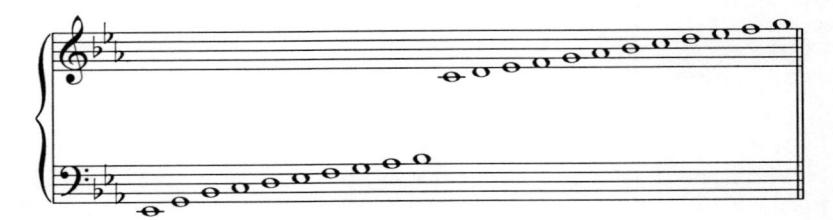

Figure 9: The tuning system of the 22-stringed *kayagŭm*.

notated sources, such as the *Cholchangmallok*, the oldest *kayagŭm* notation (1796), the *Kungnip kugagwŏnbo* (Notation of the National Center for Korean Traditional Performing Arts) of 1913, the *Pangsanhanssi kŭmbo* (String notation by Han of Pangsan) of 1916, and a *chŏngak* notation transcribed in the 1930s. The tuning system and performance techniques of *sanjo* are different from those of *chŏngak*. These differences can be summarized as follows (see Lee Chaesuk 1984 for a more complete discussion).

The *chŏngak kayagŭm*

- Tuning system: Pentatonic scale with a range of two octaves and a fourth.
- Right hand technique: Mostly pushing and flicking.
- Left hand technique: Mostly light and gentle vibrato. The tone is pulled down for a melodic descent of a major second and bent when rapidly repeating the note *imjong* in the *kyemyŏn* mode and the notes *namryŏ* and *kosŏn* in the *p'yŏng* mode.[12] A tone is pushed for a quick melodic ascent of a perfect fourth.

The *sanjo kayagŭm*

- Tuning system: Pentatonic scale with a range of two octaves and a fifth.
- Right hand technique: Mostly pushing, plucking, and flicking with the thumb, index, and middle fingers. Many double flick-

---

[12] If the central pitch (*hwangjong*) is E^b (in either mode), then *imjong* represents roughly the pitch B^b, *namryŏ* the pitch C, and *kosŏn* the pitch G.

ings are used, and there are more performance techniques to perform rapid passages than there are for *chŏngak.*
- Left hand technique: Even in the same piece, vibrato varies according to the different modes. The same note in a different mode has a distinct function, which should be expressed well through different kinds of vibrations. The function of the after-tone is important as well, and the technique of pushing the string is irregular and varied compared to that of *chŏngak.*

Contemporary Kayagŭm *Performance Techniques*

Kayagŭm performance techniques have been expanded to accommodate the use of various scales, harmonies, and rapid movements of newly composed pieces that began to appear in the 1960s. In traditional *kayagŭm* performance practice, the performer's right hand and left hand have different functions: the former plays the melody and the latter produces vibrato. New techniques, however, appeared, often making full use of the structure of the *kayagŭm*. Examples include using the right hand to produce harmonics, and con sordino as well as harmonies. The left hand can mold the tones created by vibrato or pushed notes and can produce chance notes by stroking the strings on the performer's left-hand side of the bridges. Furthermore, the left hand has begun to be used on the performer's right-hand side of the bridges to play a melodic line, to play harmony, or to accompany the main line. The expression of *kayagŭm* music is thereby expanded and the tone color of the instrument is enriched by the development of various performance techniques. The performance techniques by different *kayagŭm* are listed below.

The 12-stringed *kayagŭm*

The original *sanjo kayagŭm* is used, but new performance techniques have been explored on the traditional instrument.
- The left hand used for vibrato is also used on the performer's right-hand side of the bridges to produce melodic lines.
- Various new fingering techniques have been developed, particularly the use of arpeggiated fingering.
- Musical expressions including tenuto, glissando, and staccato are used while one or both hands are used for harmony.
- Glissando is used on the left-hand side of the bridges as well as the right-hand side.
- Several strings on the left-hand side of the bridges are pressed by fingers or the palm to create a variety of sounds.

- The use of con sordino or harmonics in traditional performances has greatly increased.
- Fingernails are used for scratching the strings, successive flicking, or glissando.
- Glissando and tremolo are used at the same time.

A detailed description of the above performance techniques is presented in Lee Chaesuk 1984.

The 15-stringed *kayagŭm*

The pieces composed by Sŏng Kŭmyŏn for the 15-stringed *kayagŭm* were based on traditional folk music idioms, and the music was mostly melodic. Thus, the performance techniques of the 15-stringed *kayagŭm* are almost similar to those of *sanjo*.

The 21-stringed *kayagŭm*

Along with the new performance techniques of the 12-stringed *kayagŭm*, more techniques are added for rapid progressions and leaping progressions because of the expanded register. Performance techniques that appeared in newly composed pieces for this *kayagŭm* are listed below.

- Both hands are used on the performer's right-hand side of the bridges; the right hand performs the melody and the left hand the harmony (figure 10), and vice versa (figure 11). Or both hands perform the melody in turn (figure 12) or at the same time (figure 13).
- The left hand performs rapid staccato passages (figure 14).
- Harmonic intervals are expanded because of the added number of strings (figure 15).
- Western music with large registers can be arranged and performed (figure 16).

The 18-stringed *kayagŭm*

The techniques are similar to those of the 21-stringed *kayagŭm*. Both hands play rapid passages, and there are difficult techniques played by the left hand in particular (figure 17).

The 17-stringed *kayagŭm*

Similar to the 21- and 18-stringed *kayagŭm*, the 17-stringed *kayagŭm* uses the techniques that appear in the pieces for the 12-stringed *kayagŭm* and the 21-stringed *kayagŭm* (figure 18).

The 22-stringed *kayagŭm*

The tuning system employs a seven-tone scale unlike that of the 21-, 18-, and 17-stringed *kayagŭm*, which use a pentatonic scale (figure 19).

Construction and Performance Techniques of the *Kayagŭm*   115

Figure 10: Yi Sŏngch'ŏn, "Chŏnyŏk kido" (The evening prayer) in "Pada" (The sea).

Figure 11: Yi Sŏngch'ŏn, "Pyŏl hana na hana" (One for the star, one for me) in "Na hana" (One for me).

Figure 12: Yi Sŏngch'ŏn, "Tcholbudŭl nŏ chalnatta" (The overnight millionaires, yeah you!) in "Pŏlgŏbŏkkin Sŏul" (Naked Seoul).

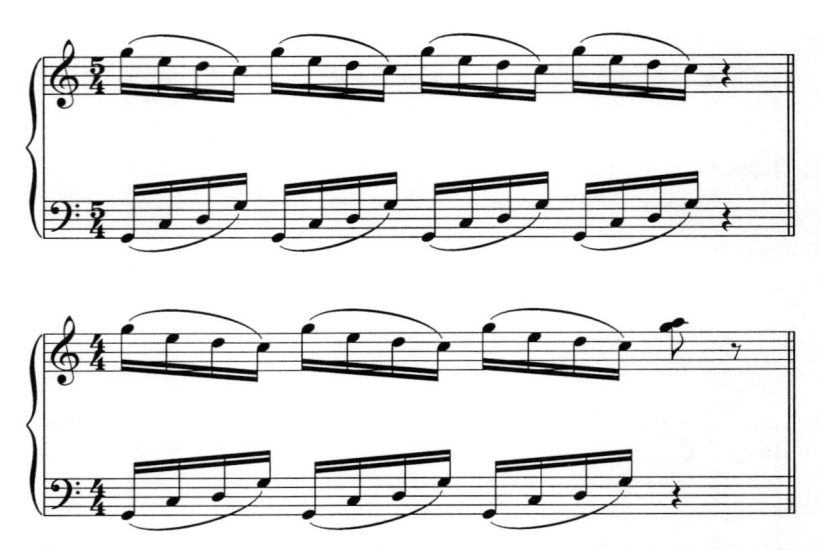

Figure 13: Yi Sŏngch'ŏn, "Poshint'ang chip-e ungk'ŭrin kaegirŭm shinsa" (Greasy man in a dog-soup restaurant) in "Pŏlgŏbŏkkin Sŏul" (Naked Seoul).

Figure 14: Yi Sŏngch'ŏn, "Mikkuraji ŭi sesang" (The world of a mudfish) in "Mikkuraji nondurŏng-e ppajida" (Mudfish falls into a rice paddy).

Conclusion

The *kayagŭm* has essentially been constructed in three basic forms throughout its two-thousand-year history. The *p'ungnyu kayagŭm* has a *yangidu,* and it is carved out from a single paulownia log. This *kayagŭm* can be traced back to the *shillagŭm* at the Shōsōin repository in Japan, through the *kayagŭm* shown in the treatise the *Akhak kwebŏm,* and through today's *p'ungnyu kayagŭm* used in *chŏngak*. The *sanjo kayagŭm* has no *yangidu,* and the

Construction and Performance Techniques of the Kayagŭm   117

Figure 15: Yi Sŏngch'ŏn, "Haessal hana na hana" (One for the sunlight, one for me) in "Na hana" (One for me).

Figure 16: Yi Sŏngch'ŏn, Solo Op. 29 ([Beethoven's] Sonata in C# Minor, op. 27, no. 2, 1st movement).

Figure 17: Yi Haeshik, "Kŭmp'uri" (Exorcism of strings).

Figure 18: Hwang Pyŏnggi, "Tal hanop'igom" (Oh the moon, rise high and shine brightly).

Figure 19: Pak Pŏmhun, "Ishibihyŏn kayagŭm-ŭl wihan hyŏpchugok 'Sae sanjo' (Concerto for 21-stringed *kayagŭm* 'New *sanjo*').

material of the front and the back of the soundboard is different. Also, it has a reduced width and length compared to that of the *p'ungnyu kayagŭm* and has been used in folk music since the nineteenth century. Contemporary *kayagŭm* began to appear in the mid-twentieth century. The structure is the same as that of the *sanjo kayagŭm,* but the number of strings has increased to 15, 17, 18, 21, and 22. Furthermore, polyester strings have replaced the silk ones to enhance the volume, and pegs have been employed for tuning.

In summary, performance techniques have developed according to the construction of the *kayagŭm*. Contemporary *kayagŭm* in particular have broken with the conventional division of labor between the two hands, that is, the right hand on the right side of the bridges and the left hand on the left side of the bridges used by the *sanjo kayagŭm*. Furthermore, with contemporary *kayagŭm,* the techniques of the left hand have developed to include arpeggios, accompaniment to the right-hand melody, and playing the melody together with the right hand using tremolo.

References

Chang Sahun. 1976. *Han'guk ŭmaksa* [Korean music history]. Seoul: Chŏngŭmsa.

———. 1993. *Han'guk ŭmak-kwa muyong-e kwanhan yŏn'gu* [A study on Korean music and dance]. Seoul: Segwang ŭmak ch'ulp'ansa.

Hayashi Kenzō. 1964. *Shōsōin gakki no kenkyū* [A study on the musical instruments at the Shōsōin repository]. Tokyo: Kazama shobō.

———. 1984. "Shillagŭm (kayagŭm) ŭi saengsŏng" [The origin of the *shillagŭm*], trans. Hwang Chunyŏn. *Minjok ŭmakhak* 6:135–40.

Howard, Keith. 1994. "The Korean *Kayagŭm*: The Making of a Zither." *Papers of the British Association of Korean Studies* 5:1–22.

Hwang Pyŏngju. 1990. "Shipch'ilhyŏn kayagŭm ŭi kaeryang-e kwanhan yŏn'gu" [A study on the modification of the 17-stringed *kayagŭm*]. *Kugagwŏn nonmunjip* 2:33–53.

Kim Ujin. 1989. "Akki hyŏngt'ae pyŏnhwa-e taehan yŏn'gu: Chinyŏn ŭigwe ŭi akkido-rŭl chungshim-ŭro" [A study on the development of the structure of musical instruments: As appeared in the *Chinyŏn ŭigwe*]. *Han'guk ŭmak yŏn'gu* 17.18:79–107.

Kugakki kaeryang wiwŏnhoe [The Committee of Modified Korean Instruments]. 1989. *Kugakki kaeryang chonghap pogosŏ* [Report on modified Korean instruments]. Seoul: Kugakki kaeryang wiwŏnhoe.

Kungnip kugagwŏn [The National Center for Korean Traditional Performing Arts]. 1996. *Kaeryang kugakkijŏn* [Modified Korean instruments exhibition]. Seoul: Yeaktang kaegwan kinyŏm haengsa torok.

Lee Chaesuk [Yi Chaesuk]. 1984. "Kŭnse kayagŭm yŏnjubŏp ŭi pyŏnch'ŏn" [The development of *kayagŭm* performance techniques in the twentieth century]. *Minjok ŭmakhak* 6:17–29.

Pak Hŭngsu. 1980. "Toryanghyŏng" [Weights and measures]. In *Toryanghyŏng-kwa kugak nonch'ong* [Weights and measures and a collection of Korean music essays], 183–200. Seoul: Taebang munhwasa.

Pak Hyŏngsŏp. 1994. *Chosŏn minjok akki* [The instruments of the Chosŏn (North Korean) people]. P'yŏngyang: Munye ch'ulp'ansa.

Pak Pŏmhun. 1994. *Chakkok p'yŏn'gok-ŭl wihan kugakki ihae* [An appreciation of Korean instruments for composition and arrangement]. Seoul: Segwang ŭmak ch'ulp'ansa.

Song Bangsong [Song Pangsong]. 1984. *Han'guk ŭmak t'ongsa* [Korean music history]. Seoul: Ilchogak.

SIX

"Recycling" an Oral Tradition Transnationally

CHAN E. PARK

The focus of this chapter is performance of an oral tradition in intercultural context, experientially based on my own innovation as a performing researcher. The object of investigation is *p'ansori,* a solo-singer art of story-singing that has survived massive sociocultural, linguistic, political, and aesthetic shifts in recent Korean history. Insofar as *p'ansori* is an oral tradition, presentation outside its familiar milieu requires not only the singer's mastery of what has been handed down as tradition, but its effective delivery; for instance, can one stage an interpretive performance without resorting to interpretive writing, such as subtitles? The spectrum of challenges ranges from embracing the collective "folk" consciousness of modern Koreans developed in their sociopolitical context to cultivating a cross-cultural rapport in performance.

"Folk Music" in the Modern Era

Early in the 1980s in Seoul, I attended as fieldwork a seminar held at Korea University on *p'ansori,* which was then being rediscovered among urban intellectual circles. On the wooden platform in an old-fashioned classroom where the lectern had been removed to provide a stage a legendary team—my late teacher Chŏng Kwŏnjin, with his favorite drummer, the late Kim Myŏnghwan—gave a performance. Questions and answers followed. A student charged, "Traditional *p'ansori* is too quaint and difficult for our generation to enjoy. Could you not simplify the

---
This chapter is a revision of an earlier publication (Park 1998).

tunes to compose new pieces with?" Seated cross-legged on the platform in his meditative posture, Mr. Chŏng responded, "Not knowing the old ones, why learn a new one?" Of his numerous legacies, this one in particular helped shape my own attitudes toward "recycling" tradition into modern contexts, namely, that tradition is a treasure-house buried under the modern and postmodern "forward" and "extrovert" movements, and to study it is to humbly turn our focus "backward" and "inward"; that traditional performance is first and foremost a process of self-discipline, and creativity is the process of "packaging" old materials for new audiences in new contexts rather than a new concoction in place of discipline; and that in the absence of knowledge, "fusion"[1] is often a truncation of tradition, a hasty "genetic engineering" where the third dimension, the depth, is yet unfathomed.

Recently, the conservation of cultural heritage as an antidote to mechanization has loomed up as a new discourse, prompting inquiries into our modern and postmodern constructions of "the past." Korea in the past three decades has experienced a dynamic change that has profoundly affected the shaping of modern perspectives. In the aftermath of the Korean War (1950–53), the long-established folk culture was either being lost or reconstructed in the sweeping encounters with the foreign, sociopolitically dominant cultural expressions. The excavation of precapitalistic "authenticity" began where connection between the past and the present was severed and "being native" meant estrangement from "being modern." One of the material manifestations was the formation of districts of antique shops, which in the beginning catered mostly to foreign sojourners and dealers. Urban nationals followed by collecting and literally "re-placing" the "antiques" in their Westernized living and commercial quarters: old doors as screens, blanket chests for coffee tables, wooden mangers for indoor plants, stone mills as table stands, pages torn from old books to cover walls in ethnic taverns called *minsok chujŏm*, chipped rice bowls unearthed from a grave site for tea, or a porcelain chamber pot for a flower vase.

The excavation of the vestiges of Old Korea extended into the realm of the intangible. Categorized as "the untouchables," especially since the dissemination of neo-Confucianism in the

---

[1] I refer here to the frequent experiments conducted by modern artists in the use of traditional styles, movements, and concepts.

thirteenth century, folk and ritual performance traditions were abruptly unearthed on modern stage as icons of native culture. Various intellectual, commercial, and political sectors have focused on preserving and recycling sacred and secular stage acts long considered "vulgar" or "superstitious." What exactly is "folk performance" to a modern Korean in this sociocultural context? How is it linked to one's consciousness psychologically? What sort of cultural manifestation is "performance"? A performance is often studied as the reflection of the central meanings, values, and goals of a culture in action, as they shape and explain behavior (Turner 1990:1). Stage acts often serve as meta-commentaries on societal happenings while also influencing the course of social change. Can we still find cultural continuum in the reenactments of traditional music, dance, or oral narrative seemingly nonsynchronous with the times? What journeys lie between the present and the past, what future redemption in training, performance, reception, or research?

To reiterate, Koreans' attitude toward native performance and performers has more or less been self-deprecatory and self-condescending. Entrenched in neo-Confucian social hierarchy and Sinocentric subservience, followed by the recent occidentalism and still more recent import of Japanese popular culture, Korean elitism seems to have adopted as its social mores divergence from native sentiment. The history of literary dualism—persisting long after King Sejong's promulgation in 1446 of what is now regarded as a linguistic prodigy, *han'gŭl* (literally, "Korean writing")—is a witness to this. Such an attitude catalyzed the Westernization of the Korean peninsula—at least south of the demilitarized zone—and the subsequent loss of folk heritage, almost complete in less than a century.

Complex is the Korean construction of folk music's sociological stand, crossed between new recognition and old condescension that lingers. Following the Korean independence from Japanese colonial rule, the term "national music" (*kugak*) loomed up as a metonymy for "folk music" (*minsogak*), a calling for national identity. During the postwar reconstruction era of the 1960s, the Korean government assumed the role of lawful patron of traditional culture and launched its program of preservation. Traditional folk music became designated as important intangible cultural assets (*chungyo muhyŏng munhwajae*) and its musicians as "holders" (*poyuja*)[2] of the tradition. While the nation's standard curriculum embraces the Western musical canon, numerous institutions of higher learning have joined in establishing degree programs in folk music. A major in Korean music is much more acceptable today than in previous decades, though it is sought largely by women and confined to such "milder" genres as dance or *kayagŭm* (12-stringed plucked zither). With Korean music dubbed a cultural asset and legitimized as an academic discipline, private lesson fees have soared astronomically in competition with those of imported genres. The mass media's stand on folk music, however, remains passive and seemingly aimless. Entertainments, mostly imitations of Western and Japanese show business, are mildly dabbed with folk music frequently fused with Western instruments or tunes, as if in response to the "globalization" drive first proposed by the Kim Youngsam regime as the national motto of the 1990s.

Ambivalence characterized the public impression of folk music during the intense antigovernment movement of the 1970s and 1980s. Performative elements of such outdoor genres as the mask dance (*t'al ch'um*), farmers' band music (*nongak*), and the native shaman ritual *kut* became drafted as the spectacle of resistance in street demonstrations and marches. In the structuralist context of modern theater, they were deconstructed on stage in vaudevillian *madangguk*, the proletariat-spirited, open-air theater that emerged in the late 1960s.

> The word literally means "open square" or "meeting place" and, applied to the South Korean theater scene, it refers to agitational street theater based on traditional folk drama and western agit-prop. The word "agitational" should be taken quite literally here: many *madang* performances succeed in getting the audience in such a state of ecstatic frenzy that they are spontaneously transformed from spectators into slogan-chanting political demonstrators. Many mass demonstrations are therefore initiated or animated by *madang* performances. (Van Erven 1992:98)

The obtuse manifestation of political agendas in this theater's adoption of folk expression widened an already substantial gap between "public" and "folk." Politicized as a reflection of the gruesome social drama unfolding, the public image of folk music—however heroic it might have been—suffered. As the

---

[2] In popular lore they are often referred to as human cultural assets (*in'gan munhwajae*).

military regime further tightened its grip, the sounds of resistance grew proportionately louder. Weary of the daily ritual of student demonstrations heralded with native percussion, hurled rocks, and tear gas, the citizens responded with cynicism, *"Tto chŏnom ŭi sori!"* ("That damned noise!"). The painful memory of the military regime is quickly fading today, but will folk music continue to mirror Korean society through the IMF (International Monetary Fund), environmental peril, and beyond?

One of the debates in Korean musical aesthetics lingers on the question of *han,* commonly translated as "grievance," "unrequited desire," or "regrets." Singling out a set of sorrowful melodic patterns typically referred to as *kyemyŏn* mode, some claim *han* has "the" essence of Korean music. The recent movie *Sŏp'yŏnje,* a film based on a short novel by Yi Ch'ŏngjun, has imprinted the story-singing tradition of *p'ansori* in the hearts of modern Koreans. The main character, a broken singer, deliberately blinds his daughter so she can acquire a "truly *han*-filled" *p'ansori* voice. The "art for art's sake" aestheticism built into the theme had a nostalgic appeal to Koreans in their belated search for their lost culture, as witnessed by the film's box office success. The magnitude of its popularity despite the morbid plot leads to an intriguing revelation: the film on one hand helped elevate *p'ansori*'s social status, but on the other hand confirmed it as a practice by the *han*-crazed "Other," who for art's sake would physically maim his own child.

Breaking the Insider/Outsider Boundary

Insofar as every ethnic group has its own musical tradition, the purpose of interethnic exchange should reach beyond a mere display of heritage to celebrating the commonality uniquely contained in the differences. Korea's cultural exchanges with neighboring kingdoms, mainly China, Japan, and northern tribal states, date back to ancient times. Despite Sinocentric oversimplification that all aspects of Korean culture were "Chinese," or Japan's nationalistic denial of Korean influence on the shaping of its own, Korea remains the crossroad of exchange on the East Asian cultural map. In the process of exchange, Korea has assimilated what was transmitted from abroad and has in turn transmitted what had been Koreanized. In the modern era, the arena of exchange has been expanded to involve the West as a main contributor.

Following the intellectual trend of the past several decades in pursuit of the nature and patterning of primordial humanity, interested researchers have ventured to the remotest areas of the world, far away from the industrialized West. Korea, too, has seen its heritage surface in serious levels of folkloristic studies, participated in by outsiders as much as insiders, on stage and in academia. Beyond the level of intellectual "tourism" and its "required" or "permitted" level of familiarization, and challenging the insider/outsider boundary, some "went native."[3] Buried between the nationalistic recount and scholarly historicity of folk music's development is an unusual "insider" experience of an "outsider" and her lore. In the spring of 1973, Jan McQuain, a Peace Corps member from Seattle, organized a professional farmers' band troupe (*nongaktan*) with the late Yi Chŏngbŏm and Kim Pyŏngsŏp and toured through the villages and towns of Kyŏngsang and Chŏlla provinces. "Our playing season began with rice planting and ended with the harvest.... The idea of going to the countryside to do nothing but drum all day was too beautiful" (McQuain 1973–74:46). Her ethnography, "Traveling in a Farmers' Band," begins,

> "Farmer's music and dance is from the heart of Korea," our announcer proudly states every time he opens the show.... "When those Japanese were here, we couldn't even bring our instruments outside; we weren't allowed to play.... And play we do! We have some famous people here today, old-timers.... Plus, from far away across the Pacific, comes a woman, a foreigner, an American who drums with us. Sometimes her friends show up too: two American men who play the *jing* [*ching*] (big gong) and *hojok* [*hojŏk*] (horn). Now when have you ever seen a foreigner in a farmers' band? That's why we're called the Korean-American Women's Farmers' Band." (McQuain 1973–74:43)

Imagine the incredulity of the country folks, witnessing a Caucasian female in broad daylight twirling and circling the village square playing the *sŏlchanggo* drum dance! The better a drummer she became, the wilder their conjectures became:

> "Why did she join a farmer's band?" "I don't know; is she a good person?"... "I hear she went to college and teaches English in Seoul."... "That's a lie! Who ever heard of a teacher joining a band?"... "I think she's a prostitute."... "She's an orphan; her mother was a *kisaeng*, her father, American." And one time when I was having trouble with my neck, "Look, they've brought in a

---

[3] The concept of "going native" in folklore as a bridging of the gap between academia and field was explored in the conference "Going Native," held at The Ohio State University, May 1999.

retarded girl from America to dance in the band." (McQuain 1973-74:48)

Visiting her at the riverbank of Masan, I observed them crowd the back of the tent to watch her eat barley rice and young radish kimchee amidst the swarm of blowflies intent on partaking of her modest lunch. The "outsider" cross-racial, cross-cultural, and cross-societal adventures such as McQuain's—a far cry from "mainstream" accounts—were also part and parcel of the overall shaping of the face of Korean folk music today.

Crossing the Temporal, Cultural, and Linguistic Boundary

A performance is a declaration of our shared humanity that at the same time utters the uniqueness of particular cultures (Turner 1990:1). Discussion of a folk performance in a modern context aims at a diachronic understanding of the folk consciousness within a culture. Discussion of a performance in a cross-cultural context is a probing of what form and content interculturally matter. Such internal inquiry embraces the domain of cross-cultural consciousness to determine how the performance tradition could best be translated. Here I focus on *p'ansori,* an oral tradition that remains from premodern times; it was designated Important Intangible Cultural Asset No. 5 in the 1960s. Its physical space is the shape and size of a straw mat, framed by the audience at flexible settings. Its narrative reality, unbound by elaborate theatrical setup, is invoked in the intricate interplay of voice and drum. Wielding its innate flexibility as storyteller's stage and unfettered by an imaginary "fourth wall,"[4] its *p'an,* the psycho-physical performative context, allows a range of performer-audience intertextuality not permissible in the theater of realism. The remaining anecdotes (Pak Hwang 1987, 1974; Chŏng Noshik 1940) indicate that this intimacy between performer and audience shaped and characterized *p'ansori* during its emergence and proliferation. Today, the remaining narratives continue to unfold on straw mat but are mounted on the modern stage and distanced from the audience; they are to be revered as a "cultural asset" and not to

---

[4] The design and use of proscenium arch and curtain reflects the segregation of stage from auditorium, where the audience is barred from participating in the performers' reality except via theatrical illusion by the imaginary wall of proscenium, frequently referred to by theatricians as "the fourth wall."

be "tampered" with. *P'ansori* has been stopped in its development to be preserved as a museum display.

The narrative structure of *p'ansori*, crafted mostly in the old dialects and musical and vocal styles of Chŏlla province, stylistically alternates between speech (*aniri*) and singing (*sori*); the former moves plot, the latter poetically details thoughts and actions. Accompanied by the drum, the voice moves through an intricate set of melodic and rhythmic paths, like a paintbrush revealing a deeper meaning of the language. The structural coordination between singing and speaking in *p'ansori* provides yet another example of the Bakhtinian distinction of "discourse that conjures" and "discourse about the conjuring," or the narrated and the narrative world (Bakhtin 1981:255). The structural relationship between the signifier and the signified, voice and meaning, is emically and metaphorically described as "drawing the picture within" (*imyŏn kŭrigi*). Its vocal tradition has been handed down stroke by stroke from master to apprentice, matured with individual flavor, and polished through lifelong practice.

Despite its sociocultural elevation as a national keepsake, how many Koreans would enjoy *p'ansori* as active storytelling? How many outside its close-knit world would savor the aphorisms "Correct mind, correct sound" (*chŏngshim chŏngŭm*) or "If you wish to be a singer, be a human first"?[5] How many would seriously heed the moral message in the "Song of Filial Piety" ("Hyodoga"), one of the remaining *tan'ga,* or *p'ansori* warm-up songs?

> The root for all human conduct
>   is none but love for your country and parents, is it not?
> Wangsang, frozen, prayed on ice,
>   out from the fishing hole caught a carp;
> Maengjong, on his knees, prayed and wept in the
>   bamboo grove,
>   under snow deep found a bamboo sprout,
> With his utmost served his parents.
> Another ancient man named Kwakkŏ,
> Whenever he had a special dish prepared for his parents,
>   his own child would eat it, so to bury his child away,
> Was digging a site when a pot of gold he found,
>   all to serve his parents better.

---

[5] This was an adage handed down from previous generations of singers, given to me by Chŏng Kwŏnjin during my study.

In today's court of law, burying a child alive would most certainly be considered a heinous crime, and "all to serve his parents better" as an insane reason at best. In a traditional context, however, Kwakkŏ's action was lauded as exemplary, endorsed by Heaven, which rewarded him with a pot of gold. In the great schism between the past and the present lies *p'ansori*'s challenge of representing sounds and semantics of the past in the present.

Beyond the transtemporal challenge mentioned above, in the past several decades, *p'ansori* has been presented abroad along with other Korean musical genres. Global networking of Korean performance is not merely a postwar phenomenon nor is it confined to the East-West crossing only; it has actively begun to converge and diverge with performances of neighboring countries since the Three Kingdoms era (37 B.C.E.–C.E. 668). The exchanges of the twentieth century are merely the latest developments in this historical continuity: following his retirement performance, the legendary singer Yi Tongbaek led his troupe in 1939 on a performative expedition through Manchuria (Pak Hwang 1987:221), while a variety-acts troupe called Taedong kagŭktan, which included the singers Yi Hwajungsŏn and Im Pangul, made its second tour to Japan in 1943 (Pak Hwang 1987:198). Catering mostly to Korean communities, the expeditions seemed not so much cross-cultural as cross-border, covering coal mines and munitions factories where Korean draftees were forced into labor under Japanese military rule. Cross-cultural exchange as we know it began in the 1960s, when the names of the late female virtuosos, Kim Sohŭi, Pak Nokchu, and Pak Ch'owŏl, began appearing in the proceedings of festivals and academic demonstrations in Europe and the United States.

If art is a reflection of society, it is bound to evolve as society changes. Insofar as society is a world in process and not an end, performative expression as a metaphor of societal life should also evolve as a process. Is the performance of an oral narrative in another sociolinguistic context possible at all? What sort of "process" is an intercultural stage? With its complex system of signs, the signifier, and the signified, language to oral tradition "functions as a material substance similar to paint in painting, stone in sculpture, and sound in music" (Lotman 1976:17). What structural adjustments should be made when delivering an oral tradition outside its own language territory, that is, where the essential "material" fails? My own creation of an intercultural performance of *p'ansori* starts with deconstructing some of the fixations and practices that have shaped the world of *p'ansori*, which, under the pretext of storytelling, has been developed as refined vocal music.

Insofar as *p'ansori* has maintained its stance somewhere between the realm of vocal music and storytelling, it imaginably was innovated by those who assumed their roles between the two poles, that is, "singer" and "storyteller." In the bursts of aristocratic patronage that galvanized extensive musical and lyrical revision in the nineteenth century, *p'ansori* moved further from storytelling toward an increasingly self-conscious musical and lyrical genre, its singers becoming "vocal artists" or "singing poets." The status quo narrative structure of *p'ansori*—alternation between lengthy singing and brief speaking—leads to the conclusion that singing has been cultivated as the art's raison d'être, while speaking has been truncated as connector, "prose summary in a word or two...relaxation from the tension of singing" (Kim Hŭnggyu 1978:116–18). Singers who were inclined to expanding the speaking part were often dismissed as *chaedam kwangdae* (singers who tell witty stories) or *ttorang kwangdae* (wishy-washy singers). Could *p'ansori* be rehabilitated to a storytellers' stage where "telling" and "singing" were equally legitimate?

Second, *p'ansori* is not merely a voice, but a language as well. From a musical perspective, its essence is customarily invoked not as much in lexical correctness as in vocal metaphor, the poetic signs within the vocal expression. Such signs, often crossing sociolinguistic boundaries, facilitate communication by producing a richer set of messages than language itself, and their striving for maximal saturation underlies the structure of the artistic text (Lotman 1976:40). For example, the poetic tension and relaxation in the rhythmic heaving and dropping of the shoulders in *salp'uri* dance transmits a feeling of longing; equally telling is the accompanying *shinawi* musical movement.[6] These are poetry in motion and in music, a complex of visual and aural images "whose elements are not discrete units like words" (Smith 1989:150). A dance or instrumental music works within a less arbitrary sign system, thus less mediation between object and image. An oral tradition, however, grows on a language, an arbitrary, cultivated, and discrete system of signs. It articulates, for example, in metaphorically or metonymically structured words the image of

---

[6] *Shinawi* is the musical ensemble developed as accompaniment to shamanistic rituals of the southern provinces. *Salp'uri* (dance of purge) is an artistic version of shaman ritual exorcist dance.

longing, like "autumn rain falling on paulownia leaves" (*ch'uu odong*), an antique sign still capable of conjuring forlornness. In oral tradition, language is the soma that carries poetic communication, the soul. History witnesses that the staunch nineteenth-century Confucian ethnographers of *p'ansori* wielded the very idea of "poetic" deliverance in language to inject neo-Confucian morality into the proliferating art. With literary fluency, they collaborated with singers' musical fluency, seeking ethical as well as poetic enterprise in their selection and revision of narratives.[7]

Third, what sort of presence is *p'ansori* to assume when it departs from the familiar setting to stand trial interculturally? Shall it be a "Korean treasure" or "Korean storytelling"? In the twentieth-century vortex of cultural transition, the process of creating *p'ansori* narrative came to a standstill, and the remaining versions became fixed as cultural assets (*munhwajae*) and archetypes (*wŏnhyŏng*). Discovered as part of a shifting marketplace variety show three centuries ago, *p'ansori* has through various stages of development evolved into a national emblem, fixed and lineally preserved by "holders" and "holder-designates." Neither in form nor in content is *p'ansori* a flexible context for storytelling; instead, it has become a ritual of nostalgic invocation of national identity. But as "The Emperor's New Clothes" teaches us, all performances are naked when placed before an audience whose perceptions are yet uncluttered by social, political, and gender hierarchies. Placed before a foreign audience, *p'ansori* would be no more or no less than a performance subject to the rules of good stage citizenry. The organizers of intercultural events, however, in their effort to "educate" the audience about *p'ansori*'s distinction and provide a safety blanket for the road, invariably begin their program notes with the mention of the art's status as a cultural asset. Can a performance be impressive without impressing?

Fourth, according to the testimonies by a number of living master singers, the standard format of *p'ansori* performance has traditionally been *t'omak sori* (performance by piece). Mandated by its status as an asset, however, a book-length performance

---

[7] It has been established that the scholar-connoisseurs and aristocratic patrons of the nineteenth century contributed to the selection and edition of five exemplary narratives from a total existing repertoire of twelve, based on moral and aesthetic merit. The five are "The Song of Sim Ch'ŏng" ("Shimch'ŏngga"), "The Song of Ch'unhyang" ("Ch'unhyangga"), "The Song of the Underwater Palace" ("Sugungga"), "The Song of Hŭngbu" ("Hŭngbuga"), and "The Song of the Red Cliff" ("Chŏkpyŏkka").

format referred to as *wanch'ang* (narrative in its entirety), came into vogue, heralded by the singer Pak Tongjin. "Without intermission, Pak in 1968 performed five hours of 'Song of Hŭngbu'... eight hours of 'Song of Ch'unhyang' shortly after... 'Song of Shim Ch'ŏng' in 1970, 'Song of the Red Cliff' in 1971, and 'Song of the Underwater Palace' in 1972" (Pak Hwang 1987:250). In competition with Pak's Herculean stamina, other singers followed lest they be regarded unworthy. For those in the audience willing to endure, the demanding length may serve as a ritual obstacle in cultural rehabilitation, and the greater the ordeal, the more genuine the result. Modern theater auditoriums—with confining chairs silenced and distanced from the stage—are natural torture chambers deserving of such an ordeal. The late singer Kim Sohŭi would confide that "discrediting the *wanch'ang* practice is one thing I would be happy accomplishing before I die."[8] In contrast to the flourishing of book-length *p'ansori* performance domestically, it has been established that transnational performances of *p'ansori* should be glimpsed for "never more than seven minutes abroad."[9] Could *p'ansori* be performed abroad as *p'ansori* and not merely as an abbreviated sampling?

In *ch'anggŭk,* a multisinger dramatization of *p'ansori,* English subtitles recently have come to be projected on screen next to the stage. The first attempt was made by the National Ch'anggŭk Company in 1987 in preparation for the 1988 Seoul Olympics, a job entrusted to my modest ability.[10] For the non-Koreans in the audience, it was a welcome respite. Their appreciation expanded further into the cross-cultural realm to find additional elements of humor and pathos, leaving their Korean neighbors wondering what discovery could exist beyond their own. During one of the evening performances of "The Story of Chief Aide Pae" ("Paebijangjŏn"), I noticed an equally interesting performance unfolding in the auditorium—bursts of "untimely" mirth among foreigners, and curiosity building among Koreans.

In subtitling *p'ansori* in English, I have encountered several challenges: linguistically, the signified condensed in the idiomatic

---

[8] This was told to me by singers Sŏng Uhyang and Han Nongsŏn on separate occasions.

[9] One of the then New York–based Korean performers I invited to perform with me for the Second Annual Asian Festival held in Columbus, Ohio, May 1996, stressed this.

[10] I provided English subtitles for "The Song of Ch'unhyang" (1987), "The Story of Chief Aide Pae" (1988), and "The Song of Shim Ch'ŏng" (1989).

phrases, ancient quotes, historical allusions, and myths must be unraveled and packed into matching signifiers in another language; culturally, the depiction of ancient characters, thoughts, and situations is not literary translation per se, but requires cross-cultural fluency at every step; temporally, the subtitle must function as simultaneous interpretation, to flow with the stage action as performance is measured in time; and spatially, the co-playing of subtitles, which splits the audience's attention between the action and its transcription, must be as unobtrusive as possible. Furthermore, synchronization is needed not only between subtitles and stage action, but between stage action and slide projection. Frequent discrepancies occurred during the performance because of the personnel's unfamiliarity with *p'ansori* on stage heard in Korean and *p'ansori* on screen read in English.

P'ansori as Orality

A performer, when creating a performance event, faces various artistic and ethical decisions in building the relationship between performance and reception with the audience. The reason for the instability of a folkloric text is the emergent, processual character in it that stresses the dialectic of innovation and tradition within community-based expressive culture, and the relations between the performer and audience (Titon 1995:439). Performance, after all, is the responsibility to an audience for a display of communicative competence (Bauman 1977:11), the ethical frame of text-making based on performer-audience intertextuality. In performance, a wide range of channels, both linguistic and metalinguistic, rehearsed and spontaneous, is implied by "communication," but "competency" is appreciated where the basic channels of communication between performer and audience are shared. In the performance of an oral tradition, its language is the primary channel, used by the performer and understood by the audience simultaneously. We have at hand an emergent challenge of text making in an intercultural performance of an oral tradition, yet unmentioned in folklore to the best of my knowledge. Situated before the audience with hardly a means to share the linguistic and sociocultural specificity, what sort of "text" shall *p'ansori* choose to be? An asset "politically correct" from a foreign land, or an event ethically textualized for audience accessibility?

I propose it exit the conventional frame when necessary to interpret the tradition in performance. Where a linguistic channel of understanding stands at practically nil, the performer of an oral tradition could get creative with inventing a working channel of communication. In this process of reconstruction, tradition encounters novel innovation, and that between the poles lies the "range of emergent text structures to be found in empirical performance" (Bauman 1977:40). With a modest level of bilingual fluency in Korean and English and modest familiarity with *p'ansori* singing acquired during my research in Korea in the 1970s and 1980s, I have in the 1990s journeyed into the unknown beyond the national boundaries in search of the living *p'an* the performances of the past are known to have exuded.

Ethnography of Creating a "Metatext" of *P'ansori*

Back in Honolulu from a decade-long field study in Korea, I found the initiative for creating an interpretive *p'ansori* manifesting itself in performative urgency. It took two unsatisfying performances for me to realize the need for a yet undiscovered channel of communication with the local audiences of Hawai'i. The application of the nineteenth-century ethnographer Shin Chaehyo's (1812–84) much revered theory of "appearance, words, vocal achievement, and the dramatic gesture as the four basic elements of *p'ansori*"[11] in his *Kwangdaega* (Song of the *kwangdae*) was shifting in me. The scope of words (*sasŏl*) was expanding beyond the mere concept of poetic diction to embrace an account or storytelling in an intercultural context. Compelled by the need to reach the audience, I set out to creating a *p'ansori* about *p'ansori*, a *p'ansori* metatext, a means of delivering a tradition intact with its unpacking made easier. It is primarily *sori*, "singing," the traditional vocal style, that stimulates in the minds of the audience corresponding audio-visual images, the fundamental source of poetic communication. *Aniri*, "speaking," is where textual interpretation could find room to expand, a freer-flowing channel of verbal communication. The structural alternation between expository *aniri* and descriptive *sori* inherent in *p'ansori* (with expanded usage of the former) was my path to follow. Wherever

---

[11] Kang Hanyŏng (1956) introduces these four elements as "the golden rules of *p'ansori* theory"; Marshall Pihl (1994:96–100) in his translation reconstructs one of the four elements, *inmul* (appearance) as "presence," "considering the word 'appearance' may sound too commercial" (recollection from one of our debates at University of Hawai'i in the early 1990s). Kang's and Pihl's recognition help authenticate Shin Chaehyo's utterance as primary theoretical canon.

out of the latter an event, a character, or situation clamors to be heard cross-culturally, I would first expound in the audience's language, then illustrate in singing. In the process, I came up with a metastructure that alternates between newly composed *aniri* in English and selected *sori* in a language of its own, between verbal act of interpretation and musical reenactment of tradition.

When presenting a long-established tradition, one's ethical responsibility does not end with communication but involves "authentic" representation, an act of balancing entertainment with education. In handling a tradition, the performer is "positioned at a complex nexus of responsibility...[and must] keep faith with the past, with their deceased teachers, and with the present, the mumbling members of the audience who seek engagement now" (Glassie 1995:402). The *p'ansori* narratives and their stylistic renditions have been established as an artistically salient and culturally potent tradition over many generations. Paramount is the historical responsibility of educating the audience while creatively perpetuating tradition by breaking the tradition.

In conclusion, how may I characterize in folkloristic terms my modest labor in creating a *p'ansori* metatext? Some assert that "while folklorists commonly work from performances to texts, interpreters commonly work from texts to performances" (Fine 1984:2). Crossing between research and performance, my lonely labor affords no room for binary division but begins and ends in both. Creativity in behavioral science is defined as "a process by which a symbolic domain in the culture is changed," since it is the result of the interaction between a sociocultural context and an individual within (Csikszentmihalyi 1996:8–23). Attempts at cultural preservation, however, inevitably alter, reconstruct, or invent the traditions that they are intended to fix (Handler and Linnekin 1984:288). *P'ansori* metatext is a counterattempt that focuses on reliving the concept of *p'an*, the flexible context of performer-audience intertextuality seemingly abandoned in the art's elevated status. Performance that constructs the community ideologically and emotionally also strengthens or changes the shape of networks by promoting interaction (Noyes 1995:471). Ironically enough, far away from the hub of *p'ansori*, in small towns in Kentucky, Mississippi, Montana, and Hawai'i, I discover soil fertile for retextualization of the *p'an*. Where *p'ansori* is merely storytelling and the singer is simply a storyteller, tradition can be creatively de-traditionalized to be reunited with the timeless but now forgotten current. Given an unassuming performer-audience relationship and room for creative emergence, *p'ansori* expands its network transnationally.

The Story of Hŭngbu and Nolbu Retold

In the summer of 1993, I was back in Korea for research and a continuous supply of Korean food. I also acquired from Han Nongsŏn, protégé and heir of the late Pak Nokchu, her version of the "Song of Hŭngbu," constructed in energetic *tongp'yŏnje,* or "eastern-style singing." The following is an abridged version I prepared and performed for the one-day symposium "Korean Folk Music Engages the Modern World," held on the University of California, Berkeley campus, May 1, 1999.[12] I take liberty to weave into dialogs colloquial expressions uncharacteristic of belles lettres in most printed forms.

[Drum]

Aniri

In this world, the law of karma dictates that the good is rewarded and the bad is punished—so the story of Hŭngbu and Nolbu begins. According to the Confucian code of inheritance, the older son Nolbu inherits the family assets at the time of the father's death so that he can take care of his extended family. Nolbu is unfit for such responsibility. He has a personality most unreasonable, greedy and perverted, and rumor has it that he has an extra organ the size of a large chess piece right below his rib cage, producing rancor and enmity. He rejoices in causing the sufferings of others. Listen to the song "Nolbu's Entrail of Perversion."

Chajinmori [13]

> He'd cut trees in the direction of *taejanggunbang*,
> Recommend relocation toward *samsalbang*,
> Build a house in *ogwibang*,[14]

---

[12] The spoken narratives are my own construction, and I have translated the songs so that each translated line more or less corresponds to the prescribed rhythmic cycle.

[13] This is a four-beat rhythmic cycle, frequently used in enumerating things, actions, or physical or mental characteristics.

[14] *Taejanggunbang* in ancient Korean cosmology refers to one of the eight directions guarded by eight spirits. It is believed that cutting trees within its perimeter invites disaster. *Samsalbang* is a direction that invites three kinds of damnation:

Fan so fire spreads,
Drive stakes into pumpkins yet to grow,
Invite a traveler in
to stay the night,
and turn him out when dark.

He'd attack a *ch'orani* actor[15]
and tear his mask to bits,
Steal the drum from a minstrel,
Steal needles from an acupuncturist,
Approach a gentleman and rip his horsehair cap,
Rape a young girl,
Spread false rumors about a chaste widow,
Give a hungry baby a smelly toe to suck,
Knock down a defecating man right on his release,
Urinate into a ceremonial wine bottle,
Pour poison in a *soju*[16] bottle,
Cut strings off a new horsehair headband,
Wrestle a cripple to the ground,
Thump a hunchback on his back,
Smear feces on a blind man,
Kick a pregnant belly,
Dig hollows on a busy road,
Whip his horse through a pottery shop,
Shoot a watergun at the silk shop display...

[Singing without drum]

These are just a few examples,
Would the villain know the Three Bonds,
Or the Five Human Relations?[17]
Such a brutish and obnoxious knave,
Would there be another one like him?

---

sudden death, bad timing, and other disasters. *Ogwibang* is geomantically avoided as the most ominous and unnatural direction.

[15] This is a cross-dressed actor of the traditional era, dressed in a red jacket and a blue-and-green skirt, wearing a grotesque female mask and carrying a flag on a pole.

[16] *Soju* is an inexpensive Korean liquor.

[17] The Confucian cardinal virtues, which are as follows: the three bonds are the relationships between sovereign and subject, father and son, and husband and wife; the five relations additionally include faith between friends and respect for sibling order.

Aniri

On the other hand, Hŭngbu is fiercely moral and furiously compassionate, and despite unbearable mistreatment from Nolbu, does his utmost to love and respect his older brother. With all his heart Nolbu hates Hŭngbu, because Hŭngbu is a good man, a popular man, happily married to a beautiful woman with eleven wonderful children and another one on its way, an inevitable result of a good yin-yang match. One cold winter morning, Nolbu chases Hŭngbu and his famiiy out to live by themselves with nothing but the shirts on their backs.

Cold, hungry, and homeless, Hŭngbu and his family suffer unspeakable poverty and humiliation. In old Korea, if you are a *yangban* (aristocrat), your life's job is to compose poetry and recite prose; you're never to do physical labor even if you are starving. Such trends have continued until today, and some say this was one of the contributing factors of the current IMF crisis. Hŭngbu has been working on his dissertation for the past fifteen years and has no life skills to make a living. But he and his family remain kind and compassionate, and in the end, Heaven rewards them with great wealth and happiness. I will tell you how it happened.

One day, a pair of swallows flies in and builds a nest under Hŭngbu's eave. Soon two baby swallows hatch. The first one flies away; the other one, while practicing flying, falls and breaks its legs, and is about to die. Kind Hŭngbu treats it with utmost care, and it survives. Next spring, Hŭngbu's swallow returns from the Swallow Kingdom in the south carrying a gourd seed in its mouth. With a thankful heart Hŭngbu plants it in his backyard. In the fall, three huge gourds are ready for harvest. One fine day, tightening their hungry stomachs, the whole family gathers to saw them one by one, singing, "Dear gourd, give us a pot of rice to go on."

Chinyang[18]

Shirirŏng shilgŏn,
Pull (the saw).
E-e-yŏ-ru,
Pull it.
"When this gourd is open,
I wish nothing except
A pot of rice to come out.

---

[18] This rhythmic cycle is made up of six slow beats.

Rice is my whole life's wish yet unfulfilled.
E-e-yŏ-ru, pull it."
"Look here, Wife,
Come on, Wife, a tune for sawing, please."
"A tune for sawing, I would give gladly,
But too hungry to sing."
"If you are that hungry,
Tighten your waist sash.
E-e-yŏ-ru
Pull it.
Little ones, stay that side,
Big ones, come to my side.
We will open this gourd,
Boil and eat the meat inside,
Sell the shell outside,
Survive we will, so pull it.
The boat floating on the river yonder,
Is pregnant with many thousand *sŏm*[19] of grain,
So what, I envy not,
For it is nearly as full as this gourd of mine.
Shirirŏng shilgŏn,
Shirirŏng-hŏ-hŏ-ng shirirŏng,
Shirirŏng shilgŏ-ŏn,
Pull, pull the saw."

Hwimori[20]

Shirirŏng shirirŏng
shirirŏng shirirŏng
Shirirŏng shirirŏng
shikssak t'okkwaek!

Aniri

The first gourd opens—it is empty! You know what they say: "Unlucky ones crack eggs to find bones in them." "Look, there is a chest—no, two!" Cautiously, Hŭngbu lifts a corner; it is full of money! He peeps into the other; it is all rice! Ecstatic with joy, Hŭngbu unloads the chests with amazing speed. Money and rice stream out and pile up like mountains.

---

[19] This refers to a straw sack of grain, equivalent to 5.12 U.S. bushels.
[20] This rhythmic cycle is made up of four fast beats, descriptive of urgent, sweeping movements.

Hwimori

> Hŭngbu's ecstatic,
> Hŭngbu's ecstatic,
> He empties the two chests but
> Full to the brim,
> He empties the chests, turns and looks
> Full to the brim,
> Turns and looks,
> Rice and money piled up high,
> Turns and looks,
> Full to the brim again,
> Turns and looks,
> Rice and money piled up high,
> Up to the brim,
> *Aigu*, I love it to death!
> [Without drum]
> Three hundred sixty-five days a year,
> *Kkuyŏk kkuyŏk,* more, more, come out!

Aniri

They become the richest family in the country. From the second gourd, rolls and rolls of rare silk slide out. Everyone, including servants, neighbors, dogs, cats, pigs, and even rats, is now dressed in single, double, triple layers of silk. From the third gourd comes a nationally acclaimed construction crew with master builders carrying blueprints and tools. Voila! A beautiful mansion is built.

Chungmori[21]

> One more gourd is brought in,
> *Shirirŏng shilgŏn,* saw it.
> *Shirirŏng shirirŏ-ŏ-ŏŏŏŏŏng shilgŏn*
> *Shilgŏn shilgŏn,* saw it.
> With the treasures from this gourd,
> Buy ten thousand acres in Kimje and the fertile land of Owemi,
> Spend a fortune, buy them.
> For the land of Soswettŭl in Ch'ungch'ŏng province,
>   offer a fortune,
> Let capital yield more capital.
> *Shirirŏng shilgŏn,* saw it.

---

[21] *Chungmori* is a medium tempo, 12-beat rhythmic cycle.

Hwimori

> *Shirirŏng shirirŏng*
> *shirirŏng shirirŏng*
> The gourd opens halfway.
> From within, human voices,
> Fellows with big saws, small axes,
> chisels, hoes,
> hammers, rakes,
> Endless, endless, endlessly come out
> Build Hŭngbu a mansion.

Aniri

From this point on, all of Hŭngbu's capitalistic moves reap huge successes: stocks, bonds, real estate, Wendy's, MacDonald's, Victoria's Secret...

Hŭngbu's success story is dear to all hard-working Koreans. The gourd-opening scene is usually interrupted by big applause from the audience. Nolbu, a specimen yet to appear in Freudian psychoanalysis, is also popular among the postmodern, deconstructionist literary critics as well as many small-business owners in Korea. They praise Nolbu as a role model in a capitalist society. Many restaurants in Korea are named "The House of Nolbu," but never "The House of Hŭngbu" for all his scholarship.

Nolbu hears on the wind that Hŭngbu now owns Wall Street. Some say his poor relation won a ten million dollar lottery ticket from a corner store somewhere in Ohio. Others say some goblins mistakenly left a treasure bag in front of his house. Nolbu wants to see for himself, so one day he walks over to Hŭngbu's house. Where a tiny mud hole used to be towers a dazzling mansion. Sizzling with jealousy, he calls:

"Hŭngbu-ya!"
"My dear Older Brother!"
"Whose house is this?"
"Mine, Older Brother."
"Nice, let's swap houses."
"Sure, dear Older Brother."
"I hear you prowl the night."
"Older Brother???"
"Don't think you can fool me! The policemen are all around looking for you. Leave all your keys and house papers with me and run to Manchuria, don't come back for five years; I will care for your home and assets."

Hŭngbu tells Nolbu the story of the swallow's broken leg and the magic gourd seed. Nolbu listens with great interest and says, "It's that easy to be rich! You broke one swallow's leg—I'll break several dozens'! You'll see, I'll be far richer than you!"

The news of Nolbu's visit reaches the ladies' quarter. Setting aside her embroidery, Hŭngbu's wife shudders at the prospect of confronting Nolbu. Like a good Confucian wife, however, she comes out to greet him, accompanied by her daughters-in-law. The swishing of their silken dresses and perfumes, my, it is like watching a fashion show.

Chungjungmori

> Hŭngbu's wife comes out,
> Hŭngbu's wife comes out.
> Once undernourished, ill-dressed,
> Impoverished so,
> Now she has everything: silk,
> Money, rice, silver, gold, gems,
> Deer antlers, and ginseng.
> Her daughters-in-law all in luxuriant attire
> Hŭngbu's wife herself,
> In finest Hansan ramie,
> Dyed in delicate blue,
> Her skirt pleated closely
> Her upper waistband widened boldly,
> Daintily, daintily, she promenades.

Aniri

> "Welcome, dear Older Brother-in-Law."
> Her daughters-in-law follow in unison.
> "Welcome, dear Great Uncle-in-Law."
> "Whoa! Look at your wife, Hŭngbu. Isn't she a darling in silk, so different from when she had her ass kicked! Yesterday's mudfish is today's dragon, how magical!"

In the next song, the ladies prepare a special table for Nolbu. Fresh *namul*[22] and soups, gourmet stews, pickled delicacies, kimchee, and the Korean barbecue, yum! Dip a sizzling piece in seasoned soy sauce, *ch'iiiiiiii!*

---

[22] Steamed vegetables.

Chajinmori

>They are preparing dishes,
>Porcelain plates from Ansŏng,
>Lacquerware table from T'onyŏng,
>Silver spoons and copper chopsticks,
>Placed neatly, like two rows of petty officers standing
>   in waiting
>in the district office courtyard.
>On a black bamboo tray with a flower painting,
>On chinaware engraved with a turtle,
>Steamed nonglutinous rice cake and shell cake steamed
>   on pine needles,
>Square cake imprinted with flower,
>Steamed red bean cake,
>Peeled apple, processed honey, wild honey,
>Egg-coated shish kebab,
>Tripe sashimi, sauced cow liver and kidney,
>Placed symmetrically.
>Dumplings, honey-dipped, *maximowiczia chinensis*–soaked,
>Cookies coated with pine nuts,
>Roots of ginseng and platycodon, shredded and garnished,
>Octopus jerky, with bean oil dipping,
>Rare spices and flavors,
>Mountain herbs, ferns, watercress,
>Mung bean stems, soaked in delicious bean soup
>Of generous portion,
>*Cock-a-doodle-doo,* steamed chicken,
>*Kurururu,* quail soup.
>Ouch! It's hot, not copper chopsticks,
>Use wooden chopsticks.
>Pick a piece of meat from the grill,
>In soy sauce flavored with sesame oil,
>Splash! Dip it,
>*Ch'iiiii . . .*

Aniri

>"Have a drink, dear Older Brother-in-Law."
>"Hŭngbu, you know damn well that I never drink unless accompanied by a drinking song by a *kisaeng*, not even at a funeral. You have dressed your wife well. Have her sing me a drinking song."

Hŭngbu's wife explodes: "How dare you ask a sister-in-law to sing you a drinking song! Go ahead, boast away how wealthy you are! Well, we happen to have more than you could ever dream of. How I loathe the sight of you, get out of my house! You won't leave? Then I retire!"

Chinyang

"Older Brother-in-Law, look here, Older Brother
  of my husband,
Asking your own younger sister-in-law to sing
  a drinking song,
Wherever did you hear such blasphemy?
In the frozen chilly winter morning,
With our little ones lined up,
Driven away in such humiliation,
Even in my casket, I would never forget!
I abhor the sight of you! Get out!
Why, except to disturb us, would you ever come to my house?
If you don't leave, I leave!"

Aniri

"Hŭngbu, your wife is no good. Throw her out, I will match you with a new one."

"......"

"Ya, Hŭngbu, what is that reddish stuff standing in that corner?"

"That is a *hwach'ojang*, an antique chest with flower engravings."

"That's a beauty, I'll take it."

"It's heavy, I will have a servant deliver it to your house tomorrow morning."

"Sly jerk! All night long you want to take out all the treasures and give me the empty chest. No thanks, I'll carry it myself 'as is.'"

Nolbu loads the chest on his back.

"Hello, everyone, sing along with me, so I won't forget. Hwach'ojang......"

Chungjungmori

"*Hwach'ojang, hwach'ojang, hwach'ojang,*
I've got one *hwach'ojang,*
I've got it, I've got it,
I've got one *hwach'ojang.*"

He jumps over a brook.
"Now I forgot!
Ch'ojang (soy sauce with vinegar)? *Ch'ojang*? No!
Pangjang (abbot)? *Ch'ŏnjang* (ceiling)? No!
Koch'ojang (chili pepper paste)? *Toenjang* (soy bean paste)? No!
Songjang (corpse)? *Kudŭlchang* (hypocaust)? No!"
He tries these words backwards.
"*Changhwa-ch'o,
Ch'ojang-hwa,
Aigu,* what is it?
So frustrating, I am going crazy!
Aigu, what on earth is it?"
Entering his house,
"Look here, Wife!
When the master of the house
Returns home from outside,
You should be dashing out
To receive him with due respect,
But you don't even budge!
What a wench!"
Nolbu's wife comes out,
Nolbu's wife comes out.
"*Aigu,* dear, dear Husband!
I didn't know you've returned,
I really didn't know you've returned.
Come here, Husband, come to me."

Aniri

"Wife, what is this I have here?"
"My, wherever did you get this precious thing? It's a *hwach'ojang!*"
"O Mommy, Mommy, that's it!"
"He is getting senile. Yesterday he called me his daughter."

Engrossed in swallow hunting from that day on, Nolbu manufactures several dozen traps of different shapes and sizes: some are round, some are long, some wide, some narrow, and some resemble spaceships. He nails them on the house, and the house tilts to the side under their weight. But swallows are too simple to enter such a complex maze. Tired of waiting, Nolbu one day goes out to catch swallows with a net, with his wife behind him with a six-pack and a bottle of *soju*.

"Swallows, swallows, don't go there, come into my net, come on in."

Chungjungmori

    T'was the time, following three moons of spring,
    When began summer, the Eighth of the Fourth Moon,[23]
    Swallows flutter,
    An oriole sits in weeping willow,
    Calls out its own name,
    With the net Pokhŭi-ssi[24] crafted
    Deftly slung over his shoulder,
    To catch swallows he goes out.
    To Pangjang[25] he goes out.
    Here, Right Head Peak, there, Left Head Peak,
    Cross Peak, Counter Peak,
    Left, right, and all around,
    Aaaaaaaa, iruwŏ ...
    T'uk! He disturbs a bush and the birds resting within.
    "*Huyŏ—hŏ hŏ hŏch'a*, that swallow!"
    Entering Pangjang Mountain, *t'uk!* He kicks another bush.
    "*Huyŏ-hŏ hŏ ... ŏŏ ... up*, that swallow!
    Where are you headed?"
    Seeing a black-eared kite soaring up,
    "Is that a swallow?"
    Seeing crows and magpies heading south,
    "Is that a swallow?"
    Seeing a golden oriole on a spring day,
    "Is that a swallow?"
    Seeing a dove diving down the cliff,
    "Is that a swallow?"
    "Swallow, You, there,
    Enter not that house!
    It was built on ill-boding days!
    See the sign of fire on the columns and girders?
    Enter my house instead, come oooooon!
    I-hee-hee-hee-iruwŏ ... ... "

---

[23] The Eighth of the Fourth Moon (April) is Buddha's birthday.

[24] Pokhŭi was a legendary emperor of ancient China who first crafted nets.

[25] This is the old name for Chiri mountain, between Kyŏngsang and Chŏlla provinces.

References

Bakhtin, Mikhail. 1981. *The Dialogic Imagination*, trans. Caryl Emerson and Michael Holquist, ed. Michael Holquist. Austin: University of Texas Press.

Bauman, Richard. 1977. *Verbal Art as Performance*. Prospect Heights, Ill.: Waveland Press.

Chŏng Noshik. 1940. *Chosŏn ch'anggŭksa* [A history of Korean singing drama]. Seoul: Chosŏn ilbosa.

Csikszentmihalyi, Mihalyi. 1996. *Creativity: Flow and the Psychology of Discovery and Invention*. New York: Harper Collins.

Fine, Elizabeth. 1984. *The Folklore Text: From Performance to Print*. Bloomington and Indianapolis: Indiana University Press.

Glassie, Henry. 1995. "Tradition." *Journal of American Folklore* 108: 395–412.

Handler, Richard, and Jocelyn Linnekin. 1984. "Tradition, Genuine or Spurious." *Journal of American Folklore* 97: 273–90.

Kang Hanyŏng. 1956. "Kwangdaega haesŏl" [Commentary on the *Song of the* Kwangdae]. *Hyŏndae munhak* [Modern literature] 2.8:146–57.

Kim Hŭnggyu. 1978. "P'ansori ŭi sŏsajŏk kujo" [The narrative structure of *p'ansori*]. In *P'ansori ŭi ihae* [Understanding *p'ansori*], ed. Cho Tongil et al., 103–27. Seoul: Ch'angjak-kwa pip'yŏngsa.

Lotman, Yuri. 1976. *Analysis of Poetic Text*, trans. and ed. D. Barton Johnson. Ann Arbor, Mich.: Ardis.

McQuain, Jan. 1973–74. "Traveling in a Farmers' Band." *AWC Journal* 2:43–48.

Noyes, Dorothy. 1995. "Group." *Journal of American Folklore* 108: 449–78.

Pak Hwang. 1974. *P'ansori sosa* [A short history of *p'ansori*]. Seoul: Shin'gu munhwasa.

———. 1987. *P'ansori ibaengnyŏnsa* [A two-hundred-year history of *p'ansori*]. Seoul: Sasang sahoe yŏn'guso.

Park, Chan E. 1998. "P'ansori in Trans-National Context: The Global Transmission of a Korean Performance Tradition." *Korean Culture,* Summer/Fall, 14–21.

Pihl, Marshall R. 1994. *The Korean Singer of Tales*. Cambridge: Harvard University Press.

Smith, Hazel. 1989. "Image, Text and Performance: Inter-artistic Relationships in Contemporary Poetry." In *Literary Theory and*

Poetry: Extending the Canon, ed. David Murray, 149–66. London: B. T. Batsford.

Titon, Jeff. 1995. "Text." *Journal of American Folklore* 108:432–48.

Turner, Victor. 1990. "Introduction." In *By Means of Performance*, ed. Richard Schechner and Willa Appel, 1–7. Cambridge: Cambridge University Press.

Van Erven, Eugène. 1992. *The Playful Revolution: Theatre and Literation in Asia*. Bloomington and Indianapolis: Indiana University Press.

SEVEN

Korean Folk Songs for a Contemporary World

KEITH HOWARD

> Sipping a liqueur in the piano bar of an international hotel. The pianist improvises, adding wordless scat vocals. The scene changes, as drums and bass join in, the slow and languid introduction gaining a regular beat: we are now in a dim, smoke-filled jazz bar. The singer intones, a slight reverb coloring his voice: *Arirang, arirang, arariyo.* As the rhythm intensifies, the familiar refrain is replaced by a verse: *This hill, it is far to go, My hometown is over there, but even if I want to I can't get there...*

In the beginning was "Arirang." Well, not exactly. This is the beginning of a track from a 1998 release titled "T'ongil arirang" (Unification *arirang*), sung by Yong Woo Kim (Kim Yongu).[1] Clearly, in style and presentation, it is very different from the folk song known as "Arirang." The words of this first verse are pertinent to today's divided Korea and are written as if the author is looking across the demilitarized zone. It looks to a time when the peninsula will be reunited, yet echoes the late nineteenth century, when "Arirang" lyrics told of migrant workers brought to Seoul to rebuild the royal palace under the rule of the prince regent, the Taewŏn'gun. They looked from the capital toward their distant homes, across the mountains and hills; there is still an Arirang hill in a northeastern suburb.

"Arirang," the only Korean folk song known worldwide, has an intriguing and multifarious history. In terms of musical structure, and in respect to one well-known text that tells of a woman waiting forlornly for her lover on the banks of a river, the song is said to have roots in the mountainous regions around Chŏngsŏn several hundred kilometers to the east of Seoul (Kang Tŭnghak

---

[1] Track 4 on *Kwenari* (Samsung SCO-165KYW, 1998).

1988; Kim Yŏlgyu 1987). The structures of some "Arirang" lyrics suggest greater antiquity, some telling about legendary rulers of the Three Kingdoms period (37 B.C.E.–C.E. 668), while others, at least in terms of metric construction, apparently date back to the fifteenth century (see McCann 1979:43–56). The first mention of "Arirang" is in a 1756 manuscript (see Kim Yŏn'gap 1986: frontispiece). The most common stanzas nonetheless seem to hail from the late nineteenth century or the early twentieth. The first known transcription was published only in 1896, accompanying translations of lyrics in an article by Homer B. Hulbert in the third volume of the *Korea Repository*, a journal largely sponsored by the missionary fraternity (1896:45–53).

Only in the twentieth century did regional versions begin to appear; Kim Kyohwan, in his 1929 *Chōsen min'yō shū* (J)/*Chosŏn minyo chip* (Collection of Korean folk songs), states that many such versions were now well established (1929:275, cited in Im Tonggwŏn 1974:374–76). By then, "Arirang" itself was considered worthy of study, as Kim Chiyŏn's *Chōsen min'yō shū: Arirang I* in the June 1930 edition of *Chōsen/Chosŏn* demonstrates. Yi Pohyŏng argues that regional versions are based on a song developed in the early twentieth century in Seoul, not the Chŏngsŏn song or any similar songs that survive in the province in which Chŏngsŏn is situated, namely Kangwŏn (1997:81–120).

The popularity of "Arirang," however, was ensured after it was sung at the screening of a silent nationalist film produced by Na Un'gyu in 1926. In 1930, a recording was made based on the film, with a monologue by Sŏng Tongho coupled to Kang Sŏgyŏn's singing of "Arirang"; in the late 1980s, the Korean Ministry of Culture and Information (Munhwa kongbobu) re-released an abbreviated version on cassette.[2] The complete recording, spanning the four sides of two standard-play records (SPs) and ending with a band playing music by Verdi, has more recently been issued by the Synnara (Shinnara) company on a compact disk with thirteen other cleaned-up SP recordings of similar vintage.[3] Synnara has deemed "Arirang" worthy of a series. The company has released four CDs containing contemporary versions of thirty-three regional variants and a single album of thirteen "Arirang" renditions sung by Koreans in China (Yanji) and Russia (primarily

---

[2] Today the Korean Ministry of Culture and Tourism (Munhwa kwan'gwangbu).

[3] See track 14 on *Arirang I: Minjok ŭi norae* (*Arirang* I: Song of the people; Synnara SYNCD-001, 1991).

Sakhalin).[4] The image given by the 1926 film, of nationalistic struggle against oppression, remains vivid for today's Koreans; hence, the original screening became the basis for a successful contemporary theater production, *Akkŭk* (Music and theater) *arirang*, devised by Kim Chat'ap and performed at the Hoam Art Hall in June 1999. Throughout Korea, "Arirang" stanzas routinely lament the injustices of the Japanese colonial rule, describing the loss of land, despairing at hardship, or crying for lost loved ones (for examples, see Howard 1989b:106–14; Chŏng Chaeho 1982:281–82; Naegojang chŏnt'ong kakkugi 1982:142–44).

"Arirang," in both its basic form and regional versions, is one of few folk songs retained without substantial change in the socialist Democratic People's Republic of Korea. Lyrics were modified in, for example, the late 1970s Sea of Blood–style "revolutionary opera" *Tell the Story, Forest* (*Millima iyagi hara*), but the inherited words generally survive, and for good reason: "The song tells with sorrow about the passing of time, about...the sad situation of the people, deprived of their homeland by the Japanese imperialists and expresses, although not clearly, protest against the Japanese imperialists' occupation of Korea, in which the Japanese are referred to as the root of all misfortunes" (*Korea Today*, March 1985).

"Arirang" has become an icon of identity, used for national celebration. It is the subject of many books.[5] It also stands in for Korea in international collections, for example in Britain being found in pentatonic songbooks, arranged for a brass band, or with an accompaniment of Orff instruments, recorders, and piano in a school workbook (e.g., Pont 1972:10–13). On one American recording, it is played by a trio of Chinese *di* flute, Japanese *shakuhachi* flute, and *shamisen* lute.[6] There are versions in English, French, and other languages; versions sung solo and versions for chorus with jazz and orchestral accompaniment. In Korea, it provides the inspiration for a CD, *The Sounds of Arirang* (Samsung SCO-100CSS, 1996), by Kwang-Soo Lee (Yi Kwangsu), formerly the

---

[4] These recordings are respectively *Hanbando ŭi Arirang* (*Arirang* of the Korean peninsula; Synnara SYNCD-089–92, 1994) and *Arirang: Chungguk, Rŏshia* (*Arirang*: China and Russia; King Records SYNCD-106, 1995). A less documented CD is also available from a different company: *Arirang moŭm kokchip* (Collected versions of *Arirang*; Hyundai HYCD-1030CD, 1997).

[5] See, for example, Kwŏn Hŭidŏk 1991, Kim Yŏn'gap 1986 and 1988, Kang Tŭnghak 1988, Minhak hoebo 1987, and Kim Yŏlgyu 1987.

[6] See *Venerated Patterns of China and Japan* (Lyrichord LSST7395, n.d.).

lead small-gong player (*sangsoe*) and vocalist with the first Samul-Nori troupe. Yi begins with a vocal improvisation during which he accompanies himself on the large gong, *ching*, damping it with his hand in the manner of a shaman ritualist. His voice is full of emotion, imparted by rapid dynamic shifts and considerable vocal ornamentation, particularly a heavy vibrato. Then, following the basic song, he gives five regional variants, the last being the popular and jolly southwestern "Chindo arirang." A second vocal improvisation bridges "Arirang" versions from Kangwŏn province in the east and Miryang in the southeast, and a third, accompanied by the plaintive sounds of the *taegŭm* bamboo flute, ends the album.

Preserving Folk Songs

"Arirang" illustrates a simple point: inherited definitions of the essence of folk culture are often at odds with historical reality. Notions of development and change are regarded as alien to the heritage industry. "Arirang," then, despite a very different reality, tends to be seen as ancient, or as timeless, as a root from which contemporary musicians can find inspiration. In a rapidly urbanizing Korea, definitions of folk culture superimpose a romantic rural idyll on reality. And, before readers react with despair, I should note that this is little different from the situation in Europe and America. In respect to folk song, Goethe once said, "We always invoke the name of folk song without knowing quite clearly what we mean by it." "Folk song," as a term, seems to have started with Herder's use of *volkslied* in the second half of the eighteenth century, but exactly what Herder initially meant has since been a matter of what Elbourne calls "tortuous debate" (Elbourne 1976).

In Korea, having borrowed the term for folk song, *minyo,* used in Japan, where it had been introduced by the novelist Mori Agai as a direct translation of the German *volkslied*,[7] scholars typically search for the authenticity of original forms or versions known as *wŏnhyŏng* and consider folk songs to have been transmitted orally by amateurs from generations long past: "Folk songs are songs of the people. They are not composed by particular individuals, but spring up from among the people and are orally transmitted.

---

[7] For the use of the term in Japan, see Hughes 1985; for Korea, see Howard 1999.

They have words fixed to tunes, but are free, because they are nonprofessional works, of complex rhythms, imageries, poetic diction, and so on" (Chŏng Chaeho 1982:261–63; see also Kwŏn Osŏng 1984:12). The author of this statement seems to have studied the phraseology adopted by the International Folk Music Council in 1954. Maud Karpeles was instrumental in encouraging the setting down of a definition that her mentor, the British folklorist Cecil Sharp, would have approved of:

> Folk music is the product of a musical tradition that has been evolved through the process of oral transmission. The factors that shape the tradition are: i) continuity which links the present with the past; ii) variation which stems from the creative impulse of the individual or the group; and iii) selection by the community, which determines the form or forms in which the music survives....
>
> The term [folk music] does not cover composed popular music that has been taken over ready-made by a community and remains unchanged, for it is the re-fashioning and recreation of the music by the community that gives it its folk character. (Anon. 1955:23)

Definitions such as these are Eurocentric and anachronistic; they should be thrown out with the trash. The timeless past is dubious, the lack of conscious composition doubtful. The definitions overlook elements that indicate "invented traditions" in Hobsbawmian terms (Hobsbawm and Ranger 1983:1–14).[8] They create Benedict Anderson's "imagined communities" (1983), manipulating comradeship by intertwining community life and cultural traditions, creating and using artificial social boundaries.[9] They also impose ideas relating to authenticity and correctness, ideas voiced in Britain in the early nineteenth century by William Wordsworth (1940–49, 2:405) and Walter Scott[10] and most

---

[8] For the application of Hobsbawm's ideas to Korea, see Kim Kwangŏk 1992:7–28.

[9] For the manipulation of boundaries in Britain, see Anthony Cohen 1982 and Sandra Wallman 1979.

[10] For a discussion of Scott, see Harker 1985:72–74. Harker also cites James Hogg: "I have in no instance puzzled myself in deciding which reading of each song is the most genuine and original, but have constantly taken the one that I thought the best" (73; from *The Jacobite Relics of Scotland*, first published 1819–21). Much the same could be said about the imposition of strict modal interpretations in the notations of Cecil Sharp and others, or the debates between Kidson and Grainger about transcribing exactly what was present in recordings of folk songs rather than "cleaning" up the melodies. A good overview is provided by Harker (1985), but note the critique of Harker presented by James Porter (1991:113–30).

famously worked out by Francis James Child in his ballad collections: "Many of the older [ballads] are mutilated, many more are miserably corrupted, but as long as any trace of their originals are left, they are worthy of attention" (Child 1861, 1:viii). Authenticity, as Shalom Staub has noted, is indeed a slippery path (Staub 1988). I should not, however, simply cast aspersions, because it should be clear from the above that these same definitions allow indigenous performance arts to be raised on pedestals as cultural icons. Noting, however, how questionable the inherited notion of "tradition" in Korean music is, it befits us all to ask how music from the past can be made relevant for a contemporary world. Making folk songs relevant is what I am exploring in this chapter.

In the Republic of Korea, the perception of folk culture as unchanging has been strengthened through a state preservation system. In respect to performance arts, the system began on October 1, 1962, when the incoming military regime of Park Chung Hee announced a law, the Cultural Asset Preservation Law (Munhwajae pohobŏp; Law 961).[11] This was promulgated early in 1963. The system operated by appointing scholars to a Cultural Assets Committee, the Munhwajae wiwŏnhoe, and charging them with research on traditional arts and crafts. Their reports were used to recommend representative genres for conservation as intangible cultural assets (*muhyŏng munhwajae*) and to appoint individuals as "holders" (*poyuja*), paying stipends in return for teaching and performance obligations. The primary series of reports was the Cumulative Research Reports on Important Intangible Cultural Assets (Chungyo muhyŏng munhwajae chosa pogosŏ), supplemented by internally circulated semiannual progress reports and publicly available regional compendia. By 1985, 165 volumes of the primary series had been completed. The system was overseen by the Office for Cultural Asset Management (Munhwajae kwalliguk); by 1997, 102 Intangible Cultural Assets had been appointed.[12]

---

[11] The law and the system it set up divides heritage into tangible buildings and structures, natural monuments, folk customs, and intangible arts and crafts. The system developed over time; hence the law was amended some fifteen times by 1990. For details, see Howard 1989b:241–62. Note that a system for maintaining and preserving buildings and monuments had been established during the Japanese colonial period—see Maliangkay 1999.

[12] I have used the past tense in the preceding sentences because at the time of writing, 1999, a review of the system that is likely to introduce sweeping changes is under way.

The mechanisms for both preliminary research and postappointment maintenance focused on securing the conservation of the oldest, most authentic form of any given art or craft. Change was thus interpreted as retrogressive; hence archetypes were promoted over developed or damaged forms. It was as if items of folk culture—and, more widely, the entire corpus of Korea's cultural heritage—were to be preserved as museum objects. The original law, though, aimed both to conserve and to promote. Promotion marked an effort to develop arts and crafts as icons of national identity, echoing the culturalism of the 1920s—and into this I can fit the example of Na Un'gyu's film—and National Assembly debates through the 1950s. Indeed, according to article 1 of the 1962 law, the system would both "contrive the cultural progress of the people and contribute to the development of human culture."[13] It was, then, designed to enhance pride in Koreanness. Promotion required that folk performance arts be put on urban stages and be broadcast over the state-controlled media.

Much of the impetus for the system came from Ye Yonghae, a journalist working at the *Korean Daily News* (*Han'guk ilbo*), and reflected Ye's landmark 1963 volume, *In'gan munhwajae* (Human cultural assets). Ye, talking to me on August 13, 1991, related his story:

> I petitioned the government strongly. I wanted Human Cultural Assets recognized because they knew the old things that had been passed down to us but were considered part of a base culture to be despised. Koreans thought it shameful that the lowest people, the *ch'ŏnmin*, had the best knowledge of our music, drama, and crafts. But they also felt shameful because they didn't know the arts and crafts themselves. We risked losing our heritage. We needed to raise the status of the *ch'ŏnmin*, and I thought this could be done if the government honored them. Giving them an honor would function as part of the rehabilitation of the arts and crafts as well as the rehabilitation of performers and artisans.

Ye coined the term "Human Cultural Assets" to stand for the government's "holders."

The two core aims of conservation and promotion are reflected in the seven folk song genres to date appointed as Intangible Cultural Assets. Three are from a popular and professional category, linked to genres that were already in some way staged, by

---

[13] This was echoed in a later five-year cultural plan. Note, too, the title of the first chapter in Kim Yersu's *Cultural Policy in the Republic of Korea*, written for UNESCO: "The Problem of Cultural Identity" (Kim 1976:10–13).

entertainment girls and their male counterparts, *kisaeng* and *kwangdae*, and their successors: *Sŏnsori san t'aryŏng*, songs once sung by itinerant bands (asset no. 19; appointed in 1968), *Sŏdo sori*, songs from the northwest preserved by migrants in Seoul (no. 29; 1969), and *Kyŏnggi minyo* from the central region (no. 57; 1975). Two come from the southwest of the peninsula: the women's song-and-dance genre, *kanggangsullae* (no. 8; 1965), and rice-planting songs, *Namdo tŭllorae* (no. 51; 1973).[14] The final two are indisputably local: *nongyo* farming songs (no. 84; 1985), and *Cheju minyo*, folk songs from Cheju island (no. 95; 1990).

After much research, conducted principally by Yi Sora, a musicologist and staff member at the Office for Cultural Assets, two localities, Kosŏng and Yech'ŏn, were chosen to represent *nongyo*.[15] It was, however, recognized that national promotion hampered the maintenance of local identity:

> Korean folk songs have special characteristics in each district, and those who know the songs in each district would like to be nominated as holders. We could nominate many more [folk song] repertories as Intangible Cultural Assets, but how many more do we want to appoint? The more we appoint, the less of our cultural heritage we will lose. But the more local [folk songs] are performed in the national arena the more they lose their local identity. It is not desirable to go on making more and more nominations. (Yi Pohyŏng, personal interview, August 1990)

The converse is also a potential problem: how can songs from just two areas be considered representative? They can surely be no more than symbolic of the songs of many hundreds of districts that could have been chosen.[16]

Beyond Korea, some would reject the notion that music can be preserved. The American ethnomusicologist Bruno Nettl questions the "imposition of artificially static forms" that the Korean system requires (Nettl 1985:126), and, in a broader context, John Blacking states that "there is a...perennial problem in using traditional art forms as vital parts of programs of social and technological change: unless they are socially reconstructed as well as

---

[14] I have considered these genres at length elsewhere—see Howard 1989a and 1989b.

[15] Since the nominations, Yi has published five volumes of farming song notations (1985, 1986, 1989, 1990, and 1992).

[16] Note the massive MBC folk song collection project, conducted between 1989 and 1995, which resulted in 103 CDs recorded in local villages (published between 1991 and 1996).

technically developed, their use can hold back, rather than enhance, change" (1987:112). Similar perspectives can be found in Korea where, beyond the state system, the need for change has long been recognized. Initially linked to the ascendant *minjung munhwa*, the culture of the masses promoted largely through student demonstrations for democracy, folk songs began to be appropriated and developed in the 1970s. University students began to visit villages during vacations, learning local songs.[17]

Imaging Folk Songs

Yong Woo Kim (b. 1968), the singer of "T'ongil arirang," was one such student:

> From 1987 until 1994, I traveled to the countryside to work with old people. I wanted to learn local folk songs. I met Cho Ŭlsŏn in Cheju in 1990, and studied with her. I went to Chindo, where I met Cho Kongnye. I guess I worked with her more than anybody else. I visited her during university vacations. I went to Chindo for my holidays, and when the semester began again, I would return to Seoul. I enjoy traveling, and I was able to join my two interests together by studying local songs.... Generally, I would stay for a week or so in one place. I studied face-to-face with my teachers, the singers, and also made cassette tapes and videos so that I could continue to practice back in Seoul. (Personal interview, June 1, 1999)

Cho Ŭlsŏn (b. 1915) is the sole holder of *Cheju minyo*; Cho Kongnye (1930–97) was holder of *Namdo tŭllorae*.[18]

As a student majoring in Korean traditional music, *kugak*, Kim had begun to study the literati lyric song style of *shibi kasa* in 1986, working for five years with Yi Yanggyo (b. 1928), one holder of the relevant asset, no. 41.[19] He also fused his vocal style with that of professional singers, notably studying for two years with O Pongnyŏ (b. 1913), holder of asset no. 29, *Sŏdo sori*, and from 1995

---

[17] Some publications exist that attest to this, such as *Chindo minsok chosa charyojip* (Anon. 1983), a private publication issued by Seoul students.

[18] Cho Kongnye always maintained that she was born in either 1924 or 1925; as was common for girls during the colonial period, her parents delayed registering her birth. She was registered in 1930, and this, therefore, remained her official birth date.

[19] The five-year period is significant: it is the period laid down by the Office for Cultural Asset Management as appropriate, and in 1991 Kim graduated within the strictures of the system as a master student (*isuja*).

working for a year on shaman vocalization with Pak Pyŏngch'ŏn, holder of asset no. 72, the southwestern *Chindo ssikkim kut*. The disparate influences did not, according to Kim, cause him any difficulty:

> When I learnt from singers, I learnt first with my body. Then, as I studied on my own, I could change what I had learnt to suit my vocal style. When I first studied lyric songs, my voice developed in an appropriate way for that repertory. When I first studied folk songs, my voice wasn't like that of my teachers. But I was able to add balance. If you listen to singers from Kyŏnggi province, they have their own special vocal style, just as if you listen to singers of *p'ansori*, Korea's solo operatic genre, they have their own special style. Professional singers of these genres cannot switch styles. Because I have a soft voice, I can adapt my voice to sing different styles, switching as needed.
>
> People say that mine is a familiar way of singing. My voice is easy to listen to, easy to appreciate. To make music easier to listen to is essential work for all contemporary musicians, and so my ability to do this is a merit. I focus on my listeners, not on what professional musicians think I should do. I was, however, influenced by scholars [because I studied music at university], and that is why I set out to master each traditional style, so that scholars would respect me. (Personal interview, June 1, 1999)

Kim's first album, *Chige sori* (Seoul Records SRCD-1354, 1996), named after the A-frame used until recently to carry heavy things on one's back, illustrates how he has developed what he learned. One track, "Pongjiga," was learned from Cho Ŭlsŏn. Cho laments that, despite the government's preservation system, old songs are dying:

> People older than I can sing Cheju folk songs and still like them. I want to teach younger people, but they aren't interested. This is difficult, since I am expected by the government to teach people in their twenties or thirties. I will teach anybody who comes to me to learn, but I can't force people. If it rains, a few people come to sing with me, but young people don't want to know. (Personal interview, August 18, 1990)

When I first met her in 1982, Cho lived in a small gatehouse at the edge of the compound of her son-in-law, eking out a living selling instant noodles. By 1990, her appointment had made her life more comfortable, and the village in which she lived, Sŏngŭp, had been designated a folk village, putting it on the island tourist trail. Many of her songs, including "Pongjiga," descend from a long-lost past. "Pongjiga" had originally been sung during the weaving of men's black hats. The hats, which held the traditional male topknot in place, had been common until the 1890s, when a decree passed as part of 1895 reforms ordered men's hair to be cut. Nobody needs a hat anymore except, perhaps, collectors. The craft itself is time-consuming. Horsehair is woven over a frame of finely split bamboo. The journalist Ye Yonghae looked at the craft and talks in his 1963 book about one Mo Manhwan (b. 1885?) who by then was "the only survivor who can split bamboo [for the brim] into yarn finer than human hair." Ye adds that Mo "is wasting his superhuman skill" (1963:35–36).[20] In Cho's song she employs a falsetto yodel in each refrain to imitate the weaving.[21]

A photograph of Kim sitting proudly beside the elderly Cho on the small veranda of her son-in-law's house illustrates the insert for Kim's album. His version of "Pongjiga" is slowed down, effectively losing the point of the in-and-out weaving motion in the refrain. A flute, the *tanso,* provides an introduction, a feature lifted from folk songs of the central Kyŏnggi region, and something alien to Cheju. Supporting Kim, a synthesizer replaces the crickets and the rustle of wind for which Cheju is famous. And, as the song progresses, the synthesizer elaborates a simple harmonic frame. The pace gradually increases, something impossible during the work that the original song was designed to accompany, and the faster pace allows the entrance of an hourglass drum (the *changgo*). The drum sets up a *kukkŏri* rhythmic cycle, a regular 12/8 pattern. Cheju islanders claim that no hourglass drums were used on the island until after the Pacific War;[22] besides this, metric songs are rare.[23]

A second track features the women's song-and-dance genre, *kanggangsullae.* Here, the connection is with Cho Kongnye:

> When I was seven years old, some of the village elders heard me sing. They discovered my talent.... When I was twelve and the sixth full moon came around, [village] women gathered together to

---

[20] Ye used a micrometer to measure frame yarn at 0.00032" and body yarn at 0.00012". Human hair is about 0.00025".

[21] A recording has been issued by MBC in their *Han'guk minyo taejŏn* series (Collection of Korean folk songs; see track 8 of *Chejudo p'yŏn* [Volume on Cheju] 4, 1991).

[22] This is based on a personal interview with the late An Sain in 1983. An was a renowned shaman who, until his death, was the holder of asset no. 71, *Cheju ch'ilmŏri tang kut.*

[23] See Ch'oe Chongmin (1984).

sing *kanggangsullae* and play. When the singers forgot the words, I piped up. That's how they discovered that I knew all the words. (Personal interview for the BBC, August 1990)

Cho's version of *kanggangsullae* is well known.[24] The genre was once widely distributed along the south and west coasts, although the *kanggangsullae* asset recognizes just two villages—and two subteams—adjacent to mountains where legend has it that women gathered and danced to the light of the moon to scare off the Japanese navy under Hideyoshi in the late 1590s. The villages, Usuyŏng on the mainland and Tunjŏn on Chindo, face each other across a narrow strait.[25] Cho, who lived at the opposite side of Chindo, helped teach a team of women from Chindo before the nomination of a suitable old woman from Tunjŏn as the asset's holder (Ch'oe Soshim). To Cho, *kanggangsullae* consisted of a basic song in very slow, medium, and fast paces—matching dance steps—and a series of illustrative songs, in which the dancers pass through an arch formed by a pair of arms, chase around as if they are baby mice hanging on to their mother's tail, weave patterns, and so on. In the past, the duration of *kanggangsullae* would have been open-ended, relying on the improvisation of topical texts, but in asset performances it typically lasts twenty to thirty minutes. It has always been a women's genre, held when village women gather after dusk and enjoy themselves; in most places, men are excluded.[26]

Yong Woo Kim's version is shorter, lasting barely seven minutes. He is accompanied by a chorus of men; no women are present. The chorus adds a second part underneath some of his stanzas, alternating between pitches a fourth and a fifth lower; in the women's genre, there is no second part. The series of illustrative songs are pared back, leaving something that can be and is sung as a one-man dance. The album insert has a photo of Kim walking with Cho; Kim is listed as the arranger of *kanggangsullae*, while Cho Yŏngbae is responsible for the "Pongjiga" arrangement. There are, then, significant differences between the old and new versions:

---

[24] See, for example, *Ppuri kip'ŭn namu hanbando ŭi sŭlp'ŭn sori* (The deep-rooted-tree collection of Korean songs of sorrow), first LP, side A (SELRO-138, 1989).

[25] The Usuyŏng holder and two of her senior disciples sing *kanggangsullae* on *Corée: Chants rituels de l'isle de Chindo* (VDE-Gallo CD-756, 1993).

[26] This is based on my discussions with Cho Kongnye, Kim Kirim (b. 1927, holder, Usuyŏng), and Ch'oe Soshim (1908–1991; former holder, Tunjŏn).

When I sing old folk songs, my style is different from that of old singers. Our culture has changed as times have changed. Old people grew up in the past, so they are my source, the source I must use, but it is a source I must adapt to create my own personal style. I respect my teachers, and they have beautiful ways of singing. I have studied with them and rehearsed with them. When I sing solo, I can use a traditional vocal style, but I have to adjust my voice to fit with the forces I am using. I work with different instruments and different voices, so if I don't adjust the way I sing, things easily become unbalanced. (Personal interview, June 1, 1999)

Kim's audience is not local villagers, but urban youth. He perceives the need to change as a way to reach this large audience, to communicate old Korean cultural experiences yet make them relevant to today. "T'ongil arirang" on his second album is an example of this. The first track on this same release arranges the folk song "Ch'ŏnando samgŏri" for piano and string quartet. Kim "adjusts" his voice by reducing dynamic contrasts, lightening vocal ornamentation, and keeping to a steady pulse. Several tracks on the album mix in a capella singing, fusing Kim's voice to a group called Sollisŭt'ŭ. A capella was fashionable in Korea during the 1990s. In 1993 and 1994, the weekly pop charts of *Han'guk kayo* featured the six-man close harmony In'gong wisŏng, offering a different take on the standard subject matter of love;[27] Sollisŭt'ŭ are a newer group, known best for arrangements of European classical music.[28] One of the collaborations is "Kun pam t'aryŏng" (Roast chestnut song), a cover version of a lyrical folk song composed probably in the early twentieth century and made popular by professional singers in and around Seoul. A capella singing provides a strong rhythmic underpinning, replacing the drum that would have been a feature of many performances of old, but also adds harmony, which of necessity enforces a rigid pentatonicism. The words remain traditional, with the exception of a single slow phrase at the half-way point, as can be seen in the following table, comparing this version to that sung by Muk Kyewŏl (b. 1921) and Yi Ŭnju (b. 1922), the holder and "future holder" respectively of *Kyŏnggi minyo*, asset no. 57:

---

[27] Their first album was released by SKC (YDCD-125, 1993).

[28] Partly reflecting the success of their collaboration with Kim, they were invited to perform at the National Center for Korean Traditional Performing Arts (Kungnip kugagwŏn) at a concert to celebrate Tano Day on June 18, 1999.

"Kun pam t'aryŏng"	
Yong Woo Kim	"Traditional"[29]
(Samsung SCO-165KYW,	(Meari, SISCD-013,
1998)	1988)
1 The wind blows, the wind blows,	1
In Yŏnp'yŏng Sea west of Inch'ŏn the money wind blows.	
2 You are a bachelor, I am a virgin,	4
Girl and boy—*Olssa!*—should play around together.	
3 The cock crows, the cock crows	5
Over in that beautiful place—*Olssa!*—the cock crows.	
4 Without any reason the dog barks, the dog barks,	3
Olssa!—The dog barks without any reason.	

Kwang-Soo Lee has also experimented with what for want of a better word I will call "fusions." Lee (b. 1952) joined the first SamulNori team, a four-man percussion team, within a year of its founding in 1978. SamulNori, in addition to setting down a repertory based on the traditional local and professional percussion music known as *nongak* or *p'ungmul*,[30] collaborated with many musicians. In 1983, the first concerto was commissioned for SamulNori and orchestra; in 1987, the first SamulNori and jazz album was released; in 1988, SamulNori released an album in which they built pieces from shaman rhythms; and SamulNori have worked with pop musicians, including Cho Yong Pil in the 1980s and the rap artist Seo Taiji in the 1990s.[31] In 1997, Lee issued two albums. One, *Kwang-Soo Lee and Red Sun*, was with long-term SamulNori collaborators (Samsung SCO-139CSS, 1997). The other celebrates Lee's forty years as a performer and presents two extended vocal repertories, the shaman-and-Buddhist-influenced

---

[29] This is already halfway toward something new, since the singers are supported by an instrumental ensemble. The date of the recording, despite the CD stating 1988, appears to be the late 1960s or the early 1970s, since two musicians who migrated to Hawai'i, the husband and wife Sŏng Kŭmyŏn and Chi Yŏnghŭi, are both present.

[30] Most Korean scholars still refer to this percussion music using the all-encompassing term *nongak*. Local terms, reflecting band activities in ritual, work, and entertainment contexts, include *kut*, *maegut*, *kŏllip*, *kŏlgung*, and *p'an kut*. Increasingly, students and performers are returning to the term *p'ungmul*, arguing that *nongak* should be abandoned because it was introduced during the Japanese colonial period.

[31] See, for example, *SXL Live in Japan* (CBS Sony, Tokyo, 32DH824, 1987), *Record of Changes* (CMP, New York, CD3002, 1988 and Rhizome Sketch, Tokyo, RZF 1002, 1989), "Hwangsangsok ŭi kŭdae" (You, like royalty) and "Hayŏga" (Anyway song) on *Taiji Boys: Live and Techno Mix* (Bando BDCD-015, 1992), and *Seo Taiji and Boys II* (Bando BDCD-017, 1993).

"Hoeshimgok" and "Poryŏm," plus two shorter tracks.[32] Lee accompanies himself on the small gong, and on the cover photograph wears a cloak and sash suggesting a shaman costume worn when calling the Buddhist spirit Chesŏk. On the second track, a drummer joins him, and Lee replaces his gong with a temple block; on the third, we hear a temple gong, left to resonate. The Buddhist intimations increase, and on the final track Lee is joined by chanting monks.

Both Lee and Kim resonate with nationalist appeal. Where Lee takes his audience to Buddhism, shamanism, and the percussion bands that were so much a feature of the Korean countryside in the past, Kim focuses on folk songs. The link between them, then, is vocal quality. According to Kim,

> I put much emotion into my voice. My voice is good for singing sad songs. If I watch TV or radio, I cry when I hear sad music. Tears flow down. In folk music, songs express the trials of life, which we in Korea refer to as our *han*. *Han* is built into the texts and the music of folk songs. When I sing, I am able to put *han* into my voice. I want to express exactly what the song is meant to be about. When my listeners share my feelings, I am happy. (Personal interview, June 1, 1999)

Han is normally explained by Koreans as a resentment or grudge, the result of oppression during six centuries as a suzerain state of China, thirty-five years as a Japanese colony, the Korean War, and several decades living under a military dictatorship. In terms of literature, the notion of distinct Korean aesthetics has been debunked in a recent article (O'Rourke 1998:34–41), but contemporary musicians remain inseparable from the concept.[33] Both Kim and Lee have developed peculiar vocal styles that they consider redolent of *han*. Both involve emotion, much as was once the preserve of southwestern folksingers and the vocal quality known as *aewan ch'ŏng* (sad voice). But neither comes from the southwest; Lee was born in Yesan, South Ch'ungch'ŏng province, and Kim in Yŏngdong, North Ch'ungch'ŏng province. Emotion, then, is imparted by favoring slow-paced songs, adding vibrato and pre- and post-tone ornamentation, and—but only in the case of Lee—sudden dynamic contrasts.

---

[32] See *Yi Kwangsu 40* (Seoul Records SRCD-1388, 1997).

[33] One recent book, titled *Han*, by Kim Myŏnggon, contains twenty-eight interviews with musicians (1994).

Rebadging Korean Music

If the development of folk songs began as student protest, Yong Woo Kim is evidence that it has been achieved by harnessing the success of the government's preservation drive. It is as if two opposed political colors have fused, and such a fusion was surely necessary, given that the state system attempted to maintain folk songs that had little place in contemporary life. Land reform in the 1950s negated the raison d'être of farming songs; the use of outboard motors meant that fishing songs were gradually abandoned; and *kisaeng* and *kwangdae* are not part of modern life. Further, singers who remember folk songs as sung in work or entertainment contexts are becoming fewer as time passes, and preservation relies increasingly on those with no direct link to the cultural contexts of the past.

The reality, though, is complex. At the student level, my consideration needs to start at Seoul National University, where the acoustic guitar ballads of Kim Min'gi (b. 1951) and others, which led in the 1970s to the dissident "song movement" (*norae undong*) and in 1977 to the association Echo (Meari), were a music of protest.[34] Contemporary songs drawing on Korean music, written and arranged by composers such as Kim Young Dong (Kim Yŏngdong; b. 1951), parallel the song movement. Just as there was a nationalistic undercurrent arguing against copying American and European ballads in the movement, so Kim Young Dong was challenged for mixing the worlds of Western music and Korean traditional music. Kim, nonetheless, proved immensely successful; he has written incidental music for theater, film, and TV and in the last few years has toured the country with his "music for meditation" (*myŏngsang ŭmak*);[35] his lead allowed Kim Suchol (Kim

---

[34] In 1981, Echo secretly printed 149 songs with lyrics dissecting Korean social and political issues, including thirty-eight by Kim. For a discussion, see Hwang Okon 1996.

[35] I have discussed this in Howard 1998:521–24. Kim Young Dong's recordings include *Kim Yŏngdong chakkok* (Compositions by Kim Young Dong; Seoul Records SECD-3011, originally Seorabul SRB-0079, 1982); *Maegut-kwa Tan'gun shinhwa* (Ritual to a falcon and The story of Tan'gun; Seoul Records SRCD-3010, originally Seorabul SRB-0091, 1983); *Mŏn'gil* (Long road; Seoul Records SRCD-3012, originally SPEC-057, 1987); *Kim Yŏngdong Sŭlgidung norae chip* (Songs by Kim Young Dong and Seulgidoong; Seorabul SRB-0219, 1988); *Sŏn* (Zen meditation; Seoul Records SRCD-3013, 1990); *Kim Yŏngdong ŭi myŏngsang ŭmak: Sŏn 2* (Meditation music of Kim Young Dong, Zen 2; Seoul Records SRCD-3012, originally SOER-050, 1991); *Ŭmak segye 1: Aegukka* (Music world 1: National anthem; King KSC4036A, 1993); *Ŏrŭndŭrŭn we kŭraeyo?* (Children, why is it so?; Seoul Records SRCD-1403, 1997); and *Param ŭi sori* (Wind songs; YDKim/Ungjin mujik WJCC0276, 1999).

Such'ŏl) and Yi Byung Uk (Yi Pyŏnguk) to achieve fame for similar mixes.[36]

The song movement increasingly shifted focus to social consciousness, as can be seen on a retrospective album issued in 1997, *Hŭkpaek sajin* (Black-and-white photographs; Samsung SCO-122MIN, 1997). This has the subtitle "Photographic Songs of the Last Memories of the Twentieth Century." The first song, "A Day to Go to Buy Flowers," by Ch'oe Sŏngho, was written in the mid-1980s to mark the forced bulldozing of a street of vinyl shops selling flowers in southern Seoul to make way for new and expensive apartments. Here it is arranged in a harmonica-backed country-and-Western style reminiscent of the pop singer Kim Kwangŏk.[37] Two songs from the 1970s talk about contemporary official corruption, alluding to the nineteenth-century Tonghak rebellion—"New Biography of Nolbu" and "Drought"—with the second by the dissident singer and poet Kim Min'gi. One song by Paek Ch'angu, sung by the *p'ansori* expert An Suksŏn, looks forward to the unification of North and South Korea. The entire album uses a pop backing of guitars, keyboards, bass, and drums, plus a battery of Korean percussion and melodic instruments. The styles shift, from pop, through folk songs supported by a heavily accented rhythmic cycle played by the *changgo* drum (e.g., track 6), to a foxtrot—the old-style pop style of *yuhaengga* introduced to Korea from Japan in the 1920s—in "Kimch'i t'aryŏng" (Ballad of Korean pickled cabbage; track 11).

---

[36] The albums of Kim Suchol/Kim Soochul (Kim Such'ŏl) include *Hwangch'ŏn kil* (The road to Hwangch'ŏn; Samsung SCO-057KSC, 1994); *Sŏp'yŏnje* (Western style; Samsung SCO-046KSC, 1994); *Pullim sori* (*Sori* for invocation; Samsung SCO-059KSC, 1994); *Taebaek sanmaek* (Taebaek range of mountains; Samsung Nices 1994); *Ch'ukche* (Festival; Samsung SCO-099KSC, 1996); *Best Music for Films 1* (Samsung SCO-124KSC, 1997); and *Best Music for Films 2* (Samsung SCO-125KSC, 1997). The first three 1994 releases had been issued previously on Seoul Records. Yi's albums include *Meditation: Yi Pyŏnguk myŏngsang kagok II* (Yi Byunguk songs for meditation 2; Synnara SYNCD-037, 1993); *Ŏullim V: Norae moŭm* (Song collection of Ŏullim; King Records SYNCD-097, 1994); *Ŏullim "Ensemble"* (Seoul Records SRCD-1205, 1994); *Seroum 1 "New Music"* (Cantabile SRCD-1221, 1994); *Seroum 2 "New Music"* (Cantabile SRCD-1223, 1994); *Ttangullim: '95 KBS Ch'angsa t'ŭkchip tŭrama* (Earth resonating: 1995 special drama for the founding of KBS; Seoul Records SRCD-1273, 1995); *Ŏullim shilhwang "Ch'ŏng"* (Ŏullim live, volume 1, "Ch'ŏng"; Cantabile SRCD-1334, 1996); *Ŏullim shilhwang "Hŭng"* (Ŏullim live, volume 2, "Hŭng"; Cantabile SRCD-1349, 1996); and *Tungji* (Tungji ŭmak—Family ensemble; Top, TOPCD-016, 1999). These are all on CD; some titles were previously released on LP.

[37] See *Tashi purŭgi II* (Singing again II; King KSC 4139-A, 1995), track 1, "Param-kwa na" (The wind and me).

Against this, and in keeping with the preservation system, many scholars argued for the maintenance of tradition. Mediation between the two poles, one nationalistic/conservative/Korean and the other international/progressive/Korean, came in a number of articles by the academic-critic Lee Kang Sook (Yi Kangsuk) (1977, 1980) and the composer-critic Yi Kŏnyong (1987). These argued for Korean identity to be imposed in all musical creation, by establishing a musical democracy that would use and unify all musics as a Korean product. Essentially, this vision of democracy blurs the boundaries between Western music and Korean music and between Korean court and folk music. This, then, is the context into which Yong Woo Kim fits.

Further, Kim's development as a singer is tied to one group that absorbed the ideas of Lee and Yi and the music of Kim Young Dong. This is Seulgidoong (Sŭlgidung),[38] founded in 1985 by Hojoong Kang (Kang Hojung; b. 1960). Kang, incidentally, was, like Kim Yong Woo, born in Yŏngdong:

> Most Koreans don't know how to appreciate our traditional music.... I decided to make a new [Korean] music. When I was in my second year of university, I took a simple pentatonic folk song from Chŏnju, North Chŏlla province, and sang it for the university song festival (*taehak kayoje*) on MBC TV. I played the guitar as I sang, and was accompanied by a traditional flute, the *tanso*. This was how I started to adapt Korean music to popular song styles. In those days, if you wore a Korean costume on TV, watchers would switch to another channel. You had to wear more Western clothes....
>
> I established Seulgidoong with some alumni friends and with colleagues who were playing with me in the KBS Traditional Music Orchestra (KBS kugak kwanhyŏn aktan). We thought that we would not be successful if we kept faithfully to the tradition. Our best hope would be to generate a style using folk songs and songs from *p'ansori*, and we called this style *kugak kayo*. We added guitars and synthesizers to Korean instruments. By using traditional songs, but changing the arrangements, we allowed people to understand [Korean] music. We began to accumulate lots of fans.
>
> Then, my mother died. We were due to perform on TV the same week. The song we were to sing, with words [collected] by [the folklorist] Shim Usŏng, asked where mother had gone, describing the scene at her graveside. This was to be a live broadcast. As I sang, I cried. People connected with my sorrow, and

---

[38] The name is an onomatopoeic term for a three-tone ornament used on the *kayagŭm* in literati and court repertories.

through this with the music. People wrote in asking for more. (Personal interview, June 1, 1999)

The group's identity was formed. Seulgidoong was courted by the media, and a radio station paid to record their first album of songs, believing, correctly, that the songs would be popular on radio. Actually, this album set songs to very regular meters, designing them for dance. The second album, again sponsored by a radio station, was a tribute to Kim Young Dong. Kim had spent four years studying in Germany, and returned to Korea with no job. He willingly collaborated, his songs appearing on the A side, and Seulgidoong's on the B side. The next album took Korean scenery as its theme, after the short warm-up songs known as *tan'ga* associated with *p'ansori*. Again, the next two albums were also devoted to songs.[39] A concert in Japan led to regular invitations, and soon Seulgidoong was running music camps, including one in Denver for Korean Americans. Success brought opportunity, and members began to take other jobs; Kang himself became a lecturer at Chugye Arts University. From 1992 on, a new team began to crystallize; by 1994 it consisted of ten graduate musicians.[40] The new team appeared on stage in restyled ramie and hemp farmers' costumes, lined up almost as if they were a pop band, with a battery of percussion instruments and synthesizers raised behind a bank of amplified Korean instruments. They began to move toward instrumental arrangements rather than just concentrate on songs, but they continued to give pieces titles, texts, and melodies that linked each to the folk tradition or to the mass culture ethic of *minjung munhwa*. They never allowed abstract pieces a place in their concerts. This second team disbanded in 1999. At the time of this writing, a new and younger third team has been recruited, still under Kang's leadership.

---

[39] See Seorabul SRB-0129, 1988, SRB-0226, 1988, SRB-0247, 1990, SRB-0278, 1991, and SRB-0285, 1991.

[40] The members were Junho Lee (Yi Chunho) (*taegŭm* [large transverse bamboo flute] and *sogŭm* [small transverse bamboo flute]), Hojoong Kang (Kang Hojung) (*p'iri* [oboe]), Kyunghee Oh (O Kyŏnghŭi) (*kayagŭm* [12-stringed half-tube zither]), Soonyon Chung (Chŏng Sunyŏn) (*haegŭm* [2-stringed fiddle]), Yoonjung Huh (Hŏ Yunjŏng) (*kŏmun'go* [6-stringed half-tube zither], *ajaeng* [bowed half-tube zither], *kkwaenggwari* [small gong]), Il Won (Wŏn Il) (*kkwaenggwari, p'iri, t'aep'yŏngso* [shawm]), Sungtaek Kwon (Kwŏn Sŏngt'aek) (*kayagŭm, puk* [barrel drum]), Dongki Hong (Hong Tonggi) (piano, synthesizer), Yong Woo Kim (Kim Yongu) (*changgo* [double-headed hourglass drum]), and Youngchi Min (Min Yŏngch'i) (*taegŭm*, percussion).

Yong Woo Kim, as the main singer for the second team, is not alone in having found success as a solo musician. Two members have emerged as leading composers, the pianist Dongki Hong (Hong Tonggi; b. 1967), who concentrates on dance and theater music, and the oboist and percussionist Il Won (Wŏn Il; b. 1967), on film scores. Won describes his relationship with Seulgidoong in the following way:

> I joined Seulgidoong in 1993. At that time, the main focus of traditional music performances was on orchestras or small chamber groups of solely traditional instruments. No group was particularly successful. I thought we needed to have something like a guerrilla group, with all the composers actually performing. Merely reviving tradition has little meaning in the contemporary world, but we must keep the silhouette of the old while creating something unique. Seulgidoong had blended together Korean and Western instruments in their songs, but from the point when I joined, we began to concentrate more on rhythmic aspects. I left again because Seulgidoong became a kind of vacation job for its members; we all developed our own work outside the group, and just moonlighted within it. (Personal interview, June 22, 1999)

Won helped devise new drums for the ensemble—kits of oversize *puk* barrel drums, drums turned on end and mounted on frames like massive snare drums, and sets of tuned drums used like congas—to allow percussion riffs and solos to be performed, much as would be expected from a jazz drummer. Won's first success as a composer came in 1993 with an orchestral updating of a fishing song, "Shin paennorae" (New boat song). It was performed to great acclaim on TV, then recorded in several versions, one combining a small ensemble with a jazz group, and another with the complete Seulgidoong.[41] It has become a popular piece with Korean traditional orchestras. Success comes partly from accessibility, notably the familiarity of the folk-song melody. More, though, the piece inspires because of the percussion involved: when performed, people respond enthusiastically in exactly the same way as they do after a jazz or pop drummer has executed a tremendous solo.

---

[41] The first combined the groups Puri (P'uri), TriBe-HEaM, and a traditional ensemble, and appears as track 8 on *3 ilgan ŭi chŏlmŭn ŭmakhoe* (Young musicians association three-day concert; Samsung Music SCO-098MUN, 1996). The second is track 8 on *Seulgidoong: From the Evening Tide Till the Coming Dawn* (Samsung Music SCO-127TAC, 1996).

Folk Songs as Pop

Won now has four albums to his credit, three devoted to film scores.[42] The first, released in 1996, was his soundtrack to *Kkonip* (A petal), a film directed by Jang Sun Woo (U Changsŏn). The film, winner of the Grand Bell award, concerns the brutal suppression of a 1980 civilian uprising in the southern city of Kwangju by the South Korean military under Chun Doo Hwan. It is told from the perspective of a fifteen-year-old girl. By the summer of 1999, the album had sold more than forty thousand copies (an average CD of traditional music sells about a thousand copies).[43] Folk music has, finally, become pop music:

> The theme begins with string pizzicato chords and a single gong, damped after each note, just as the gong is damped by shamans when they call the spirits of the dead. Above this, a Korean fiddle, the *haegŭm,* is heard, soon supported by string chords. The musician is Soonyon Chung from Seulgidoong. The fiddle has a peculiarly nasal quality; it pleads for attention and, perhaps for this reason, it holds a central place in shaman ritual ensembles throughout the west of Korea, notably around Seoul. Next a female voice, wordless, echoes the fiddle, much as in the shamanic *kuŭm*. Later, the theme returns, sung by the heroine, Lee Jung Hyun (Yi Chŏnghyŏn). Now, the accompaniment is electric guitars, synthesizers, and a high-hat cymbal. The world of Korean folk music has been transformed.

References

Anderson, Benedict. 1983. *Imagined Communities: Reflections on the Origin and Spread of Nationalism.* London: Verso.

Anonymous. 1955. "Definition of Folk Music." *Journal of the International Folk Music Council* 7:23–31.

———. 1983. *Chindo minsok chosa charyojip* [Collected data on the folk customs of Chindo]. Seoul: Private publication.

Blacking, John. 1987. "A Commonsense View of All Music":

---

[42] These include *Kkonip* (A petal; Samsung Music SCO-088WIN, 1996); *Asura* (Samsung Music SCO-144WIN, 1997); *Arŭmdaun shijŏl* (Spring in my hometown; Paektudaegan [Korean Film Art Centre], n.d.); and *Ijaesu ŭinan* (*Les Insurges;* Sony Music CLK 9062, 1999).

[43] This is according to Pak Sŭngwŏn at Seoul Records (personal interview, June 2, 1999). During 1998, Seoul Records sold a total 100,121 copies of its 163 traditional music albums.

Reflections on Percy Grainger's Contribution to Ethnomusicology and Music Education. Cambridge: Cambridge University Press.

Child, Francis James. 1861. *English and Scottish Ballads*. 1956 reprint. New York: Folklore Press.

Ch'oe Chongmin, ed. 1984. *Han'guk ŭi minsok ŭmak: Chejudo minyo p'yŏn* [Folk music of Korea: Volume on Cheju folk songs]. Sŏngnam: Han'guk chŏngshin munhwa yŏn'guwŏn.

Chŏng Chaeho. 1982. "Minyo" [Folk song]. In *Han'guk minsok taegye 6* [Survey of Korean folk culture 6], 261–353. Seoul: Koryŏ taehakkyo minjok munhwa yŏn'guso ch'ulp'anbu.

Cohen, Anthony, ed. 1982. *Belonging: Identity and Social Organisation in British Rural Cultures*. Manchester: Manchester University Press.

Elbourne, R. P. 1976. "The Question of Definition." *Yearbook of the International Folk Music Council* 7:9–29.

Han Chungmo and Chŏng Sŏngmu. 1983. *Chuch'e ŭi munye iron yŏn'gu* [A study of chuch'e philosophy culture and arts theory]. P'yŏngyang: Sahoe kwahak ch'ulp'ansa.

Harker, Dave. 1985. *Fakesong: The Manufacture of British "Folk Song" from 1700 to the Present Day*. Milton Keynes: Open University Press.

Hobsbawm, Eric, and Terrence O. Ranger. 1983. *The Invention of Tradition*. Cambridge: Cambridge University Press.

Howard, Keith. 1989a. "*Namdo tŭl norae*: Ritual and the Intangible Cultural Asset System." *Journal of Ritual Studies* 3.2:203–16.

———. 1989b. *Bands, Songs, and Shamanistic Rituals: Folk Music in Korean Society*. Seoul: Korea Branch of the Royal Asiatic Society.

———. 1998. "Blending the Wine and Stretching the Wineskins: New Korean Music for Old Korean Instruments." In *Essays in Musicology: An Offering in Celebration of Lee Hye-ku on his Ninetieth Birthday*, ed. Yi Sŏngch'ŏn, 501–36. Seoul: Seoul National University.

———. 1999. "Minyo in Korea: Songs of the People and Songs for the People." *Asian Music* 30.2:1–37.

Hughes, David. 1985. "The Heart's Hometown: Folksongs in Modern Japan." Ph.D. diss., University of Michigan.

Hulbert, Homer B. 1896. "Korean Vocal Music." *Korean Repository* 3:45–53.

Hwang Okon. 1996. "The Birth of Academic Inquiries into Korean Popular Music." Paper presented at the National Meeting of the Society for Ethnomusicology, Toronto, November.

Im Tonggwŏn. 1974. *Han'guk minyo yŏn'gu* [A study of Korean folk songs]. Seoul: Chimmundang.
Kang Tŭnghak. 1988. *Chŏngsŏn arirang yŏn'gu* [A study of Chŏngsŏn-area *Arirang*]. Seoul: Chimmundang.
Kim Kwangŏk. 1992. "Socio-Cultural Implications of the Recent Invention of Tradition in Korea: An Overview." *Papers of the British Association for Korean Studies* 1:7–28.
Kim Myŏnggon. 1994. *Han: Kim Myŏnggon ŭi kwangdae kihaeng* [*Han*: Kim Myŏnggon's travels of the *kwangdae*]. Seoul: Tosŏ ch'ulp'an sanha.
Kim, Yersu. 1976. *Cultural Policy in the Republic of Korea: Studies and Documents on Cultural Policies*. Paris: UNESCO.
Kim Yŏlgyu. 1987. *Arirang... yŏksayŏ, kyŏreyŏ, soriyŏ* [*Arirang*... history, nation, song]. Seoul: Chosŏn ilbosa.
Kim Yŏn'gap. 1988. *Arirang—kŭ mat, mŏt kŭrigo* [*Arirang*—its flavor and essence]. Seoul: Chimmundang.
———, ed. 1986. *Minjok ŭi sumgyŏl, kŭrigo palchaguk sori—Arirang* [Breath of the folk, sound of footsteps—*Arirang*]. Seoul: Hyŏndae munhwasa.
Kwŏn Hŭidŏk. 1991. *Arirang minjok yesulsa* [A folk arts history of *Arirang*]. Seoul: Samho ch'ulp'ansa.
Kwŏn Osŏng. 1984. "Minyo-nŭn minjung ŭi noraeida" [Folk songs are the songs of the people]. In *Ppuri kip'ŭn namu p'alto sori 1* [The deep-rooted-tree songs of Korea 1], 7–20. Seoul: Korea Britannica.
Lee Kang Sook [Yi Kangsuk]. 1977. "Korean Music Culture: Genuine and Quasi-Korean Music." *Korea Journal* 17.8:4–10.
———. 1980. "Today's Korean Music." *Korea Journal* 20.11:70–77.
McCann, David R. 1979. "*Arirang*, the National Folk Song of Korea." In *Studies on Korea in Transition*, ed. David R. McCann, J. Middleton, and E. J. Shultz, 43–56. Honolulu: Center for Korean Studies/University of Hawai'i Press.
Maliangkay, Roald Heber. 1999. "Handling the Intangible: The Protection of Folksong Traditions in Korea." Ph.D. diss., School of Oriental and African Studies, University of London.
Minhak hoebo. 1987. *Folkism 15: T'ŭkchip—Arirang* [Folkism 15: Special edition—*Arirang*]. Seoul: Minhak hoebo.
Naegojang chŏnt'ong kakkugi, comps. 1982. *Okchu ŭi ŏl* [The spirit of Chindo]. Chindo: Chindo kunji p'yŏnjip wiwŏnhoe/Kwangju: Chŏnil ch'ulp'ansa.
Nettl, Bruno. 1985. *The Western Impact on World Music*. New York: Schirmer Books.

O'Rourke, Kevin. 1998. "Demythologizing 'Mŏt.'" *Koreana* 12.3: 34-41.
Pont, Kenneth, arranger. 1972. *Music Workshop Books 1*. Oxford: Oxford University Press.
Porter, James. 1991. "Muddying the Crystal Spring: From Idealism and Realism to Marxism in the Study of English and American Folk Song." In *Comparative Musicology and Anthropology of Music: Essays on the History of Ethnomusicology*, ed. Bruno Nettl and Philip V. Bohlman, 113-30. Chicago: University of Chicago Press.
Staub, Shalom. 1988. "Folklore and Authenticity: A Myopic Marriage in Public Sector Programs." In *The Conservation of Culture: Folklorists and the Public Sector*, ed. Bert Feintuch, 166-79. Lexington: University Press of Kentucky.
Wallman, Sandra, ed. 1979. *Ethnicity at Work*. London: Macmillan.
Wordsworth, William. 1940-49. *The Poetical Works of William Wordsworth*, ed. E. de Selincourt. Oxford: Oxford University Press.
Ye Yonghae. 1963. *In'gan munhwajae* [Human cultural assets]. Seoul: Han'guk ilbosa.
Yi Kŏnyong. 1987. *Han'guk ŭmak ŭi nolli-wa yulli* [The logic and principles of Korean music]. Seoul: Segwang ŭmak ch'ulp'ansa.
Yi Pohyŏng. 1997. "Arirang sori ŭi kŭnwŏn-kwa pyŏnch'ŏn-e kwanhan ŭmakchŏk yŏn'gu" [A musical study of *Arirang*'s origin and changes]. In *Han'guk minyohak 5* [Studies in Korean folk song 5], 81-120. Seoul: Han'guk minyo hakhoe.
Yi Sora. 1985, 1986, 1989, 1990, 1992. *Han'guk ŭi nongyo 1-5* [Korean farming songs 1-5]. Seoul: Hyŏnamsa.

EIGHT

The Script, Sound, and Sense of the Seoul Olympic Ceremonies

MARGARET DILLING

An early version of the scenario for the Seoul Olympic ceremonies posed three questions as working principles. First, does this script include a subject fit for a world festival? Second, is the specific character of Korea today realized in this script? Third, does it have the fresh shock of the avant garde? The alliterative language fell away as the script passed through revisions into production. But the three guidelines remained operative. I would paraphrase subject as "universal," specific as "distinctively Korean," and shock as "new." The music subsequently commissioned, composed, and selected for the ceremonies was likewise measured by these three criteria. I will use them as markers to discuss how music implemented the scenario or, to put it another way, how the design of the ceremonies became audible.

I am grateful to Kang Shinbyo and John MacAloon for inviting me to participate in the Seoul Olympiad Anniversary Conference and for prompting this formulation of my research on the music of the Seoul Olympic Ceremonies. All of the information on which this study depends—official documents, musical scores, and interviews—owes to the generosity of the people cited in appendix A. Composers of music not treated in this chapter will be discussed in forthcoming monographs on the music. It was the high quality of that music and its relation to Korean traditional music that first drew my attention to the ceremonies.

My research in Korea has been supported in part by a Jacob Javits Fellowship from the U.S. Department of Education and has been made pleasant and possible in Seoul through the hospitality of my community, the Religious of the Sacred Heart (Sŏng shim sunyŏwŏn), and by friends and research assistants: Sŏ Chŏnghwa, Kim Ajŏng, Gary Rector, Pak Chongshik, and Kim Chŏngŭn; and in Berkeley by Cho Sŏngt'aek, Yi Sŏnggŭn, and the Center for Korean Studies at the University of California. With the exception of the English final program, the translations are my own, with the help of research assistants listed above.

Before composers, music advisers, or scenario writers could begin work on their specific projects, they had to enter a process of interpreting the Korea they wished to present to the world and of translating that concept into a performance. This hermeneutical task of self-reflection and creation carried a corresponding effort to imagine the effect of Korean cultural forms on a world audience. If the world was coming to Seoul, what of Seoul (Korea) could be communicated to the world?[1] For the "flower" of the cultural Olympics—the opening and closing ceremonies—art forms unique to Korea were perhaps too foreign to be accessible to outsiders. How could Korea present its traditional culture as impressive but not so exotic as to feel strange? The first section of this chapter follows the process of interpretation by the planners as they articulated it in several drafts of the scenario between 1986 and 1988 and elaborated it later during interviews. The voices in documents and conversations are arranged around scenario themes in an effort to let them explain what they were trying to do. The method in the first section is to interfere as little as possible with the information provided by juxtaposed texts, to take them first at face value.

The process by which preliminary ideas came to final form in the production revealed the planners' attitudes toward traditional Korean culture and its communicability. Moreover, the drafters of the all-controlling scenario had made a basic decision not simply to display items of folklore but to emphasize "reinterpretation and re-creation of traditional Korean arts throughout the production" (draft 6, 43).[2] This basic policy to reinterpret and re-create tradition guided the planners of music for the ceremonies as well. In presenting Korea to the world through the medium of music, they

---

[1] A contest open to the citizens of Korea produced the slogan of the Seoul Olympics: The World to Seoul, Seoul to the World ("Segye-nŭn Sŏul-lo, Sŏul-ŭn segye-ro"). The catchphrase was officially adopted by the Seoul Olympic Organizing Committee (SLOOC) on January 10, 1985.

[2] This passage by Yi Ŏryŏng above (1988:43) continues, "By reinterpretation (*chaehaesŏk*) and re-creation (*chaech'angjo*) we can give a new taste or flavor (*sae masŭl*) to those things."

The Seoul Olympic Organizing Committee was the publisher of all official documents pertaining to the opening and closing ceremonies. To simplify references within the chapter, I have devised a system of draft numbers and familiar titles to identify versions of the scenario as it passed from the early planning stages to the final program (see appendix B). While writing this manuscript, I did not have access to the original text of report number 1. Extended excerpts from the document are cited from Kim Munhwan 1988.

would not rest on the past glories of their native musical tradition. Instead, they decided to take the risk of commissioning new compositions, rooted in the tradition but not repeating it.

The second section of this chapter, less neutral in narration, presents three cases of music that exemplify this policy in diverse musical idioms: a song in pop music style designed to be universally appealing; a composition, modeled on Korean traditional art song, that was distinctively Korean; and a pair of electronic compositions generated by computer, which were considered avant garde. For various reasons, each of the three pieces became a center of controversy, stirring up heated debate and changes just weeks before, days before, even the night before the two ceremonies. In light of the sparks that flew during these interactions, it can be said that music acted as a mirror reflecting the points of view of artists, sportspeople, intellectuals, administrators, media experts, and performers. Their inside stories on the making of the ceremonies are told in their art and in their actions, in what they said and what they did not say. When these multiple voices, in addition to my own, are set in conversation with each other in the third section of the chapter, they suggest interpretations of the ceremonies that both amplify and alter the intended meaning. Concluding evaluations of the music reinsert the sound track into the larger process of the Seoul Olympic ceremonies as a whole.

Scenario

A Universal Subject: Ideas, Images, and Ideology

The theme of the Seoul Olympic Games was Harmony and Progress. While these abstract ideas underpinned the opening and closing ceremonies, the scenario planners began as if from scratch to look for a "subject fit for a world festival" along with an image capable of dramatizing the subject in the production of the ceremonies. The first image they considered as a basic symbol for the ceremonies appeared in report number 1 (draft 1), written by members of the initial planning board for the scenario. It was a drawing of a celadon bowl with the description "Heaven-sent peaches, flowers, clouds, and doves in a round bowl. They symbolize the harmony of heaven, earth, and humans; and the two peaches and three doves suggest the five yin-yang principles of the cosmos." The image continued as frontispiece for the next version of the scenario, published as report number 2 (draft 3). Two months later, in the version of the scenario that I call the working script (draft 5), the celadon bowl with its images from earth and sky had disappeared, but the reference to heaven, earth, and humans remained. These interdependent elements from an East Asian worldview, known as *samjae sasang* (the idea of triple foundation), formed the basis for the Olympic ceremonies from first conception to final production.[3]

Scenario planners and advisers explained this basic idea with different nuances. Pak Yonggu referred to heaven, earth, and humans in the context of *madang nori,* "a ritual ceremony that starts before heaven and ends with blessing from heaven." Of the ways he suggests that *madang nori* style could shape the performance activities of the ceremonies, several figured in the final production two years later: the Han Riverside Festival beforehand, the *killori* (literally, "road play" or "procession") to cleanse the ritual space; a solemn dance to greet the sun; and the folk game of *konori* (knot game) as symbol of Korea's desire for harmony (draft 3).[4]

Yi Ŏryŏng offered a second explanation of the three cosmic principles using spatial dimensions:

> If we make the Olympic field a space like the archetype of God's city it will become a place of common feeling for connecting our space with the world's. Moreover, modern people, who have lost

---

[3] The Sino-Korean characters for these elements read *ch'ŏn-chi-in* (heaven, earth, and humans). The Korean and Chinese words for the third character, *saram* and *in* respectively, do not have the exclusively male connotation of "man." Hence, I will use "humans" throughout, although these principles are usually translated heaven, earth, and man. Gender-exclusive pronouns are not a major problem in narrating the music process since all the planners were men except one, Han Yangsun. The artist for the drawing of the celadon bowl was Pyŏn Chongha. He was one of the original trio, with Kim Ch'igon and Pak Yonggu, who began official work on the scenario earlier in 1986. He was also a member of the later Steering/Executive Committee for the ceremonies, but ill health forced him to withdraw from involvement in ceremony preparations.

[4] Pak Yonggu was the seminal thinker and organizer of early ideas for the scenario. In 1981, when Seoul was chosen as host city for the twenty-fourth Olympiad, Pak was president of the newly founded Art Critics Association (Yesul p'yŏngnon'ga hyŏbŭihoe), which included critics from the fields of art, literature, drama, dance, and music. "When our country was chosen, I thought that, as president of that association, I should gather some ideas for the opening and closing ceremonies. Therefore we started that job on the scenario in 1982. Each one had his assignment. I collected ideas from the different fields and we presented them. At that time I thought of the harmonizing of *ch'ŏn-chi-in*" (personal interview, October 11, 1989).

The Script, Sound, and Sense of the Seoul Olympic Ceremonies 177

the sense of vertical space, live only in secular, horizontal space. By reviving the sublime, transcendental, and cosmological dimensions, we can make sacred space as if the world were being created anew. People all over the world will feel utter nobility because heaven, earth, and humans now harmonize with each other in the fresh morning of God's city. (draft 1, 23)[5]

Han Manyŏng gave a third explanation of *samjae sasang* (he used the terms *sam t'aegŭk sasang*, or the idea of the threefold ultimate) with reference to the staging of the Olympic event and its success or failure:

> Our national flag was originally not only red and blue but red, blue, and yellow. That is *sam t'aegŭk sasang*. It implies heaven, earth, and humans. And peace or reconciliation or reunification means these three meet in one place and this creates happiness. Although humans think of something and plan something, if heaven is not in agreement with that, then it must fail. And if humans are thinking about something, but the atmosphere—the social or economic conditions—is not suitable for that idea, then it must fail. And if heaven and earth are in agreement with everything and all is good, but humans are not adjusted to that, then it cannot succeed. This is *sam t'aegŭk sasang*. So heaven means timing, earth means support—power to support such things in the political, economic, social realms—and human means the hero or leader. When these three meet in one place everything succeeds. This is the idea.[6]

---

[5] Yi Ŏryŏng is a writer and critic well known for his astute interpretations of Korean as well as of Japanese culture. He has taught in the Korean Language and Literature Department of Ehwa Women's University in Seoul. At the time of writing, December 1989, he had just been appointed minister of culture for Korea with acknowledgment of his pivotal contribution to the Olympic Ceremonies.

Kim Munhwan is professor of aesthetics at Seoul National University. He joined the reorganized Scenario Planning Committee in February 1987, was a member of the six-member Steering/Executive Committee, and had a pivotal role, with Yi Ŏryŏng, in drafting the working script and final version of the scenario. Kim wrote the Korean translation of the official song, "Hand in Hand," and also a "genetic" study of the scenario from which these citations from report number 1 are taken.

[6] Han Manyŏng served on six of the committees preparing the ceremonies. He is professor of musicology at Seoul National University, former president of the National Classical Music Institute (currently the National Center for Korean Traditional Performing Arts), and a cultural adviser in Korea. He has been my initial and ongoing informant for Olympic Ceremony material, providing many hours of personal interview and conversation before, during, and after the Olympics. His explanation of *sam t'aegŭk sasang* was given during an interview on October 4, 1988.

Between the publication of report number 1 in December 1986 and the final program for the opening ceremony on September 17, 1988, the idea of harmonizing heaven, earth, and humans went through several transformations. In the final production it was most clearly enacted during the prelude to the official ceremony called "Greeting the Sun." A sequence of scenes dramatized the three-part structure of the basic ritual of Korean folk religion, a shamanistic *kut:* purification of the site, which turns ordinary ground into sacred space (the scenes titled "The Passage at Dawn" and "The Dragon Drum Procession"); the descent of the deity ("Heaven, Earth, and Humans" and "Prayer of Blessings"); and a joyous festival in a renewed space and time ("The Light of Genesis" and "A Great Day"). The vertical dimension uniting heaven and earth was additionally depicted by the twenty-two-meter Olympic torch holder, at one moment suggesting the sacred tree of world religions linking heaven and earth, the next moment changing back into its Olympic function of awaiting the torch.

While the idea of heaven, earth, and humans remained the fundamental idea informing both ceremonies, neither the celadon bowl nor the world tree became the primary image guiding the plan or production. The scenario planners spent a month of meetings in search of a word capable of signifying this basic idea as well as the Olympiad theme, asking themselves What is the present reality of Korea? How is our reality common to the whole world? Do we dare name the hard fact of division between North and South Korea? How do we reconcile harsh realities with the occasion of a joyous festival? A motif running through all versions of the scenario is the tension between presenting a spectacle entertaining to the eye and a ceremony provocative of thought for those people "who think deeply about the origin of the cosmos and the crisis of peace" (draft 3). The core image finally chosen by scenario committee members reflected their basic decision to "say it like it is" with a word so real and concrete it could be realized dramatically and applied universally. The word was wall (*pyŏk*).

In the final scenario several walls would be named: race, ideology, economics. The first phrasing of the wall image, "breaking down the wall" (*changbyŏk-ŭl hŏmulgo*), was placed above the table of contents in the write-up of report number 1 as a scenario (draft 2). There it was combined with the Olympic theme, "breaking down the wall and uniting heaven, earth, and humans." By draft 3, "*Changbyŏk-ŭl hŏmulgo*" stood alone as the title. But the act of breaking down a wall was considered too violent for a nation trying to project a counterimage to one under siege during the Japanese occupation, at war with itself in the Korean War, and more recently disturbed from within by student demonstrations. After discussion inside and outside the committee, the phrasing and emphasis were shifted to "going over the wall" (*pyŏk-ŭl nŏmŏsŏ*), or, as it was translated less literally, "beyond all barriers." The working script carried this title, and wall or barrier persisted to the end as the guiding image of the ceremonies, holding together both the challenge and the hoped-for outcome of the Seoul Olympics. In both working script and final program the ceremony theme is followed by a synopsis:

Beyond All Barriers

Barriers of race, ideology, and wealth—moving beyond the numerous barriers that set us apart, we all gather together in one place, Seoul. Seoul, a sanctuary for the world: a place where mankind becomes one family again united with heaven and earth, a place where broken barriers result in new beginnings, old wounds heal, and the divine rapture of creation leads us to the future of the universe. (draft 6, 3)

This condensed "vision statement" shows that the scenario planners had translated the secular religion of Olympic ideals into a sacred realm of time and space. In the Seoul Olympics, the world's people would come together in a moment of time to a point in space to perform a ritual effectively harmonizing humankind with heaven and earth. When it came time to act out the ideas, images, and ideology in the ceremony production, the square boards of Korean martial art, taekwondo (*t'aegwŏndo*), would become a metaphor for walls as they were split by the fists and feet of the players. The boards as broken walls in the performances following the official IOC ceremony served a function similar to that of the torch holder as world tree in the performances preceding the official ceremony. The moment the sun rose from the sacred tree climaxed the ritual enactment of the vertical and spatial linking of heaven, earth, and humans. The breaking of boards climaxed the depiction of Korean/human history through the horizontal line of time. Broken walls and the harmony of heaven, earth, and humans thus had their corresponding image and dramatization, which turned the static theme of Harmony and Progress into a dynamic subject fit for a world festival—by overcoming the barriers that divide us we can meet in harmony and move together toward our common destiny in the global village.

The discovery of a subject for the ceremonies provided the planners with not only a content but a way of proceeding. According to the final scenario, the Seoul Olympics would begin "with a festival on the Han River, outside the main stadium. The idea is to avoid starting the Games in a space confined by walls. Connected to the oceans of the world, rivers provide an image in contrast and opposition to barriers" (draft 6, 42). The effort to go beyond barriers in structuring the ceremonies resulted in a dissolving of ordinary boundaries. Instead of two events separated by sixteen days of athletic competition, with each ceremony divided into a series of thematically connected scenes, the opening and closing ceremonies were conceived as a continuum in time and space, a single gesture in two motions: beginning on the river, ending on the river, passing inside and outside the stadium, on the ground and in the sky. This "Korean perception of time as a continuous flow rather than a collection of segments" (draft 6, 43) raises the second question of the working script: Is the specific character of Korea itself realized in this scenario?

Specifically Korean: Folklore Familiar and Foreign

> The ceremony itself proceeds in a uniquely Korean manner. Conforming to the philosophy of yin and yang, the opening ceremony is based on "Greeting the Sun" and the closing ceremony on "Greeting the Moon." (draft 6, 43)

The principle of yin-yang as the interaction of complementary opposites and the concept of time as a continuum is, of course, not uniquely Korean. Earlier versions of the scenario locate Korean thought within the context of Eastern (*tongyang*) philosophy. Comparisons there between East and West imply a superiority of Eastern spiritual civilization based on natural law over Western materialistic culture based on science. These comparisons disappeared in the process of revision. Setting up an ideological wall between East and West was hardly in the friendly spirit of global village neighbors that the planners wished to project. While the working script reiterated a comparison between "Western logos with its linear thinking" and "the polyvalent and circular structure of Oriental thought," the planners found a way to "improve" on Western linear thinking by drawing on intellectual resources from within Western culture itself. "We tried to create [the ceremonies within] the contemporary trend of thinking, the avant garde of deconstruction" (draft 5, 51). Neither Derrida nor deconstruction is mentioned in the final version, but writers Yi Ŏryŏng and Kim Munhwan make explicit reference elsewhere to their conceptual sources. Practical application of principles of deconstruction and yin-yang was evident primarily in the blurring of structural borders of time and space in the ceremony production, while the working script links consciousness of such ideas congenial with Korean ways of thought with an effort to "consider more profoundly the Korean people's unique taste a little bit more."

In both working script and final scenario the section on the specific (*koyusang*) character of Korea begins with a metaphor: "There used to be among the pot stands a hidden unopened pot carefully kept for the day of a guest's arrival." In such a pot would be stored the bean paste or *chang* so central to Korean cooking. "On the occasion of the opening and closing ceremonies we Koreans should show to our world guests the hidden and secret taste of *chang*" (draft 5, 50).[7] In the metaphor of the unique *chang* of Korea's traditional culture, the increment of "fresh" taste in the unopened jar of paste is analogous to the "recreation and reinterpretation of traditional Korean arts" that the planners prepared for the Olympic guests. The imagery is probably the work of writer Yi Ŏryŏng. During a KBS interview broadcast three days after the Games ended, he made explicit the nuance of secret and hidden found in the scenario's Korean text: "For the Olympics we showed our secret treasures to the world." He is referring not only to the philosophical riches in Korean culture and to the subtleties of society in "the best-kept secret in Asia," as the travel posters refer to Korea, but also to traditions from Korean life and ritual, some now codified in genres of music, dance, and theater.[8] However, as early as 1986, Yi had warned against making the ceremonies simply "an exhibition enumerating our folklore.... If we try to show Korean things to an excessive degree it will be as lifeless as a folk doll" (draft 1, 28).

---

[7] Aside from a change of the insider reference—"our people's taste" to "Korean people's taste"—the only difference in the Korean text of the two versions is a double negative for emphasis in the earlier version: "It would not do not to show our...taste of *chang*" (draft 5, 50).

[8] Government sponsorship has made modern versions of these traditions public and available to Koreans. Established in the 1960s, the National Cultural Asset System directs and funds an elaborate network of research, designation, revivals, performances, contests, festivals, and evaluations of traditional arts. Few countries would have at the ready such a storehouse of performance genres to draw on when they wanted to present their cultural treasures to outsiders.

The ceremonies for the Tenth Asian Games staged by Korea in the fall of 1986 were an example in recent memory of displaying items of folklore. They contained royal processions (two), a wedding, and a military band procession; court and folk dances: crane, fan (two), cymbal, flower crown, drum, lantern, and *salp'uri*; farmers' band music, *konori* mass game, women's circle dance, children's games, and folk songs. Actually the Seoul Olympic ceremonies included many of the same genres, but in 1988 nothing was just itself. It was always reinterpreted in a creative context, offering the fresh taste of the unopened pot of *chang* instead of a *pibimbap* of folklore items.[9] The Olympic scenario mentioned several ways the organizers tried to reinterpret and re-create their traditional culture. The royal procession from the Yi dynasty was turned into a procession of drums. The dragon drum in place of the king would have power, when struck from the foot of the sacred tree, to make the sun rise. In addition, "By having many people twirling the *sangmo* [a Korean hat with a long white paper streamer] we emphasized the rhythmic beauty of the line... matching them with the modern ribbon of rhythmic gymnastics. 'A Great Day' was invented by changing the fluttering parachutes into the tents and canopies used on days of Korean festivals" (draft 6, 43). The planners sought constant metamorphosis of traditional arts. The purpose was to give not a stale but a fresh taste, to break through habitual ways of perception of both cultural insiders and foreigners. "Both entertaining and thought provoking," the ceremonies were designed to startle people into seeing Korea in a new way.

The Fresh Shock of the Avant Garde: Cultural Competition

> The opening and closing ceremonies of the Seoul Olympics will be presented to the entire world. For an event of this magnitude only something that will make a great impact will suit the occasion. (draft 6, 43)

The third criterion for the scenario aimed at an effect commensurate with the scale of the occasion and the size of the audience. The magic medium for achieving that effect—bringing humanity to one point in time and space in Seoul, overcoming the

---

[9] *Pibimbap* is a favorite Korean dish composed of rice, slivered meat, and cut vegetables of many kinds crowned with an egg, all stirred together just before eating.

boundaries of distance between peoples, making visible the hidden treasures of Korean traditional culture—was television:

> Now there is a new media generation. So the Olympics can produce a miracle. Four billion people of the world, their eyes and ears focused on one place, can make one heart. The sun will be the spotlight, the wind the sound effects, all of this controlled by the hands of the Korean people in Seoul. (draft 5, 4)[10]

In this penultimate draft, the TV screen becomes the stage of a puppet theater, the Korean people the puppeteer. The metaphor of all the world as a stage changes, through the power of TV, to Seoul as the stage of the world. This puppet theater image did not survive beyond the working script. The equation of world population with the number of ceremony viewers was generalized to expressions like "worldwide audience." But the scope of the exposure remained a daunting fact in the planners' list of challenges:

> The Seoul Olympiad is the greatest festival for the Korean people since the beginning of history. And who knows when this big a festival will come again in the future. Given this opportunity we cannot stop with mere entertainment. The event should provide freshness and shock together with joy. (draft 3, 2)

"Shock" in English, the third of the "S" factors, was softened to "surprise and lasting impression" in the official translation of the final program, but the word for shock or impact (*ch'unggyŏksŏng*) remained in the Korean text and other internal documents.[11] To convey Korea's particular feeling and culture to

---

[10] This excerpt is from a three-page essay introducing the working script. It is signed by the the SLOOC president, Pak Sejik, and dated March 1987. Like most of the documents relative to the scenario, it represents the collective thinking of the planning committee though prefaced by an administrator. One member of the planning committee said good-naturedly, "We told him what to say." However, Pak was far from being a distant administrator, and several sections of the essay echo his characteristic ideas as they were heard both in private and in public. He followed the development of the scenario in close detail. For instance, he attended every meeting of the pivotal series, March 8–15, 1987, at the Plaza Hotel, when the revision committee hammered out the details of each unit of the ceremony in marathon sessions.

[11] Twice during our many hours of conversation about the ceremonies, Han Manyŏng insisted on "surprise not shock," but without further explanation of the reasons for his objection to the original word. A manual for broadcasters in Korean, undated but probably assembled shortly before the ceremonies, also changes the goal of "shock" to "surprise," as if the planners had toned down an abrasive connotation for public relations reasons.

the world audience, "there must be shock in the meeting of science, especially new technology, and art. By fresh conceptions, trite and fixed ideas will be broken and people can see" (draft 5, 1). This effort to make a great impact was thought of in terms of a competition (*kyŏnggi*: draft 6; *kyŏngju*: draft 5): "In the Olympiad not only athletes have competitions to break world records but also, through the performance of the opening and closing ceremonies we [will] set some cultural world records for humanity of new imagination and scientific technology" (draft 5, 50). An earlier draft carries through on the analogy between cultural and bodily Olympics: "Therefore in the contest of wisdom if we imitate others or stick to and repeat our own way of doing things we immediately fall behind. Only if the Seoul Olympiad gives visual, auditory, and cultural shock with ideas that have never been tried can it win an eternal record" (draft 5, 51).[12] The aggressive imagery of competition was diffused in the final version, but even the "application of the most advanced technology" would be "done in a uniquely Korean way."

How to accomplish the third goal was worked out in the production plans of the working script and the final program. Both drafts mention the opening ceremony scene with the world tree, the later scenario more succinctly:

> One example [of new production ideas] is the use of the flame holder as a theatrical device. Shortly before the official ceremony, the camouflaged world tree is dismantled to unveil the flame holder. Highly advanced technology was essential to make the huge structure vanish instantly and reveal the flame holder. (draft 6, 43)

An early production idea of devising an enormous curtain that would hide the torch holder and then fall away was scrapped because of technical demands. The idea eventually used was in line with the theme of metamorphosis and fluid boundaries. Through laser technology the S-shaped symbols of heaven, earth, and humans atop the sacred tree would separate and rise with the sun, revealing the flame cauldron concealed underneath: "To be transformed in a wink from a solid object to air, computer control was needed. The combination of scientific technology, dramatic effect far beyond people's expectation, and the aesthetic object of the sculpture makes for a new shock effect" (draft 5, 51). The

---

[12] *Nogoja*, or someone who falls behind, denotes one who cannot keep up with the others, as in a military exercise.

gasps of surprise from the audience at the moment, especially from those seated in the southeast corner of the stands near the cauldron, attested to the success of the startling effect, reached again later in the high-tech means by which the torchbearers rose to the heights of the cauldron to light the flame.

The scenario planners wanted the shock of surprise to come from "not only scientific technology...but also [from] the image itself" (draft 5, 52). An elaborate show of laser lights projected on the night sky at the end of the closing ceremony was planned at the time of the working script. Even though the technology was invented by "others," the idea and the selection of pictures was conceived by Koreans and planned as a first-time-ever for the Olympics. By means of random questionnaires, "We will ask the world's people what is the first image that comes to mind when you think of the whole history of humanity, from its first appearance on the planet up to the present. After selecting the top five among the submitted images we will use them in the laser show.... Or we could ask for symbols of hope for the future" (draft 5, 51). The laser show, without the public contest beforehand, was relegated to the Han Riverside Festival the night before the opening ceremony,[13] while 88 "Hodoris and Hosunis"—seven-year-olds born on the day Korea was named the host country of the 1988 Olympics—were brought into the stadium as symbols of hope.[14]

The transforming spirit of the planners extended to the official ceremony as well. According to the working script, they wanted to organize audience participation in more than the usual way of their holding placards for a mass visual design. Small wind instruments, called *pŏdŭl p'iri* in Korea, were distributed by section to all spectators to be played during the long entrance of athletes. Another method for sustaining spectator interest was to collect representative masks from all 160 participating countries and have them dance as face, body, or pole masks "to evoke surprise in the

---

[13] Proposed images of humanity became Olympic circular symbols and words (harmony, peace, progress) projected onto the side of Korea's tallest office building, the "63" building. The fierce electrical storm that night during the outdoor concert justified the planners' fear that the original plan for using laser technology during the opening ceremony did, in fact, have too many variables subject to disaster. No one could forget the downpour during the entire opening ceremony of the Asian Games near the same September date two years before.

[14] *Ho* from the name of the tiger (*horangi*) for the Seoul Olympiad mascot, Hodori, was prefixed to the affectionate nickname for boys (*-dori*) and girls (*-suni*).

participants by their curiosity in looking for their own country's mask" (draft 5, 52).[15] Stereo headsets for each of the 100,000 people in the stadium would transmit simultaneous translations into five languages of the narrative explaining the ceremonies.[16] By the time of the final program, the participation features of earphones, musical instruments, and placards are listed as means "to entertain the audience."

In the final scenario, entertainment as a goal is coupled three times with a message: (1) "both entertaining and thought-provoking"; (2) "other than the presentation of the theme, another important aspect is to entertain the audience"; and (3) "the show is entertaining and exciting but at the same time care was taken to create a universality" (draft 6, 42–43). In earlier versions, entertainment was mentioned pejoratively as "not mere entertainment" or "not only entertainment for the eye and simply game or play" (drafts 1 and 3). Scenario revisers were concerned that the ceremonies might become too heavy philosophically, too serious. In every version there was mention of the joyous spirit of a Korean festival, traditionally not separated from "serious" religious ritual, but here requiring a constant balancing act between ideology and spectacle. In the effort at synthesis the ceremonies have the quality of a consciously constructed art work, with scenarios explicitly aiming at a cohesion of theoretical factors and desired affect. "When the three S factors of subject, specific, and shock are combined organically and well transmitted to the world, the Seoul opening and closing ceremonies will be a warm and peaceful womblike place for humankind" (draft 5, 52).[17] In the English translation of the final scenario, the S's are smoothed over: "subject" becomes "theme"; "specific," "originality"; and "shock," "the impression of each piece." In contrast to the working script's daring suggestion that the Seoul Olympics could be the origin of a new "humanity as never experienced before," the

---

[15] This scene reached the production stage not as part of the official ceremony but as the scene representing "Chaos" (Hondon) in the dramatization of Korean history following the official events.

[16] For the actual ceremonies this became seven languages: Chinese, Russian, Arabic, Japanese, Spanish, French, and English.

[17] The womb imagery recalls the shape of the stadium as intended by architect Yi Manik. The opening ceremony drew on his model of the stadium as a Korean celadon vase when the parachutists, having formed the five Olympic circles in a stunning formation overhead, then fell like colored flower petals into the stadium space. During the closing ceremony, the aerial view via TV made the stadium's womblike reference visible in the black night.

final program ends with a "warm fuzzy" prediction: "As the three factors involved in the show are synthesized... the opening and closing ceremonies of the Seoul Olympics will convey a warm and peaceful feeling to the world" (draft 6, 43). A vivid aesthetic had blurred to global bliss.

A production script is obviously not meant for the public eye of either natives or foreigners. There was, however, a very public beginning to the story behind both theoretical and practical scenarios, as well as behind the sounds, in the ceremonies to open and close the Tenth Asian Games in the fall of 1986. These ceremonies functioned as a large-scale rehearsal for those of 1988. In the Asian Games, Koreans tried out on a regional stage ideas that they totally reimagined before putting their show on the world stage. There are multiple correlations of theme, structure, and cultural genre in the 1986 and 1988 ceremonies. In addition, the final version of the 1988 ceremonies serves as a kind of self-critique of their performance in 1986; what the planners included and omitted, repeated and modified, restructured and reinterpreted may be read in turn as their own evaluation document, even a progress report in taste among planners, performers, and producers. Although many structures in Korea had ostensibly changed during the political dramas of 1987–88, the dramatis personae in cultural circles were still the same people, their theaters of operation the same institutions.[18] What is remarkable is that the same set of actors could produce a play so transformed, the aesthetic tightness and rightness of 1988 far beyond the rehearsal. For instance, a sequence of scenes common to the 1986 and 1988 versions of the opening ceremony depicts a paradisaical world disrupted and then restored to harmony. In the Asian Games ceremonies, the Land of Morning Calm is darkened by storm clouds, which yield to the spring and summer of youth. By the time of the working script for the Olympic ceremonies the storm as crisis had changed to a confusion of masks, as in the final

---

[18] This is particularly true among the administrators of the two organizing committees. The director-general of the Olympic Ceremonies Operation Unit, Yi Kiha, explained his role to me: "I was involved from the time of the Asian Games. So actually I began my job in 1984. Beginning at that time I staged the Asian Games. But when the Asian Games were finished I took charge as department chief of the Olympic opening and closing ceremonies. This department had general control of the ceremonies. In 1984 the AGOC and the SLOOC were together. On paper they were separate. But, in fact, the same people did both" (personal interview, October 3, 1989).

production. The taekwondo scene in the Olympic scenario served the dramatic function of restoring order, whereas in the Asian Games ceremony it was a demonstration sport lightly disguised as representing summer in a cycle of seasons.

In the next section I will allude to this refinement of symbolic reference in examining how the music supports both the theoretical and practical scenario in three scenes: "One World" (*Han madang*) at the end of the opening ceremony; "Beyond All Barriers" (*Pyŏk-ŭl nŏmŏsŏ*), the climax scene of the same ceremony; and the pair of scenes for the lighting and extinguishing of the torch during the official ceremonies.

Music

> In an attempt to show the ideology of the Seoul Olympics and the quality of Korean music to the world we asked excellent domestic composers to write music on the basis of the scenario. We asked them to try and produce music which would harmonize Korean traditional music and Western music and have universal appeal for the world's people. (SLOOC 1988b:68)

Once the working script was in place by April 1987, a committee of four music experts selected composers according to their known compositional styles to match the style of particular scenes: Korean traditional, Western classical, or cosmopolitan popular.[19] Then began an arduous process for the composers—orientation to the scenario, discussions with music directors, a viewing of past Olympic films, collaboration with choreographers, composing, making demonstration tapes, making revisions, rehearsing, recording, making presentations to committees, making more revisions, rerecording, making substitutions for rejected works—before their work was finally included on the audio track. Like the scenario writers, the composers entered a hermeneutical process of interpreting and translating. They had to ask themselves how to represent Korea to a world audience with music that would appeal and not alienate, that would sound familiar and not too

---

[19] Members of the Music Committee were Yi Kangsuk, Han Manyŏng, Yi Sangman, and Kim Hŭijo. After they recommended the composers to the SLOOC, each composer was commissioned; the SLOOC paid the composer one half of his commission at the beginning, the second half when he turned in the composition. Even the three or four composers whose works were eventually not used in the final production were paid their full commission.

The Script, Sound, and Sense of the Seoul Olympic Ceremonies 189

foreign. Each composer reexamined Korea's musical traditions through the lens of his own compositional style and made an imaginative leap to an outsider's response. Such a translation effort was at work in the process that brought, or almost brought, to the ears of the world a pop song, an art song in traditional Korean style, and a computer composition. In attending to the single "channel" of music within the multitrack system of elements that make up Olympic ceremonies, this section of the chapter also serves a heuristic function of testing what is added to our perception of the total event by listening intently to one component.

Universal: Music as International Trade

> "The music of the Olympic ceremonies is for the world, not just for our country."
> "If we use too much traditional music most countries will have a feeling that it's unfamiliar and too urgent, you know, propagandistic. Even though we select traditional music it can be slightly arranged and some modern feeling given to it."
> "I didn't use Korean rhythm and pitch systems because I thought the Olympic music should be open to all people, not be too closed to foreigners."
> "Because it was the Olympics I used disco rhythm."

These voices of composers and a committee member during interviews suggest issues common to all, as well as some prevailing attitudes and assumptions about the unique tradition of Korean music, on one hand, and the fear that it might sound strange to foreigners on the other; the need to match the music to a functional event; and the belief that Western popular music was the most universal idiom. The last view was evident in the SLOOC's choice of a composer, lyricist, singing group, and recording company from the popular music world to create the official song of the Seoul Olympics, later called "Hand in Hand." The purpose of the song was described in the Ceremony Administration Team Report: "In November 1986 we decided to make and distribute the official song in order to heighten the festival mood and participation and to advertise the Seoul Olympics efficiently to the IOC nations. Also through the song we wished to share harmony and friendship transcending nationality with the people of the global village" (SLOOC 1988b:73). A more informal explanation is offered by the SLOOC administrator in charge of executing the contract for the song:

The SLOOC had to make an official song for domestic and overseas distribution. At that time even most Americans in the USA, Korea's closest friend, did not know about the twenty-fourth Olympiad. Also, images from the news worried people, images from thirty years ago of the Korean War, of an undeveloped country. "Are there big buildings in Seoul?" people asked. In Europe and Africa also, the Seoul Olympic Games were not known worldwide. So the best way of informing the world about the Seoul Olympic Games, of emphasizing cooperation between all the IOC countries, was to make a big famous song like "We Are the World." (Kim Ch'igon, personal interview, September 23, 1989)[20]

This popular song hit, composed for an international relief effort, was mentioned by many people as the model Koreans had in mind in imagining their own theme song. Though not directly associated with the 1984 Olympics, the composition was associated with Los Angeles. " 'We Are the World' was so perfect as a theme song I didn't see how we could do better," said one composer who had attended the Los Angeles ceremonies. This admiration may account for the resemblance of melodic contour in the opening of the chorus in both songs.

While the SLOOC officials who made arrangements for the production of the official song seemed in agreement on the use of a pop music idiom, some advisory committee members thought the official song representing Korea should not be popular music but classical music.[21] The SLOOC won out over objections of the classicists. "We imposed it," said one official. The contract stipulates pop style in view of the desired effect:

> The words of the song should include the theme of the Seoul Olympic Games and Korea and should be worldwide, universal, popular, and written in English. As for the music it should be easily singable, have universal mass appeal. It should be capable

---

[20] Kim Ch'igon was the assistant secretary-general of the SLOOC for the Ceremonies and Cultural Field. Prior to the Asian Games, he served as national minister of culture and information. Following the dissolution of the SLOOC six months after the ceremonies, he was appointed director of the National Museum of Art.

[21] Kim Ch'igon illustrated this attitude toward popular music among certain Koreans with a public incident. When one of Korea's leading pop singers, Patty Kim, was allowed to give a concert at Seoul's Sejong Cultural Center, sponsors of the center withdrew their membership. But, he argued, "Nowadays pop songs can be great songs. In the U.S. and Europe they call pop singers 'artists.' They do not make a division between classic and pop singers in designating an 'artist.'"

of heightening the festival mood of the Olympics and be written in a pop song idiom. (SLOOC 1988b:79)

Less easily settled were the strong objections raised early on from among the planners themselves about opening up "bidding" to an international slate of composers. The SLOOC's choice later of non-Koreans to write the song raised a further storm of protest from the world of Korean pop music professionals; SLOOC officials up to the president had to muster all their negotiation skills to deal with this internal reaction.

To tell the story of "Hand in Hand" I call not on composer Giorgio Moroder, lyricist Tom Whitlock, or the vocal group Koreana. Two unlikely but efficient narrators are the staff person and lawyer who drew up the music section of the Ceremony Administration Team Report and the contract. These documents contain information on the SLOOC's collective purposes and ways of proceeding plus hints about the song's reception:

> At first the SLOOC reviewed two possible methods of creating a song: one would be to compose the song in Korea and then for the SLOOC to advertise and distribute it. The second would be to hold an international contest, then select and distribute the winning song. Both of these plans were abandoned because of the enormous budget and numbers of personnel needed to carry them out. However, if a record company with worldwide credibility, skills, and professional experience would make and distribute the song, we could accomplish our purpose without any expenditure. After reviewing offers from B-M [Burson-Marsteller] Co. in the U.S., Dentsu in Japan, and Polygram [in Switzerland], already advertising agents for the SLOOC, the offer from multinational Polygram was the most reasonable and the most economical. So we made a contract with them on March 27, 1987, to produce the official song for the Seoul Olympics and distribute it with the official mark of the Seoul Olympics. (SLOOC 1988b:73)

Although no figure appears in this copy of the contract, the report says it cost Polygram 2 billion wŏn (about $2,850,000 at that time) to produce and distribute the song: "Polygram will pay all expenditures for production and distribution.... Polygram can produce the record, cassette, and CD [and video] and distribute them worldwide.... But after one million copies have been sold, Polygram must pay 5 cents [in the contract it says 3 percent] to SLOOC on each additional sale" (SLOOC 1988b:73). After April 1989, the SLOOC expected to receive a little more than 1 million wŏn (about $150,000) in royalties. Part of Polygram's mandate was to distribute the song in sufficient time before the opening of the Games to allow time for it to become a hit in various countries. Polygram president Ossie Drechsler assured Kim Ch'igon that the song would peak in popularity six weeks after its release, coinciding with the opening of the Games. However, "We wanted the peak a little earlier," Kim stated in a later interview, probably to attract tourists to Seoul. By the time of the Games, "Hand in Hand" ranked number 1 on the charts in seventeen countries and within the top 10 in thirty countries. What proportion of its success can be attributed to promotion and exposure, what amount to its inherent likableness may not be measurable even by the pros in the trade, like Polygram, who made it happen. However, in the cultural and commercial sport of going for the gold—gold record, not gold medal—the SLOOC had surely moved from amateur to professional status.

There is a warning in the contract that Polygram "should not overcommercialize the Olympic song in such a way that it violates the original purpose or undermines the pure spirit of the Olympics" (SLOOC 1988b:81). When I asked SLOOC president Pak Sejik what was behind this injunction, he said, "That was one of my policies not to commercialize, not only in the music part or cultural part but also in the other transactions. This [event] is not for making money but to promote friendship, understanding, cultural revitalization" (personal interview, September 26, 1989).[22] Pak also mentioned people's worry that such a business deal with an international record company would end up costing the SLOOC a lot of money. "But it didn't cost anything. Instead we earned money from royalties." While the transaction with Polygram was the most commercial aspect of the Olympic ceremonies, the SLOOC had grounds for self-congratulations in bringing off a coup in cost efficiency and international public relations, even if the internal price was high.

As for the song itself, Polygram was to choose "a world-class, famous composer and songwriter with the authorization of the SLOOC." Polygram chose Giorgio Moroder, who later arrived at

---

[22] Pak Sejik was the first member of the organizing committee in 1985, which was then called the Asian Games Organizing Committee and only later the Seoul Olympic Organizing Committee. By his own account, Pak became minister of sports on January 1, 1986, acting president [of the SLOOC] in March 1986, and full president on May 6, 1986. A former army general, Pak served as chief of a state utility prior to his SLOOC post. Following the Olympics, Korean president Roh Tae-woo—himself a former general, sports minister, and SLOOC president—appointed Pak as director of the National Security Planning Board.

his SLOOC interview carrying a portfolio of hit songs, including the official song from the Los Angeles Olympics, "Reach Out." According to Kim Ch'igon, Moroder came to Seoul three times to study Korean folk song and traditional music at MBC (Munhwa Broadcasting Company) and learn "how to express traditional Korean emotion" as it appears in contemporary Korean pop music.[23] His contractual mandate was to write a song "that everybody loves to sing" (SLOOC 1988b:79). Said Kim:

> Moroder tried to write a very easy song, very easily sung by anyone. For Westerners it was very easy to learn. But for Koreans it felt a little difficult to sing. Korean pop song is usually a little different.

The song went through its own set of revisions, not to make it easier for Koreans but more Korean for export. After hearing a demonstration and holding a discussion in October 1987 between Polygram officials, the SLOOC, Moroder, and "domestic experts,"

> We decided to revise the song to highlight somewhat the theme of the Olympics and the image of Korea. After reviewing the revised song in January 1988, we decided on the song with some small changes: inserting the word *"arirang"* and giving it the English title "Hand in Hand." Kim Munhwan supplied the Korean lyrics in April 1988. (SLOOC 1988b:74)

Even the title was problematic at one point. First known only as the "Official Song of the Seoul Olympics," the title "Hand in Hand" was opposed by some because it was too ordinary. The argument in its favor was that as a common expression it would seem familiar to people and be well received. There was a premiere at the press center, downtown Seoul, for a hundred national and foreign reporters on June 21, 1988, and in July, Polygram began marketing in a hundred countries. At this point in the official documents, an indication of local response is suggested:

> As soon as the song was marketed, some [people in] domestic pop music circles began to complain about the song, saying it was made by foreigners. The SLOOC worried about that somewhat. However, after understanding the real intention of the SLOOC, they agreed with us and willingly supported us. (SLOOC 1988b:74)

---

[23] According to Pak Sejik, "Moroder came to Korea in 1987 to get some kind of feeling for the country before composing. When he went up to Namsan [a mountain in Seoul] to watch the sun rise, he slapped his knee: 'Aha, now I've got the feeling.' And that feeling appears in the powerful part of the song" (1990).

This statement so condenses the number, duration, and intensity of a series of negative reactions that it misrepresents the reality. There seem to have been three or four major episodes in reaction to the SLOOC's plans for the official song. As mentioned earlier, the first was in 1986, when the SLOOC was considering three foreign record producers: B-M, Dentsu, and Polygram. Negative opinions came both from within the planning committees and from the Korean popular music field. In a 1989 interview, Pak Sejik recalled that interaction and his proposed solution, based on an appeal to the universality principle:

> Some were opposed to the open bidding since it was the Seoul Olympics and Korean music professionals should be responsible for composing an official song rather than giving the opportunity to foreigners. That would be a big disgrace for the Korean people. So I was in the middle. But I persuaded these people that the first and most important and ultimate purpose of the Olympics is harmony worldwide, not just in Korea but in the entire world. To contribute to that harmony of humankind we need some music common to everybody on earth. We cannot make people be perfectly at one but most people can sing. [As an alternative,] why not open the chance to compose to everybody, including Korean musicians? We have two more years. Volunteer to compose. If you win, OK, why not?

Kim Ch'igon seems to be describing the same incident during our 1989 conversations:

> The SLOOC called a meeting of pop song writers. [He names a few of them]. We proposed if you want to write the official song of the Olympic Games, write it, give it to us, we'll send it to Polygram. If Koreans write a good song then it will be nominated as the official song. If Polygram wants Moroder to write it maybe [it will be because] he writes the best song.

However, I heard from several domestic composers that they were not convinced they had an equal chance against those employed by the multinational. The second episode seems to have been in March 1987, when the SLOOC signed the contract with Polygram. The third extended between October 1987 and January 1988, as the SLOOC entered (apparently vexed) negotiations with Polygram to add *arirang* and the phrase "morning calm" in the second verse because there was no allusion in the lyrics to either the Seoul Olympics or to Korea. The fourth welling-up of the conflict is the one referred to in the administration report, in June or July 1988, when the marketing began. So it was not at marketing time that Korean pop music personnel first began to complain but a year or two earlier. The SLOOC's worry seems to be understated and the musicians' acquiescence overstated in official accounts. Indeed, at one point in the crisis, the SLOOC president considered canceling the contract, the ceremonies director-general almost resigned, and no less a personage than the president of the Republic of Korea himself was called in to listen to the song. He pronounced his approval, furthering a SLOOC resolve already influenced by the threat of having to compensate Polygram if the contract was broken.

The official accounts accurately name the cause of the negative reaction: the song was "made by foreigners." Not only were songwriters and producers definitely outsiders (Italian, American, Swiss), but the singers, Koreana, carried a foreign stigma. Although native Koreans, the group had acquired early show business experience singing with the U.S. Eighth Army Division. Based in Europe for decades, they were better known there than in Korea before their Olympic fame. The group is basically family: Tom, Jerry, and Cathy Lee are brothers and sister. Marrie Hong, well-known singer and bass player, was added later. Formerly called Arirang, they had changed to Koreana as easier for non-Koreans to pronounce. Neither their clothes, their singing style and mannerisms, nor even their pronunciation of the language is considered typically Korean. While many complained that they were not sufficiently Korean, others thought they were insufficiently famous. As Kim recalls,

> Some wanted an already famous singer, like Michael Jackson. But Drechsler told me that the Olympic Games were a big chance to make a Korean artist number one worldwide. And why hesitate to use them, he asked us. They were already a number one leading group in Europe. ["Almost top class," according to Pak Sejik.] The voices of opposition held that Koreana left Korea so long ago they were remembered only by older groups of Koreans. But this time we could make a Korean superstar.

Koreana's being already employed by Polygram had given the company a better chance of being chosen by the SLOOC over the two corporate rivals. Now the company's ability to make superstars out of near stars gave Koreana an advantage over "domestic" Korean singers. But it did not increase the group's Korean identity in the eyes of Koreans at home.

Koreana's recording of "Hand in Hand" was played constantly in Korea during July, August, and September 1988: piped into the subway and buses and broadcast on radio and TV, over public address systems in schools, and from hilltops in city neighborhoods. By the morning of the opening ceremonies, September 17, no one could have escaped hearing it, and often. In the weeks before the opening, it was played endlessly along the torch relay route, during climactic arrivals of the flame in all provincial cities, and at the twenty-one city festivals. During the Games it was broadcast at every sports venue before, during, and after events and always at the awards ceremonies. Koreana sang it live the night before the opening at the outdoor concert along the Han River and, in accordance with the contract between the SLOOC and Polygram, at the opening ceremony.[24] The principal performance of "Hand in Hand" was also the climax to the "One World" scene at the end of the opening ceremony. Twelve groups of folk dancers from the International Folk Festival ringed the track as representatives of the world of nations: Africa (Senegal), Oceania (New Zealand), the Middle East (Saudi Arabia, Turkey), Asia (Japan, Korea, Indonesia), Europe (France, Hungary, Italy, Poland), and the Americas (Peru, United States). Around the stage at the center of the stadium spiraled six thousand participants from the preceding scenes plus national flowers and mascots of previous Olympiad host countries, forming a massive, moving mandala of human harmony. All joined Koreana and the prerecorded sound track for two verses and two choruses, one in Korean, one in English:

> Hand in hand we stand / All across the land
> We can make this world a better place in which to live.
> Hand in hand we can / Start to understand
> Breaking down the walls that come between us for all time,
> *Arirang.*

It is hard to imagine a performance moment more universal in its reference or impressive in its color and dynamism.

But one *arirang* does not make an event Korean. The emphasis in this scene was on Korea within a family of nations, the "morning calm" helping all to live in harmony. The choice of sound and mood ("very modern, psychedelic effect") matched the function of the scene on the edge of the Games, sixteen days of youthful contest when Korea would be but one of 160 competitive nations. The taste was not of distinctively Korean *chang* but the flavor of

---

[24] "'A' [SLOOC] allows Koreana, belonging to 'B' [Polygram], to appear in the opening ceremony. Also 'A' guarantees that the words of the entire song, from beginning to end, along with the name Koreana will appear on the screen during the broadcast" (SLOOC 1988b:81).

contemporary, international cuisine. The scene does not point the gaze of the audience into the *onggi* storage jars in the courtyard of a traditional Korean house. Instead, like urban Koreans today who often store their bean-paste jars up on the flat rooftops overlooking a city, the look of all was directed up and out to a wider horizon. The categories of music for the ceremonies, as indicated by the three music committees, were traditional Korean, new composition, and popular. The planners ended the opening ceremony of the Olympics, as they had the opening of the Asian Games, with the musical lingua franca they thought would be understood by the whole world today, Western popular music.

There was a trade-off, however, for using foreign resources to manufacture a product for export. Koreana as international trade was a case of trying to market Koreans who had crossed over culturally to Western ways and, in the minds of some, could not come back as foreign goods and expect to be let in tax free. The SLOOC and Polygram had calculated well the positive foreign response to their official song. Less controllable were the ethnic ambiguities raised by Koreana as natives who are perceived as foreigners, singing in a pop idiom Koreans now find familiar and whose youth claim as their own, but not in this packaging. Koreans did not "buy" it: home sales were low, and native talent and tastes were offended, not because of the Western pop idiom but because the official song of the Seoul Olympics was too clearly labeled "not made in Korea."

Distinctively Korean: Music as National Image

> In our music committees at first we did not talk about whether or not to emphasize traditional music but we did talk about two attitudes in the history of Olympic ceremonies. One is just to present an international playground, mix up world cultures for a performance which entertains. The Los Angeles and Munich ceremonies are examples of that. The other is to show the respective country's traditional culture, as was done in Tokyo and Mexico. (Han Manyŏng, personal interview, May 5, 1989)

The choice to show Korean traditional culture, but "recreated," shaped the music policy for the Seoul ceremonies. This meant a spectrum of "Korean traditional" music: slightly arranged excerpts of actual pieces from the court music repertory (for the dragon drum procession and the flower crown dance); military music (*taech'wit'a*; the entrance of the Olympic flag); dramatic epic song (*p'ansori*; "Parting Ships"); simplified versions of folk traditions (farmers' band music [*p'ungmul/nongak*] for "Harmony," music and dance derived from shaman ritual [*kut*] for "Prayer", and folk songs [*minyo*] for "Farewell"); and arranged versions as bases for composition (boat songs [*paennori*] for the Han River Festival and the drum dance [*changgo ch'um*] for the delivery of the Olympic flag).[25] The variety and degrees of adaptation of traditional music attest to an attitude on the part of the composers that the repertories are not sacrosanct canons but living traditions open to creative transformations.

This is all the more true in the fourteen pieces making up the largest single category of music intended for the ceremonies: new compositions. For these, composers also drew on Korean traditional music for their instrumentation, rhythmic cycles, melodies, tonal relations, structures, and genres. As in most things Korean, there was a yin and yang to their confidence in Korean music, as statements by staff member Kim Kyŏngshik, composer Kim Chŏnggil, and producer P'yo Chaesun indicate:[26]

---

[25] A shadow side to these many uses of traditional music in the ceremonies is that most of them were last-minute substitutions to fill gaps left by problematic pieces. Of ten instances, only two were in the original plan: the military music and the court chamber music for *hwagwanmu* (flower crown dance). The adapted *konori, changgo ch'um,* and *arirang* medley were inserted next. Four of the scenes using traditional music had new compositions slated or completed but in the end rejected as not fitting the scene. In one case the problem seems to have been a mismatch in the selection, putting a Western-style composer with a traditional scene ("Parting Ships"). The piece for the dragon drum procession was thought too modern while that for the Han River Festival had a choral part too complicated for the singers. Traditional music was then substituted for the new compositions. Though mothered by necessity, the resulting invention balanced Korean and Western styles more evenly than the original plan had.

[26] The following three quotations are taken from interviews conducted October 10 and 14, 1988. Kim Kyŏngshik is a composer and producer currently working for KBS radio. He was brought into the SLOOC Ceremony Unit because they needed someone who could communicate with the composers on musically technical matters: read scores, deal with musicians and conductors about rehearsals, and so on. He served as the day-to-day liaison between the composers, the committees, and the SLOOC, often making the first contact with a composer. As communicator and recorder of decisions made at all meetings concerning the music, he was privy to the details of the music process and has been a most valuable and perceptive informant for this research.

Kim Chŏnggil is a composer and professor at Seoul National University and was the music director for the opening ceremony. He composed the official fanfare for both the Asian Games and the Olympic ceremonies as well as the opening piece for the Olympic closing ceremony ("Friendship").

P'yo Chaesun, a director of drama for theater and television, was general director and producer of the ceremonies.

We worried about whether Korean traditional music would sound boring to foreigners if it was used a lot. Korean music all sounds the same, not like Western music which can be easily differentiated. Therefore we decided not to use too much traditional music lest we alienate foreigners. Except for *Yŏngsan hoesang,* we decided to compose everything new. So we are proud that all the music was created by ourselves.

Not only in my piece but also in many of the other pieces we tried hard to compose original creative music. But I don't know if Westerners could hear that.... We tried to use our own musical idiom.

Even the *konori* mass game is different from the original. If someone wants to see the original let them go to museums. If we do exactly as in folk customs it is simply a presentation of folklore rather than creation from our tradition.

The distinctively Korean elements in the ceremonies were in fact not simple presentations of folklore, but creations from within the tradition, the joint result of the fear that "too much" traditional music might cause boredom for foreigners, coupled with a pride in the decision to compose "everything new." This performance policy was generated by other large ambitions. As Pak Yonggu phrased it in the very beginning,

I expect the Olympics to be fresh and surprising as well as entertaining. But more than a show, it should make people think. I would like the ceremonies to offer something to thinking people who ponder the origin of the universe or the crisis of peace. (draft 1, 77)

His plea for an intellectually and morally provocative dimension to the ceremonies was muted in the text of the final scenario, which gave the goals of "entertaining" and "thought provoking" equal status. But the planners' commitment to music that would cut across fixed ideas and invite fresh perception was demonstrated by their choice of Hwang Pyŏnggi as composer for the narratively climactic scene of the opening ceremony, "Beyond All Barriers." In assigning an elegant artist—famous for his making of new repertory for the *kayagŭm* (12-stringed zither)—to the taekwondo demonstration of martial art, they were asking for a fresh conjunction of forms. And they got it. At first, Hwang was not interested in composing for the Olympic event. Then he got an idea. From an unknown book by a Confucian scholar, Pak Sŏnghwa, he learned of an ancient vocal music with body movements called *yŏngga.* It inspired him to think of composing music that would emphasize the *do (to/-do)* or *tao* (way or art) aspect of taekwondo. When producer P'yo Chaesun asked Hwang to write for the scene, he told him that, in the context of the ceremony, taekwondo was not pure exercise. If it were it would need no music at all. As part of the ritual performance of the Olympic ceremonies the martial art itself takes on a ritual character, and the movements take on the quality of dance. P'yo gave Hwang the directives "meditative" and "without a fixed meter." The working script described the scene as "moderate" and "overflowing with vitality (*ki*)."

With all this in mind, Hwang composed a song in the style of *kagok*, a form of Korean traditional art song. Hwang had studied the singing of this genre for several years but was the first to say that his piece for the Olympics was not actual *kagok*, just in that style. He retained the vocal features of the genre by using a trained performer, giving him a score in court music notation, but removing all accompanying instruments and text for reasons of clarity and aesthetics. For the singer he wrote a series of vocables from basic Korean vowels, with each of the four musical phrases ending on *om*, the wisdom sound from eastern meditation practices. "And that *om* sound comes from Buddhist meditation. Symbolically the sounds include every vowel sound. That means they symbolize the universe of sound, universal sound" (personal interview, June 12, 1989).[27] Hwang divided his piece into four sections corresponding to the structure of the taekwondo performance: (1) *ch'amsŏn:* meditation (seated); (2) *kibon tongjak:* basic techniques (singly); (3) *piho p'umsae:* "flying tiger" action; and (4) *hanbŏn kyŏrugi:* one-step prearranged and free sparring (in pairs). The music was to cover about two-thirds of the demonstration, while the final breaking of boards, *hamkke p'asang kyŏkp'a*, was to have only the shouts, live and prerecorded. When joined together, the jutting taekwondo movements and staccato shouts create a vertical aesthetic effect while the slow undulating melody makes a contrasting horizontal line. The two forms play off each other: we watch skillfully controlled physical violence while hearing peace and a heart cry. It is electric and it is thought provoking.

---

[27] In the debate over the piece, many people will refer to Hwang's piece as being in *shijo* style. There are, however, significant stylistic differences between the two forms of art song, *shijo* and *kagok*: the relation of music to text, instrumentation, music-text relation, structure, gender-specific repertory (*kagok*), and degrees of complexity. Admittedly, the distinctions are subtle to the untrained listener. The use of the term *kagok* for Western-style art song also confuses the terminology.

From the beginning there were attempts to modify the impression of violence in the taekwondo movements, to emphasize its interior discipline, to interpret it anew within the scheme of the scenario. The planners "thought taekwondo was not just *mu* (military) but also *do* (peaceful)" (Kim Kyŏngshik, personal interview, October 14, 1989). In an effort to evoke these other meanings, the third draft of the scenario combined the martial art with the cymbal dance (*para ch'um*) from Buddhist temple tradition:

> When the taekwondo group confronts these *para ch'um* dancers during the demonstration, their ordered shouts are replaced by the strong sound of cymbals. After breaking down the walls, *para ch'um* and taekwondo performers get together to make dynamic formations. Power both in its flexible and strong aspects should be scientifically balanced and the whole structure generate a dramatic rise to the climactic moment when a synthesis of body and spirit creates an art close to fantastic beauty. (draft 3, 19–20)

By the time of the fifth draft, the cymbal dancers had been relegated to a scene in the closing ceremony, and the demonstration was integrated with the opening ceremony theme. The act of breaking the boards was interpreted positively as a breaking of barriers between nations, ideologies, ethnic groups, religions, men and women, poor and rich, nature and humans, humans and technology. In the later vision statement, the list was reduced to three: race, ideology, and wealth. A footnote in the working script acknowledges both the aggressive side ("by using hands and feet we defend against opponents' attacks and attack opponents") as well as the *do* side (by constant practice from the past to the present "it is the road that leads to human perfection"). The final program further defended the peaceful potential of Korea's national sport:

> This traditional Korean military art is not offensive but defensive, utilizing self-control, penance (*kohaeng*: self-discipline, asceticism), and spiritual power.... Strength emerging from tenderness is one of the characteristics of Korean culture. To show that the power of taekwondo is a result of a harmonious and gentle mind, poetry (*shijo*) recitation is used as background music. The powerful movements contrast sharply with the slow and deliberate rhythm.[28]

---

[28] In our June 12, 1989, interview Hwang himself had this to say about the defensive nature of taekwondo: "Many taekwondo people think it is not for fighting, just for peace. The interesting thing is that even army troops think the army is to

Poetic text is still mentioned in this final program of September 1988, although Hwang had excluded it at the time he reduced the text to vocables in his final version, completed in June 1988. Neither an early printing date for the program (it was actually completed at 1:00 A.M. the morning of the opening ceremony) nor possible miscommunications between production planners and program committee entirely explain the reference at this late date to *shijo* (*kagok*) background music. The gap between what was written and what was done is part of the drama that ensued over this piece between the rehearsal on June 30 and September 14, when its fate was finally decided. During this period, the "harmonious and gentle mind" that the practice of martial art should promote seemed more characteristic of the composer than of the taekwondo personnel who opposed Hwang's music or the SLOOC staff and music colleagues who struggled to defend it.[29] Pursuing why this *om*-centered piece became the most controversial music in the ceremonies reveals much about the vested interests of those involved as well as working procedures and modes of authority among the planners. For a song the world never heard, this art song was eloquent.

The voices of opposition to Hwang's music came from the taekwondo leadership. It was not music as such they objected to, for there are ancient and modern examples of using music with it, and they had accepted Kim Hŭijo's march for the Asian Games demonstration. It was Hwang's particular style of composition and the designers' attempt to transform the meaning and impression of taekwondo that raised their ire. Kim Unyong, an IOC member and president of everything taekwondo in the country and the world, is an articulate spokesman for the man of sport. He views the Olympic ceremonies as an international sports event as well as a cultural one:

The opening ceremony should show not only Korean customs,

---

make peace not war. Politicians, too. The United States and Russia even make missiles and nuclear weapons for peace. That's their intention. Everyone argues that way."

[29] I learned once again the dangers of defining someone too narrowly, in this case Hwang as a true aesthetic and an elegant artist, which he is. His undergraduate study was in law, although he was studying music privately. (He has referred in other contexts to the traditionally low-class status of those who perform for a living.) Recently he has been seen on Korean television playing his *kayagŭm* in a commercial advertising coffee. I learned from the producer that Hwang Pyŏnggi has his black belt (*ch'odan*) in taekwondo.

traditions, and culture, but it is also necessary to show an international dimension to the whole world.... Personally I think it was too much Korean. Our organizers were more oriented to a Korean flavor. If they had put maybe 10 percent more of the international or of sports it would have been much better. If you take out taekwondo there would have been no sport mass game, only ballet and dances. (Personal interview, June 5, 1989)

Before the battle over the music, Kim and associates had to fight for the very inclusion of taekwondo in the ceremonies. The same transforming spirit that had removed the fight (*ssaum*) from *kossaum nori* in the "Harmony" scene and directed the combatants to embrace instead of contend had also wanted to eliminate the martial art completely from the Olympic ceremonies or, failing that, to modify the aggressive image of the sport by using a challenging music. That music continued to elicit strong reactions from the sportsmen, as noted again by Kim Unyong:

These artists or scholars tried to submit taekwondo to their theme. They try to form everything in their patterns. But our people have never moved or made maneuvers to *shijo*. Taekwondo is a sport. You cannot kick, punch, move, and break to the sound of *shijo*. It was impossible for a thousand people to make these united motions in full view of the eyes of the world to *shijo*. They tried to use it. I watched once but they were like this [collapsing his shoulders and going limp].

I watched them too and they appeared to move the same way to Kim Hŭijo's march, to silence, and to Hwang's art song. But Kim Unyong was certainly right about the planners' intention. As P'yo Chaesun put it to me in October 1988: "The image of Korea has been militaristic. We directors hoped to raise the image of taekwondo into art, but the taekwondo people rejected it so strongly."

Why did the taekwondo people object so strongly? The ostensible reason, often repeated, was that the players were not accustomed to moving to that sound. Habit may justify the answer, but it does not hold up for musical reasons. Whether a march beat or a free rhythm as in *kagok* is played, taekwondo participants move not to the music but to the shouted signals. So the beat or lack of beat apparently does not affect the actual rhythm of their movements, whereas moving at variance to a strong regular beat, like a march, should be more problematic. Obviously, the sound environment can affect their mood and energy level. One composer-director, who liked Hwang's piece, conceded that the music robbed the martial art of its vital force (*ki*). Kim Unyong gives a clue to the actual reason, a mix of music and politics. "To show taekwondo to the world they have to show real taekwondo as a sport and martial art." He echoes a statement in an early internal SLOOC document: "Taekwondo is known as a symbol of Korean athletic culture and is already broadly spread to countries worldwide. Its meaning [in the Olympic ceremonies] is to advocate the future adoption of taekwondo as an official Olympic sport by demonstrating it in performance" (draft 4, 19). Taekwondo, presently an Olympic demonstration sport, is struggling to become an official Olympic-level sport, if not by 1992 at least by 1996, although recently even that seems in jeopardy [Ed. It was a medal sport for the first time in the 2000 Olympics]. Those five minutes on world television were crucial for establishing the image of the sport as tough enough to compete in the international arena. Music that would give a contrary impression, and certainly any music with a pliant melodic line and introspective character such as *kagok*, would detract from the intended image. No art music or designers' aesthetic was going to get in the way of the sportsmen's goal by feminizing their macho image.

Voices in defense of Hwang's piece came from fellow musicians and the producer, music directors, and staff of the ceremonies. Most of them loved the music and the idea of challenging preconceptions as well as the military and sports establishments. "Why should an artistic work have to be changed to fit a demonstration by military people?" "They should follow our directions. Artistry should have priority." There were also voices in the middle. The composer for the previous taekwondo exhibition in 1986 liked Hwang's piece but thought it did not fit in a sports stadium. A composer of electronic music and music director thought the idea was more original than the music. The composer's own voice was less contentious, more resigned:

> The reason they did not like my music is very simple, very, very simple. They could not understand my music. They are not accustomed to this kind of music and they did not like it. That is the only reason.

Later in the same conversation he agreed, however, with my conjecture. "Yes, yes, that's right. They wanted macho music. Macho and easy to understand" (personal interview, June 12, 1989).

During the three months the fate of the piece was being argued, it passed through several formats as the composer and ceremony staff tried to get it over the wall of objections by the taekwondo association. Kim Kyŏngshik, the staff liaison, had to carry the tapes of adjusted versions to the taekwondo leaders inside their military compound and receive firsthand their vigorous objections. From him and other sources I have deduced five stages for the sound track of the scene. The first format was Hwang's original composition, *shijo* (*kagok*) alone. Second, when the song was rejected, P'yo Chaesun persuaded Hwang to make a special recording of his *kayagŭm* composition, "Pomegranate House," as a possible substitute for the *kagok* piece. Hwang chose an animated middle section of the *kayagŭm* piece, but it too was rejected. The third arrangement was of *shijo* for the *sŏn* (*ch'an* [C] or *zen* [J]) meditation that opens the demonstration, *kayagŭm* for the rest. This version appears on one of the penultimate audio tracks for the ceremonies, prepared hastily for an early September rehearsal. The fourth option was no music at all, only sound effects. This was clearly the taekwondo association's preference. The fifth version and final compromise used the *shijo* section intended for the meditation—Kim Unyong called this a "transition" to the actual taekwondo performance and therefore acceptable—and the sound effects for the rest.

Everyone involved mentions how virulent the fights were between the critics and defenders of Hwang's composition. "At one point I thought they were going to try their art on me," said producer P'yo. "In the end they were too strong, I was too weak. We had to give in." From the taekwondo president's point of view, "These scenario writers and organizers [he names only Yi Ŏryŏng] were very reluctant. But finally they responded." Kim Unyong and others place the decision to cut Hwang's original piece about two to three months before the ceremonies, right after the June 30 preview. As to when the compromise decision was made to leave in the short section, "We were never consulted," Kim asserts. Three days before the opening ceremony a meeting was held in the basement of the stadium until after 1:00 in the morning. Several people described the meeting as particularly stressful, contentious, and late. From a collation of interviews, I gather that at least three decisions were made that night: to remake three hundred silver body suits in the *Han madang* scene considered too scanty for Korean taste; to relegate pop singer Cho Yongp'il from that scene to the Han River concert the night before, because a male pop singer for the closing scene looked "too much like [the] L.A." Olympic ceremonies; and to eliminate the *kayagŭm* substitute for Hwang's piece. In an attempt to placate both sides they would use one minute of the *kagok* piece during the *ch'amsŏn* meditation and then taekwondo sound effects for the rest of the performance. On opening day, the one minute was reduced to twenty-five seconds, overlaid by the narrator's voice reading the vision statement of the scenario about going beyond all barriers of race, ideology, and wealth. So, in actual sound, the piece was reduced to a background snippet.

Answers to why, when, and how the music was cut are within reach. Who actually made the decision is more elusive, although I asked everyone I interviewed. The composers, committee members, and music directors placed the decision somewhere in the higher reaches of the taekwondo authorities and the SLOOC administration. When I asked Kim Unyong, not only as president of sports associations but also as one of the four SLOOC vice-presidents, he kept stressing that it was the recommendation of the whole demonstration team. When I asked Yi Kiha, director-general of the ceremonies, about his role in the decision, he said that they heard and discussed the opposition of the choreographers (taekwondo coaches from the military) and concluded that "absolutely we should cut it" (personal interview, October 3, 1989). Finally, when I asked the SLOOC president, Pak Sejik, at what level the decision about the taekwondo music had been made, he responded, "Of course, as I said, for the bringing together of the ultimate vision and the form of how to depict it I chaired that. Professional people discussed that taekwondo must be such and such a music.... And I agreed" (personal interview, September 26, 1989). When I began my search for the decision maker, I had not expected a direct answer.

Generalizing from this incident, a cynical voice might argue that music in the ceremonies was simply a pawn of contending ideologies and image projection on all sides. Government and SLOOC officials wanted the music as a cultural reinforcement of modernity and sophistication appropriate to the "economic miracle on the Han." The taekwondo contingent preferred no music to any that might vitiate the strength of their world-class sport. The music planners saw it as a chance to be both traditional and new and, in the skirmish over *kagok*, perhaps to win a round with military types they had been subject to for decades. My own voice holds mostly regret at a missed opportunity. The juxtaposition of art music and martial art was potentially the most creative moment in the ceremonies for enacting the dialectic of the theme, Beyond All Barriers, and for provoking the audience to a fresh imaging of Korea. Ironically, the whole affair raised and dramatized the very walls that remain to be overcome between worlds of art and of sport, men of thought and of action, the power of insight and the workings of power.

New: Music as Creative Increment

> Even before they asked me to compose the torch music the SLOOC discussed how the Olympics should show a vision of the future to the entire world. There were many opinions, but they were not sure how to go about it. Although they were unclear in the abstract, they talked about wanting to have some new kind of music. (Kang Sŏkhŭi, personal interview, June 8, 1989)

The tradition in torch music is a triumphant mood and a regular beat, simulating the footbeat of the final torchbearer as the honored designate circles the track. In Munich, sounds of timpani with organ were projected from four directions of the stadium. The most recent model for Korea was the choral composition with Western orchestra and Korean drum written for the Asian Games ceremony. Kang, however, wanted not to impose a definite beat on the runners' rhythm but to let them establish their own pace. Although computer music had been used in previous Olympic ceremonies and electronically modified sound for the torch, as in Philip Glass's composition "The Olympian" for the 1984 Los Angeles ceremony, the use of computer-generated sound throughout the music for the lighting and extinguishing of the Olympic flame was "an idea that had never been tried before." Kang would not be following precedent in composing the torch music for the Seoul Olympics, and the SLOOC should have known that in commissioning him.

Kang Sŏkhŭi had established a reputation in Korea and abroad as a new music composer frequently working in electronic media. He was the obvious choice to provide music that would create the "fresh shock of the avant garde," as the working script mandated. While Kang thinks that "modern music must filter sounds of modern people who live in a complicated, technical civilization" (MBC 1989), he was ready to scale down his resources to match the acoustic limits and the function of the Olympic event. Whether Koreans were ready to receive the innovation Kang had been asked to provide was another matter.

Soon after Kang received the commission from the SLOOC in December 1987, he began making musical and technical preparations. To translate an ancient myth into a vision for the present and the future, he went back in imagination to the early history of the Olympics to create an atmosphere reminiscent of Greece and Greek myth. Prometheus holds several meanings for Kang: son of the Titans who stole fire from the gods, mediator of culture to humans, and model for the artist in his willingness to risk and to suffer the consequences. Fire has accumulated further meanings within the Olympic Games context. The passing of fire through time and space is enacted each Olympiad in the ritual of the torch relay from Hera Temple in Olympia, Greece, to the site of the Games. For Koreans in 1988, the Olympic fire entered their consciousness as they watched, live or via television, twenty thousand mostly Korean runners carry the flame from the southernmost island of South Korea to the capital toward the north on a serpentine route through provincial cities. When the torch finally entered the Seoul stadium, anticipation energies raised by the twenty-four-day relay and the seven years of preparation were joined to historical and archetypal forces more sensed than known. Added to this tension was local suspense about the identity of the final runner.[30] For this moment of time out of time, Kang wanted

---

[30] Who would be the final torchbearer was, supposedly, top secret until the person ran into the stadium that morning. But Japanese reporters, spying from the roof of the stadium, photographed a dawn rehearsal four days before the ceremony. The reporters sent their scoop to the Japanese newspapers, complete with photographs of Son Kijŏng, winner of the marathon in the 1936 Berlin Olympics. When the Koreans learned of the leak, they changed the whole procedure. During the official ceremony Son entered the stadium at the appointed time but passed the torch within seconds to Im Ch'unae, triple gold medalist in women's running during the 1986 Asian Games. She carried the torch the remaining length and end curve of the stadium track to the foot of the Olympic cauldron. There three Korean youths, representing achievement in sports, academics, and the arts, divided the flame before being lifted to a level with the cauldron by a technological surprise. These changes were made the day before the opening. The young people had to be called into Seoul from the countryside that night. The final rehearsal for the stadium relay was held at 4:00 in the morning of September 17, six hours before the opening ceremony. The passing of the torch from Son Kijŏng in his seventies to Im Ch'unae in her twenties was construed publicly as a symbolic transfer of the Olympic spirit from age to youth. A transfer of power from male to female seems ungrounded in Confucian Korea, although Pak Sejik mentioned the man-to-woman symbolism in his explanation to Son of why he must yield the final position to Ms. Im (*Chosŏn ilbo*, November 4, 1989). The change was also said to diffuse any excess anti-Japanese sentiment evoked by Son's role in history: a Korean hero whose national glory was diluted by having to run in Berlin under a Japanese name for a Japanese emperor. That morning at Chamshil he was a leaping, ecstatic national symbol of liberation, if only for a matter of seconds. Kang Sŏkhŭi told me that the age/youth interpretation was, in fact, a last-minute justification for a Korean media coup over Japan. The Japanese reporters ended up with a false scoop, an unprintable picture, and the practical embarrassment of having to destroy an entire edition of morning newspapers. Son Kijŏng was justifiably angry at being cheated

to bring together Olympic history and Prometheus' arrival in sounds borrowed from the universe and then returned.

To realize these ideas, Kang returned in February 1988 to Berlin, his "second home," where he had already created seven computer compositions in collaboration with Volkmar Hein, sound engineer and "true artist," according to Kang. As a team they worked intensively for fifty days on the two-movement piece for the Olympics. Keeping in mind the acoustical situation of the Chamshil stadium, with its four thousand loudspeakers, Kang confined himself to relatively simple musical sources: a trumpet for the "Fire Legend" movement during the entrance and lighting of the torch in the opening ceremony and a trumpet and a soprano voice for the "Harmony" movement during the extinguishing of the flame in the closing ceremony. Since the sound of an acoustic trumpet, heard often in the Olympic context as the instrument for fanfares, is "neither exotic nor mysterious," Kang wanted to combine the plucked articulation of a stringed zither, a characteristic instrument type of Asia, with the timbre of a Western trumpet (personal interview, June 8, 1989).[31] By giving a plucked attack to the trumpet sound he sought to unite East and West in one sound event. "To obtain the pizzicato sound, I put the trumpet sound into the VAX computer and made an enormous number of experiments. Then I selected from these."[32] The motivic material for the trumpet in "Fire Legend" also represented a fusion: from the East, pentatonic scales from Asian musical systems and allusion to a piece from Korean court music; from the West, some twentieth-

---

once more of the full taste of victory. And the international Olympic movement, dedicated to peace, again provided a safe arena for nations to fight out their rivalries indirectly.

[31] The strings of a zither are strung parallel to a horizontal wooden case that acts as the resonator for the sound. Among the plucked-string zithers of Asia are the *qin* and *zheng* of China, the *kayagŭm* and *kŏmun'go* of Korea, and the *koto* of Japan.

[32] Kang and Hein used the VAX 11/780 computer in the electronic studio at the Technical University in Berlin. Some capacities of the system useful for this piece are the phasevocoder computer program by which sounds can be elongated without lowering the pitch or the pitch can be raised without foreshortening the duration. According to Hein, "With its special digital filter the phasevocoder proved itself the most important compositional means for the Olympic music. It permits one to expand or compress tones, melodies, or sounds by absolute invariable pitch, 'pure intonation.' Thus a trumpet staccato can be expanded a thousand times or a new sound generated with fully distorted trumpet timbre." The phasevocoder is part of the CARL environment created at the Center for Music Experiment of the Department of Music, University of California, San Diego.

century serial techniques applied to a four-note motif of Gregorian chant. Programmatic references were made by sound waves in rapid crescendo/decrescendo resembling a swish of air, as of a discus, a javelin, a bicycle wheel, or the mythic act of Zeus hurling fire to the earth. Since the distance between the runner's entry into the stadium and his or her circling of the track and mounting of the torch holder could not be calculated to the second, Kang prepared a repeatable tape loop to cover the runner's extra time. For the climactic moment when the stadium torch was finally lighted, Kang had reserved the noble "Sujech'ŏn" melody, "mixed with a low trumpet, the sound reduced, altered and mixed innumerable times in the computer. This sound had the effect of fifteen hundred simultaneous trumpets performing "Sujech'ŏn."[33]

For the extinguishing of the flame on the final night, the daylight clarity of distinct trumpet pitches was blurred in the dark stadium to a kind of phantasmagorical soundscape. Like so much in the closing ceremony, the musical program was explicitly feminine in its reference. Kang envisioned the womb-shaped space of the stadium as visited by spirits from another world. The music represented a presence, not exactly Prometheus or Zeus, but more like a creative feminine spirit who descends in sound to visit earth momentarily and then departs for eternal realms from whence she came. Kang had in mind a woman, larger than life, like Mozart's Queen of the Night from *The Magic Flute*, hovering over the stadium and humanity. To create this effect, a single soprano voice and a single trumpet were transformed in the computer to nonvocal timbres and expanded to a brass ensemble and a chorus. The woman chants the text of the Olympic hymn in Italian on a monotone pitch in the manner of antiphonal monastic recitation, with the level intonation of *sprechstimme* but indecipherable as language. As with the Gregorian chant motif in the first movement, Kang intended a reference to the Greco-Roman roots of Western civilization within an Eastern religious frame of helpful, intermediary deities. The single voice widens to a duet, a trio, then quartet from the hundred, thousand, ten thousand, and hundred thousand voices representing those in the stadium to the universe of voices, all moving with the mother figure toward the

---

[33] About ten seconds of the initial tape were, in fact, needed on the day of the opening ceremony. The world's athletes broke rank and blocked Im Ch'unae's path in their effort to see and take pictures, slowing her down in her run to deliver the torch.

final "Harmony" imaged by the sea, the universe, and eternity.

The fate of Kang's second movement was less benevolent than its inception. Only one and a half of its five minutes were heard, the remainder sliced off by the music of the next scene. Actually, both pieces barely escaped the axe as late as the night before the opening and again the night before the closing. The story is best told in sequence.

Kang Sŏkhŭi was already on an advisory committee for the ceremonies when he was asked to be music director for the closing ceremony and in turn to compose music for the torch. On the way home to Korea after completing his pieces, he gathered small groups of composer colleagues in Berlin and Paris to present the results of his and Hein's three hundred hours of work. He asked his European counterparts,

> "Have you ever heard anything like this before?" They all said, "This is the first time I have heard this sound." I was very satisfied [for he had been aiming at something original and fresh, not familiar]. When I came back to Korea I had several of our own music experts listen. And they said, "I've heard something like this before. It's similar to Chinese music." But in fact, my music is absolutely, totally unlike Chinese music. Not at all the same. Not at all.... The people who spoke thus have such narrow experience of music. Therefore new music reminds them only of what they've heard in the past.

Kang's second question to professional colleagues in Europe concerned his decision not to use a definite rhythm for music accompanying the final torch runner. According to Kang, all the professional musicians outside the country spontaneously agreed with his choice. Back home, critics would want a more literal representation of footbeats. When he returned to Korea on March 5, 1988, Kang turned in the pair of pieces to the SLOOC and considered the matter closed as far as he was concerned.

But complaints about the computer compositions rose and persisted right up to the ceremonies. According to Kang, some SLOOC members and advisers "had no experience other than the Asian Games. By that standard they judged everything. They considered normal what they did for the torch music in the Asian Games: an orchestral performance with a big showy chorus." Kang had carefully observed the torch music for Los Angeles and Munich and also for the winter Olympics at Calgary:

> Any composer can basically understand these [unusual musical] elements. But in *uri nara* [our country of Korea] it cannot be understood at all. Even the day before the opening ceremony, the

day before the torch arrived, a considerable number of people were opposing my music. This committee said, "Don't do it. Don't perform this music." There were not only bureaucrats but also many artists opposed to it, choreographers and composers. "Why have such horrifying music in the Olympics?" they asked. I was so ashamed [of their ignorance of art and music at the international level].

One episode involved major figures from behind the scenes of the ceremony preparations. A certain well-known sound effects man accused Kang of plagiarizing the computer music and convinced the general producer of the same. To solve this awkward situation, the SLOOC president called a meeting of all the appropriate parties and committee members and ordered the accuser to present the music that Kang was supposed to have imitated. As the two pieces were played, all present agreed that even the first measures were different. Presider Yi Kangsuk was very angry at the whole incident; he delivered a lecture, and the committee applauded Kang's music. Kang insisted that the producer apologize for believing the accusation and doubting his integrity. If not, Kang would withdraw all of his music. The producer did apologize and Kang did not withdraw his music. But the night before the closing ceremony Kang's music was in jeopardy again:

> Around midnight a proposal from one choreographer, that such "horrible" music should not be used in the closing ceremony, caused a terrible stir in the group. "It should not be used." "It can be used." So went the discussion. "If you don't use it, I don't care. It's up to you." And I walked out. Finally, they decided to use it in its entirety. But, in fact, they deleted four minutes of the five. (Kang Sŏkhŭi, personal interview, June 8, 1989)

The ostensible reason for such opposition to Kang's piece was that the music for the opening did not provide a definite rhythm for the runner on the final lap of the torch relay. Others found it frightening, like movie music, or too long, but the composer doubted these rationales. "No, it wasn't for a practical reason. In the planning they used the whole thing. The cut [made the night before the closing] was not a matter of time or practicality." At one point Kang said that his Korean critics were too ignorant to understand his music. This remark recalls a similar conclusion of Hwang Pyŏnggi's about the taekwondo leaders: "They did not understand my music." The excuse—for it seems a cover for real reasons—that the music did not match a runner's foot rhythm seems as lame as the taekwondo officials saying that no one could keep together in their martial art without a musical beat.[34] In reflecting on the response to his piece and the decisions about it, Kang conceded that the general director/producer had many practical problems to contend with: the contract with NBC (the National Broadcasting Company, the U.S. television network broadcasting the Olympics) imposed time limits as did the fireworks display at the end of the ceremony, to name just a few. But a better explanation for the negative reaction to Kang's computer compositions lies more at the cultural than the pragmatic level. Many of those sitting in judgment on his pieces lacked exposure to contemporary music as it emerged from international art circles and new music circles in Korea. It is clear from his past work and appreciations from inside and outside the country that the commission for Kang to write a futuristic piece was well within his competence. But few people were prepared to move beyond the literal and the familiar in their habitual taste and to accept new sound for the Olympic ceremonies. The piece that was to surprise and impress foreigners with Korea's modernity ended in shocking Koreans themselves by being too new.

Interpretation

> I always thought the most important thing for the opening-closing ceremonies was sound and color. To put it simply, sound and color represent a country's tradition. Sound represents the feeling of a country. That's why I put so much money into the music. In any of the cases dealing with music, economy was not the issue. We spared no money or effort. No matter how many times it was necessary to revise or rearrange a piece I allowed for that. (Yi Kiha, personal interview, October 3, 1989)

Whether there is such a unified thing as the feeling of a country, how sound signifies feeling, in what ways music is referential—the nest of aesthetic and semiotic questions raised by this statement did not preoccupy the director-general of the ceremonies. His conviction of the communicative power of music was a working assumption that determined policy, including budget decisions. The interpretive task for administrators was not how sound can represent the feeling of a country but how to

---

[34] I have learned from several experiences that the necessity of giving reasons, even indirect or fictitious ones, is not characteristic of Korean social interaction but a Western mode of behavior that Koreans associate with efforts at democracy.

represent Korea in sound; not how much it would cost but to what degree the ceremonies could be distinctly Korean and the world reception still be favorable. Implicit in their decisions was an assumption of some kind of equivalence between sound and effect, an assertion that the sound, the music of the ceremonies, would evoke from the world audience a sympathetic resonance with the Korean spirit.

The importance given to music by the planners justifies—if justification is needed—the decidedly myopic focus of this article on music-related issues within the ceremonies. Previous neglect of the musical dimension of Olympic ceremonies in scholarship devoted to the Games as well as the inherent interest of the music used at Seoul add to a list of reasons why the music deserves attention in its own right. The interpretive task of this section is to go beyond the stated intentions and musical enactments of the planners in order to reframe transactions over the three pieces within a wider context of issues generated by my study of all the music in the ceremonies. The source is still the planners' own words—this time their own interpretations of the music process—but with an added attempt to make the tacit content articulate. Going hand in hand, over the wall, to the future—an awkward task in itself—can lead to further understanding of dynamics at work in the making of the ceremonies and to an aesthetic reading of the result within a field of social and political forces not calculated beforehand by any scenario.

Hand in Hand: Nationalism and Universalism

The operative script for the ceremonies was to present Korea to the world. While the barrier theme and Olympic rhetoric promoting harmony and progress, world peace and friendship supplied the requisite international and universal dimension, altruism on a global scale seemed to arouse less energy than nationalism as a driving force for policies and decisions. The experience of Korean observers at the Los Angeles Games was formative. Director-General Yi, echoing previously cited statements by the minister of culture, discovered that Korea's image as a distinctive country was either negative or nonexistent:

> I went to L.A. to investigate many things and found that people knew nothing about Seoul. In addition, people of the Third World thought Korea belonged to China's cultural sphere, or was part of Japan's cultural territory. Therefore I thought we should do something to make known the music, color (*saekkal*), and culture of

The Script, Sound, and Sense of the Seoul Olympic Ceremonies 215

Korea. For the Asian Games that might have been a bad idea [i.e., excessive] but we did it anyway. (Yi Kiha, personal interview, October 3, 1989)

In contrast to the overt agenda of presenting "mainly our own culture" in the Asian Games ceremonies, "We had enough confidence [by the Olympics] to change our position from a receiver of culture to a sender. Now we can look for what the world has in common" (Yi Kiha, personal interview, October 3, 1989). This widening of the organizers' worldview surely reflected broader changes in Korean self-perception prompted by domestic political dramas between 1986 and 1988. But the ceremonial expression of a shift from national to global awareness could be quite subtle and more than one way. In a different performance type, the torch relay, MacAloon and Kang found the 1988 relay in several respects more Koreanized and localized than its 1986 predecessor (1990). The use of Korean music in the Olympic ceremonies was also closer to traditional models than the hyped versions in the Asian Games ceremonies, and even the new compositions carried subtle reinterpretations. Thus, it was not the fact of self-presentation but the appearance of it that concerned organizers: "With many countries coming to Korea for the Games, if we present only our own culture it's a little strange, isn't it?"

The director-general found precedents for excessive nationalism in Olympic ceremonies of the past as he watched the available films. Nazi Germany had expressed German culture propagandistically to transform the negative meaning of Nazism. Tokyo did the same thing, he thought, presenting Japanese culture too strongly in an attempt to cover Japanese imperialism. At the Moscow Olympics, with only half the world participating, the Russians advertised themselves as pacifists, but their words and actions did not match. In L.A., a similar trend was evident. Yi did not make the logical next step, drawing a parallel to the Korean Fifth Republic's attempted use of the Olympics to distract attention from an unpopular military regime. The circular logic of not overly emphasizing Korean culture in order not to appear overly Korean was also not exposed. The lesson learned from the history of propaganda in the Olympics, said Yi, was to include the best of past Olympics—for example, the effort to combine the mass movement of Moscow with the sheer volume of Los Angeles—and to draw the most participants. Instead of a narrow nationalism, Korea would "send out to the world very wide, open images."

The instrument crafted by the planners for this universal outreach, the official song "Hand in Hand," was sent out amid a cacophony of voices: "publicize the Olympics through music," "revise the foreign lyrics," and "cancel the contract," quieted somewhat in the end by presidential "fiat." We have seen how the controversies over the song embodied in the musical sphere the larger problem of displaying Korea's cosmopolitan competence and creating an idiom of reassuring welcome for nervous foreigners. Though positioned for success as an international pop hit, the song still had to be promoted within the country. This was done in the manner of official Korean propaganda. It was repeated so often and everywhere that it became more like a slogan than a song. When this aural bombardment continued through the year following the Olympics, the recording took on the character of a cipher standing for an event that was not being allowed to pass into history with dignity but kept alive by artificial respiration. The song became a tool of the official campaign to maintain the Olympic spirit, which had held in check disruptive forces within the country among political parties, dissidents, workers, farmers, and students, at least for a few months in 1988, but seemed quickly forgotten when the guests had gone home. Understandably, SLOOC officials and government types wanted to prolong the Olympic high. On the occasion of the Seoul Olympics Anniversary Conference (SOAC), Pak Sejik announced a "system and a plan to revive the Olympic spirit in Korea... to keep it alive. Korea would establish the Seoul Olympic Spirit Enhancement Movement (Sŏul ollimp'ik chŏngshin kyesŭng palchŏn undong) to ensure that the dream goes on." The attendant announcement of the Seoul Peace Prize further reflected the Korean leadership's desire to preserve the country's new status following the Olympic success. As Pak phrased it, "It is Korea's turn to stand up as a maturing nation and give something back to the world," an echo of Korea's role as "sender not receiver" of culture voiced by the scenario planners (Pak Sejik 1989).[35]

---

[35] This quotation was taken from a paper delivered at a conference of Korean and international scholars invited to Seoul to analyze and evaluate the Olympic event. Pak's announcement of the Seoul Olympic Spirit Enhancement Movement occupied a marked position toward the end of his talk. During our two-hour interview ten days later, Pak responded to my mention of the movement:

> I badly need that kind of movement, especially in the wake of the first anniversary. We need spiritual enhancement; that is the objective, the goal of the Olympics. After the festival everybody deteriorated right away. That is a sad story. Unfortunately, we are

World events a few months later provided both the official song and the SLOOC past president with an unexpected coda and this chapter with his revisionist interpretation. Pak Sejik wrote a newspaper article on the song fresh from a conversation with Koreana, who had recently (1990) returned from East Germany. There, December 11–13, 1989, they had sung "Hand in Hand" on top of the Berlin Wall as a demonstration song co-opted by the democracy movement in East Europe. The line in the chorus, "breaking down the walls that come between us for all time, hand in hand" was so appropriate to the literal act that the threatened East German government, prior to the democratization momentum, had asked Polygram to remove the phrase "breaking down the wall." But Polygram refused, saying "It means creative destruction." The latter reason had also been used by SLOOC officials two years before in retaining the controversial line in the song when they changed the scenario title to "going over the wall" for the sake of diluting a violent national image. The irony is that the aggressive act in the phrase softened by Korea after intensive debate, says Pak, is what qualified the song as a hit "demo" song on international charts from Tiananmen Square to the Berlin Wall, selling five thousand copies a day in East Germany. "There is even a rumor that Gorbachev likes this song, too." More deeply ironic is former general Pak's interpretation of "the most important words in the song, 'breaking down the wall': they symbolize the process of democratization in the East Bloc in 1989 which demolished dictatorial power and broke down the wall of division with people power." During the waning months of the South Korean Fifth Republic in the spring and summer of 1987, those same phrases, "down with the dictatorship" and "democratic power to the people," in the mouths of ordinary citizens and students were considered seditious and cause for arrest. Among targets and critics of the protests were some of the same actors who were preparing the Seoul Olympic performance at that time and were now basking in the reflected glory of the song's role as international theme song of peace and freedom, as Koreans' contribution "not only to loosening world conflict but also to opening the doors of the communist-bloc countries through the successful Seoul Olympics." (With such peace-making power

---

confronted with a very difficult time in many ways. Perhaps the sole remedy for this kind of undesirable phenomenon in society is spiritual enhancement, which is a revival of the Olympic spirit.... To achieve harmony we have to go back to the days of the Olympics and even the days before the Olympics [to see] how we became one.

attributed to the song, one almost expects the first nominations for the Seoul Peace Prize to go to Koreana and Polygram). There is a tone of personal pain to the SLOOC past president's reflection on Koreans' lack of enthusiasm for the song then and now: "It has something to do with the phenomenon that Korea is the country that has the lowest evaluation of the Olympics and has forgotten it the fastest."

Outside Korea the pop song was thus given a new lease on its successful but naturally short life by the synchronizing of a fortuitous phrase with international dramas. In Korea the sound of the official song never did represent the "feeling of the country" nor was it intended to. Incessant playings have now given it the slick surface of a worn record as an official effort to distract attention from problems refusing to be drowned out by songs or slogans. Resist it as I may, I have to admit to liking the song from the first time I heard it at a ceremony preview in June of 1988, and now, a year and a half later after hundreds of hearings, I still find it has power to raise enthusiasm. I know I am being subjected to a programmed effect, first by well-oiled techniques of the commercial song industry, and then by a top-down, centralized campaign to invest the song with the authority of an audio icon that can make present the spiritual power of the event it celebrates. Critical and affective response to the song also go hand in hand.

Over the Wall: Revolutionary Art and Military Culture

The song that concluded the opening ceremony and the one slated for the taekwondo scene of that ceremony could hardly be farther apart in idiom: a Western-style pop song made outside the country with current technology according to cosmopolitan taste, and a Korean-style art song modeled on a native tradition of ancient origins and esoteric associations. The functions of the songs within the ceremony were also at polar extremes. For the final scene depicting a united world, "Hand in Hand" enabled everyone to sing, or at least hum and sway together, in a festive mood. The *kagok* solo was at variance with the martial display, dividing attention between excitement at synchronized skill and intuitions of other meanings. The official song was a promotional tool for attracting the world to Seoul, making people feel good while there, and later reminding native and foreigner alike of the glories of " '88" in Korea. It was an instrument of the dominant ideology of centralized power, and it was played too often. By contrast, the music suggesting a shift in imagination challenged the dominant ideology that has ruled in Korea, in this case represented by the military/sports establishment, and it was heard too little.

Yet for a song the world never heard in its entirety and one that was suppressed for being weak, the art song remains a symbol, both in its sound and purpose, of the dialectical backbone of the ceremonies. As the core image of wall holds together the central problem and solution of Korean and world history in a yin-yang kind of tension, the music for the demonstration scene in which the walls were broken was designed to restore the balance between *mu* and *do*, to highlight the less apparent aspect of the martial art: its potential as a way of inner discipline and peaceful exercise. As we have seen, the taekwondo leadership was trying to project a "real" image of the sport unmitigated by art; ceremony planners were trying to temper a military image with a layer of irony. From the roar that went up from the taekwondo people, it is clear that a sacred ox had been gored. When they were asked to entertain an alternate view of their sport, they saw it as an attempt to subvert its vigor. They refused to let their Olympic candidate be used as a function of the ceremony theme or to carry a host of meanings. Thus, the multivocal reference of the martial art when coupled with art music was flattened to a breaking of boards.

Aside from the political issues raised by the refusal to let the national symbol of taekwondo be reinterpreted, the incident exposes a tension in Olympic ceremonies themselves: Are they aligned more with art or with sport? Is a ceremony primarily an art work on a mammoth scale, or just a gala entertainment before the Games, let alone a ritual process of Olympic proportions? The binary phrasing of the question is more primitive than the answer arrived at by the Seoul planners. According to their stated intentions and performed enactments, for them the ceremonies were a calculated and dense interpretation of Korean culture. Even the constraints of the official ceremony were reimagined so that sharp divisions between art and function were blurred. In their making free with cultural forms all through the ceremonies, they made a tacit statement about the preservation of traditional lore. These cultural forms—royal processions, folk games, songs, and dances—are currently outside the life context of most Korean people, even in the countryside. The effort to restore or preserve is already an act of artifice; why not go the step further and re-create from a modern sensibility?

Hwang Pyŏnggi's composing within the *kagok* tradition was this kind of interpretation. He also went the further step of raising the function of music in the scene from mere accompaniment to equal status with the action. The audio and visual domains challenged each other instead of sight overpowering sound. Before so riveting a scene as taekwondo, the art song assumed a complementary voice, commenting on, even critiquing, the display. In its likeness to precedents in Korean art song repertory, the *kagok* piece was traditional, even conservative, but in the counterpoint it made to martial art as used in the ceremony it was radical. Thus, art music interpreting martial art was truly art in the revolutionary sense of countering the dominant definition of what is real (Marcuse 1978:ix, xi, 22). But the music was silenced for trying to usurp too powerful a role; for the moment, Goliath had defeated David in a confrontation between prowess and insight.

The long battle over the music for taekwondo also acted out tensions in Korea between civilian and military structures, as represented by the martial art performers. Perhaps to placate critics, the image of 808 soldiers from the 3d Airborne Brigade was mitigated by the addition of 200 Midong Elementary School girls, TV cameras focusing on their earnest little faces. But during interviews, I heard mostly criticism of this thinly veiled flexing of military muscle. A rare voice in defense of the military substructure to the ceremonies was raised recently by Pak Sejik in the twelfth of his thirty articles on the inside story of the "largest mobilization of people and goods since the Korean War." His interpretation of "military culture" is a study in point of view, in new attempts at public openness on a taboo topic, and in the values of a pivotal figure in the making of the Olympic ceremonies.

With the affection of a father figure for favorite sons, Pak details the unsung contributions of soldiers to the Olympics (1989).[36] As the SLOOC president, his one regret was not being able to give credit publicly before now to these soldiers for accomplishing their dangerous and difficult roles perfectly. As reason

---

[36] Soldiers constituted 15 percent (6,600) of the operations' personnel, 50 percent (55,000) of the security force, and 24 percent of the 20,000 participants in the two ceremonies. There they contributed physical strength to the air show, the "Chaos" scene, the *konori* mass game (each of the 1,400 soldiers had to be taller than 107 meters, glasses-free, and good-looking), and the taekwondo martial art demonstration in the opening ceremony. In the closing ceremony they appeared as the *para ch'um* monks (the cymbal dancers originally integrated with the taekwondo scene), the *kkach'i* birds installing the Ojak Bridge, and the mast wavers in "Parting Ships." Pak does not mention the hundreds of soldier musicians playing in the fanfare brass ensemble, the brass band orchestra, and the ancient military band escorting the Olympic flag.

for his silence, "There was a time when there was strong criticism about military culture (*kunsa munhwa*), so we could not let people know what soldiers did or their role in the Olympics." Pak does not give the reason why the situation a year later enables him to speak out publicly, but he does attribute the reason that soldiers performed so well to "the good points of military culture: the Korean army's characteristic 'can-do' spirit (*ch'ujinryŏk*), which says 'If at first you don't succeed, try, try again.'" His third reference implicates half the population:

> If you are a healthy citizen [male] of Korea, almost everyone has experienced the life of a soldier. *Whether you like it or not you were influenced by military culture.* The important thing is to eliminate military culture's drawbacks (*tanjŏm*) and for the sake of our society to receive and develop constructively the good points of military culture: the power of self-sacrifice in practice (*chagi hŭisaengjŏk shilch'ŏllyŏk*). (Pak 1989; emphasis added)

He concludes with a deft bringing together of opposing camps in current Korean society: "The two substructures that made the Seoul Olympics successful were soldiers and students. In the face of the large proposition of the Olympics these two elements, considered conflicting, became one." Despite the fact that many college students in Seoul took a position somewhere on the spectrum between protest, boycott, and indifference toward the world festival across the river,[37] Pak's ability to reconcile opposites and construe problems positively stood him in good stead in his frequent role as arbitrator during ceremony preparations.

During that process the SLOOC president was himself an example of both a revised military model and the participation objective in his slogan PHASE (see MacAloon and Kang 1990 for details). By his own description and others' reports, he "pooled all the wisdom of professionals from all walks of life." He constantly consulted, listened, and mediated. For instance, according to Pak, when the tapes of compositions were collected, "We all listened together, examined them in the group, and then made comments. For some pieces there were no complaints, some had pros and cons. But all music that was played in the ceremonies was agreed on unanimously." Meetings were constant and endless. People often mentioned staying until midnight or 1:00 in the morning; Pak said it could go as late as 3 or 4 A.M. for the

---

[37] Even the more radical national association of university students, Chŏndaehyŏp, imposed a ban on their own violent protests ("demo") during the Olympics so that they would not alienate fellow Koreans or provide grist for propaganda against their cause (see Mulling 1990).

executives. There was a decided effort to employ new modes of democratic procedure in the process of decision making in preparing the ceremonies. This was done within a basically hierarchical model of organization reminiscent of Korean social codes and lines of command and a military organization and terminology learned from the U.S. Army. But after all the discussion, there came a point in "important decision making when I had to solve most of the cases, especially toward the end."

To the extent that the curtain of discretion maintained by almost everyone can be penetrated by inquiring foreigners, Pak's managerial style and general SLOOC decision-making processes, especially after 1986, seem to have aimed at a combination of consensus and authority. As we have seen, other SLOOC administrators continued to employ more authoritarian expressions like "we just imposed it" when they met objections to "Hand in Hand," or "we decided to cut it [the *kagok* music] absolutely" when taekwondo personnel voiced their objections to the music. Pak Sejik presented his role more obliquely: "When professional people said taekwondo music must be with such and such a music, as chair I agreed" (personal interview, September 26, 1989).

Given these patterns of operation and other allusions, the final decision to cut—or severely modify—the art music for taekwondo was probably made by the SLOOC president himself after extended consultation, perhaps with music committee executive Yi Kangsuk, taekwondo chief Kim Unyong, and IOC president Juan Antonio Samaranch. Given the close association of Samaranch with both Pak and Kim, one detail took on more significance than it might otherwise merit. Han Manyŏng had argued for the inclusion of Hwang's piece because of its beauty. "Originally we deleted this taekwondo show entirely from the scenario. But the SLOOC told us that Samaranch likes taekwondo very much because his own son and grandson practice it in Spain" (personal interview, May 8, 1989). At this point I attribute the final decision to a complex of reasons including relationship with the head of the IOC, ambitions to place taekwondo among official Olympic sports, and an attitude toward martial art as "never used for aggressive purpose but as a contribution to peace and harmony." The irony is that the opportunity to highlight the peaceful dimensions of Korea's national sport was not only missed but violently opposed. The only advantage I can see in the elimination of the music is that if the sport does not finally achieve Olympic status, no blame can be laid on the lovely lyric song.

To the Future: Cultural Elites and the Harmony of the Whole

> The musicians asked for art music but I told them to compose functional music. The ceremonies are a functional work not an artistic work. It was difficult to convince the musicians of that. (Yi Kangsuk, personal interview, June 8, 1989)[38]

Some musicians never were convinced of the priority of function in their ceremony composition. While political reasons account for some of the problems, differing understandings of art and function were at the root of controversy over not only the *kagok* art music but also the torch music. Hwang, Kang, and other musicians might have anticipated the restrictions of their mandate from the fact that they were the last group selected for each scene. We have heard that sound and music were priorities in the total scheme, yet scene length and style, director, and choreographer were all chosen before the composer. Each of these composers was trained first in Western art music, many had studied contemporary composition abroad, and most had experimented with Korean traditional music in some form. Even among those distinguished for their work in Korean theater, film, and television, there were no "light music composers" (Kim Hŭijo, personal interview, October 13, 1988). For the sound track directed to a world audience, the music committee had selected from among Korea's "best" composers, who in turn wrote the highest quality music they could imagine within the limits of the event. Most of the composers mentioned to me their awareness of functional considerations but let slip elsewhere their ambitions to write music that could also be played later and last on its own merits. To require such professionals to write "not art music but accompaniment music," "adjusted to the dance with a strongly articulated beat" and "subordinate to the program," was to set up a tension.[39]

Though built into the task, an opposition between art and function is inadequate to explain the nuanced response of composers to balancing their creativity with the situation. A more appropriate analytical frame should consider the degrees of subtlety with which the music "went with" the total scene and concept—whether, according to informants' tastes, it did or "did

---

[38] Professor of music education at Seoul National University, Yi represented music interests on the six-member Steering/Executive Committee, which mediated between the SLOOC administrators and everyone else preparing the ceremonies.

[39] These spokesmen for music as function are Kim Chŏnggil, musical director for the opening ceremony; Han Manyŏng, advisory committee member; and Kim Hŭijo, senior composer and music advisory committee member.

not match" (*an majayo*). In the case of Hwang's music for "Beyond All Barriers" and Kang's music for the torch, conflict arose when critics tried to reduce the relation of sound and scene to a sonic equivalence between pulse and picture, whereas the two composers were in tune with wider implications of *piho p'umsae* and footbeats. Hwang's music articulated neglected dimensions of taekwondo, offering an alternative to the demonstration's sensational effect on spectators. Kang's music for the Olympic flame jarred expectations by its computer technology and alien sounds, yet it was "about" the torch in the time-depth of myth.

In the crisis over the torch music, artistic concerns reflected dynamics within the social structures of working relationships and alliances among the Korean professionals who planned the ceremonies. For example, the producer and the sound effects man involved in the Kang controversies come from the world of television, radio, and large-scale theatrical production. Their eyes and ears are attuned to media effects, audience response, and the clock. Kang and his composer colleagues are university professors and artists more accustomed to the concert hall than to constant compromise with people in other fields. They composed independently, but under directives to produce music that would be Korean, cosmopolitan, splendid—but not art music—and to help each other. This pact of cooperation was built on an ethos of collegiality already in place. In describing his role as music director of the closing ceremony, Kang often referred to the positive relation between colleagues in the same field, workplace, and generation. When a ceremony piece of Kang's fellow composer at Seoul National University, also a close friend and graduate of the same college, was criticized, it became apparent that the composers had already decided to band together in support of each other's music if they met opposition from a choreographer. As a group they refused to accept the rejection of their colleague's piece, although they later lost the fight because the music obviously did not fit the scene. During the battles over the very survival of Kang's music in either ceremony, his music was defended in executive committee meetings by Yi Kangsuk, another colleague in the College of Music (Yi Kangsuk, personal interview, June 8, 1989; Pak Sejik, personal interview, September 26, 1989). I learned how strong this mutual support is by the responses to my question to each composer about favorite pieces in the total sound track. I was only asking for a positive preference, but invariably each one demurred in his response. "They are my colleagues. I cannot evaluate."

The Script, Sound, and Sense of the Seoul Olympic Ceremonies 225

While they showed increasing willingness to express a critical stance toward the ceremonies as interviews continued a month, a year, or longer after the event, the lines of allegiance toward each other remained impenetrable.

By their own report, the process of preparing the ceremony music was tumultuous at times. I was given an impromptu demonstration during an interview with the ceremony producer at the stadium offices. P'yo Chaesun was explaining his acquiescence on the issue of Hwang's music for the taekwondo exhibition, even though he liked the idea very much and would like to produce it some day:

> I did not stick to my own idea. This work is not my individual work but a collaboration really shared by many people. My role was to collect and coordinate various opinions. This is not my nor only our country's performance. It will be presented to the world. (Personal interview, October 12, 1988)

Our conversation was suddenly interrupted by a noisy argument in the same room about letting a handicapped child in a wheelchair roll the hoop across the stadium diagonal during the Para-Olympic opening ceremony. The producer joined in the fray and ten minutes later returned to the interview, saying genially, "We have been working and fighting like that for a year and a half." The opening ceremony music director also mentioned quarrels frankly:

> In truly democratic fashion we fought and argued from seven in the morning to midnight in order to make the best thing possible. For me it is not important whether Westerners pronounce the ceremonies good or bad. More important, this was the first time in our history for such a big event. In the course of preparing it, all kinds of people worked together and quarreled among each other and it bore good fruit in the results. I think it was the process that was important for us, the experience. (Kim Chŏnggil, personal interview, October 11, 1988)[40]

---

[40] Months later a Korean research assistant was helping me transcribe many hours of taped interviews. As I was going over the Korean tapes and text by myself, I was startled and then intrigued to find that each time an interviewee had used *ssaum* (fight), the transcriber had substituted *nonjaeng* (argue, contend). When I chided the assistant, a highly ethical person and serious scholar, for this "cover-up," he said he feared the word "fighting" would give my readers the impression of physical combat, thus reinforcing a pugnacious image of Korea. I realized that the fallout from the boxing match incident during the Olympics, with its deep roots in the Korean capacity for shame—triggered by American prurient sensationalism—is with us still.

Of course, they cared passionately about the public reception of the ceremonies. But an explicit commitment to proceed in newly collaborative ways and to subordinate individual work to the good of the whole, as consistent with cultural code, seemed powerful enough to take precedence over concern for world fame or approval. In the context of the national task and unprecedented opportunity to construct and present Korean culture as a whole, group success at once depended on the support of artistic integrity and the severe delimitation of it. The initiator of the scenario, Pak Yonggu, had insisted that insofar as the ceremonies had the character of a performance it should be an artistic work (*chakp'um*), not only an event (*haengsa*). One interpretation of Pak's friction with the SLOOC president and his subsequent resignation from the committee is that he may have considered the scenario as his own creation and the work of the planning board as supplementary to his efforts, whereas "from an objective point of view, cooperative creative work (*kongdong ch'angjak*) was more appropriate than individual creative work (*kaein ch'angjak*)" (Kim Munhwan 1988:269-70). While the contribution of individual creativity to the ceremonies is undeniable, we have seen that altruism was not the only factor in decisions nor self-effacement the only response of composers when they thought their creations were being mishandled. Of all those interviewed, the most vocal proponent of artistic integrity and independence was Kang Sŏkhŭi, who composed the torch music:

> I was angry at the atmosphere in Korean society where people don't understand that an artist has to strive for what he sees is best. But they don't believe that nor are they able to recognize it when they see it. But whether they recognize it or not, it should be done. If they select someone as a composer and ask him to write, they should believe him. In our Korean society we have a lot of experiences like that. (Personal interview, June 6, 1989)

Yet, while Kang resented others' power to pronounce compositions inadequate, to fire composers, or to make them rearrange their music, even he conceded, "Of course, it was necessary to do so in order to harmonize the whole."

"To harmonize the whole" may be the best naming so far of the basic challenge in creating the music of the ceremonies. Coordinating the effort and output of more than twenty composers who were writing the score for a two-movement epic work spanning five hours was a task of enormous proportions. "The most important thing," said Pak Sejik, sounding rather like an artistic director himself, "was for the music to be in harmony, not only with the movement, but with the whole sequence of sound. From beginning to end it had to be in harmony with itself." He went on to describe sitting with ceremony committee members on the benches of the empty stadium months before the opening to listen to the sound track all the way through. There is a certain pathos to the circle of those attending to a cohesion of sound in the audio track at the end of the process instead of at the beginning, when it was needed. Only studio editing could now make transitions between divergent styles, and that by contrivance instead of design. It is a case of otherwise competent professionals facing the one-time-only, gargantuan task of staging Olympic ceremonies: suddenly everyone becomes an amateur. Yet this circle of listeners in the empty stadium—their focus on sound "in harmony with itself," sounds "harmonizing with each other"— becomes emblematic of the overall effort of the ceremonies and the process that brought them to completion.

From the perspective of music, the primary gesture of the Seoul Olympic ceremonies—the preparation and the performance—was aesthetic. Beyond the stress and strain, the multiple elements and massive scale, the politics of setting a public image, the conflicts of taste—beyond all these centrifugal factors was a shared impulse to hold things together. It was operative in the working relationships and the ethos of a common cause and, most of all, in the effort to turn Olympic ceremonies into art. The impulse to unity had its visual correlative in the circle motif: the five Olympic rings in the sky, the little boy's hoop, the twirling ribbons, and the mandala of spiraling performers in the "One World" scene. Perhaps most symbolic of aesthetic forces at work in the ceremonies was the inward-outward spin of the red, blue, and yellow *t'aegŭk* in the Seoul Olympic emblem. The harmony enacted and operative in the ceremonies was not motion in a single direction but complementary movement in seemingly opposite directions.

Combining art music with martial art was an aborted attempt toward that kind of strong beauty. A computerized soundscape of "Harmony" projected torch music of cosmic dimensions. However, in the voice of East Asian wisdom, "If humans are thinking about something, but the atmosphere—the social or economic [political or cultural] conditions—is not suitable for that idea, then it must fail."[41] The Korean cultural elites making decisions about

---

[41] See footnote 6.

the ceremony music were not quite ready for a leap into the future of sound; thus, the integrity of the fire music was compromised in the end. The one incident, however, does not nullify the basic impulse in the ceremonies toward aesthetic harmony.

Conclusion

> By heaven's favor and God's help the Seoul Olympics received the highest praise as being the most brilliant in history.... But for this experience of magnificent scenes we had to pay the price of undergoing innumerable difficulties of every kind. (SLOOC 1988b:i)

The director-general's overview statement summarizes the ceremonies and their reception: magnificent scenes, highest praise, and innumerable difficulties. There was a kind of just proportion between the brilliance of the ceremonies and the pains taken to achieve that success: "Whenever we faced situations like that we would feel the historical responsibility laid on us for the Olympic opening and closing ceremonies as the flower of the Olympics and the most important means for bringing success or failure to the Olympics. If the ceremonies should fail it would bring frustration to the Korean people and be a regrettable lost opportunity" (SLOOC 1988b:i).

In the burden of individual responsibility for the success or failure—more likely failure—of the whole people, even this official document conveys a tone of distinctively Korean *han*. A flip side of the fear of failure was surprise when it turned out so well. Koreans who had shown little enthusiasm for the Olympic project beforehand expressed to me their amazement that Korea could bring off such a world-class performance. From interviews with Korean composers, committee members, directors, staff, and administrators, I learned that the term "evaluation" is understood not as analysis but as faultfinding with political implications. "On an evaluation committee, of course your job is to be critical. Under the Fifth Republic to be critical was considered disloyal, but not now."[42] What a Korean might say to a foreigner, even one he has known and seems to trust, is generally limited by the ethos of

---

[42] Evaluations of the ceremonies appeared in several formats: the official report from the SLOOC to the IOC; symposium reports by members of the Olympic Cultural Festival Evaluation Committee; the evaluation report on the work of the SLOOC by a committee of international sports experts; papers delivered at the SOAC conference's two sessions on cultural aspects of the Seoul Olympic Games; and the report by the Ceremony Administration Team, to which I have frequently referred.

keeping problems within the family. Since several of the planners expressed preferences and criticisms to me quite frankly, I present their comments collated and anonymous in order to leave them free to speak without possible embarrassment.

Although composers would not evaluate the work of another colleague directly, they had plenty to say about the musical level and general problems in the ceremonies. Several mentioned the long-range benefits of collaborating with other composers, getting to know their work, and hearing others' orchestration. But some composers overreached themselves and wrote music that was too complicated; others were too casual about the project, just imagining the dance in their heads, thus requiring much revision or eventual withdrawal of their music. Some of Korea's best composers were not chosen to write for the ceremonies; there was overrepresentation from the composition department of the national university. Since university professors write and teach mostly contemporary art music, there was some fear that they would not be able to compose ceremonial music, and relief at what was eventually produced. While coordinating with the dance was a serious problem for some ("Choreographers speak in such an abstract language!"), all composers suffered from premature deadlines and the late firming up of the scenario. Some felt they should have been selected and commissioned "at least two years ahead," instead of the spring and summer of 1987. The cost to composers in personal and creative pain was high when the scenario changed and dances were revised. Perhaps the most crucial omission affecting the aesthetic cohesion of the music was the disparity between a scenario's being conceived as a dramatic whole and the musical score being created piece by piece. Involving so many good Korean composers showcased a spectrum of native talent, but it may also have been a case of "too many sailors and the boat ends up on dry land."[43] I noted, after many conversations with composers, that there seemed to be a need for a single artistic director of the paired ceremonies with authority to make decisions affecting the whole. One official charged with music agreed: "You're sharp."

However, an artistic director might have conflicted with the centralized SLOOC authority structure, which operated as a unifying force. Western organizational models do exist for shared

---

[43] This is literally "If there are too many sailors, the boat goes to the mountain" (*Sagong-i manŭmyŏn, pae-ka san-ŭro kanda*).

authority between artistic and executive agencies, but it may be questioned whether such an approach would have delivered any more power to the artists than did the SLOOC president's respect for the opinions of Korean art professionals and his habit of extensive consultation. Modes of decision making customary in a Confucian society ruled by former generals yield reluctantly to alternative models by consensus, and the admirable attempts made to proceed in a more democratic fashion during the ceremony preparations were perhaps already "state of the art" in a country accustomed to authoritarian models. Moreover, committee consensus as a way of arriving at artistic decisions might produce more camels than great performances; the priority of group opinion over individual insight may reduce originality to a common denominator. On the other hand, consensus and majority opinion can rub off the sharp edges of idiosyncratic ideas. The ceremony process showed traces of the latter dynamics as those involved acted out transitional interplays between democracy and artistry in the larger social drama of the relation of group to individual. Meanwhile, Korea is currently experimenting with its own perestroika in every field. Institutions for art and culture are being put under the control of the nongovernmental sector, for economic as well as political reasons. Efforts to dissociate government from military control and art and culture from government control echo the tension we have witnessed between the *mu* and *do* aspects of the national sport. Just as the *do* of taekwondo did not fare well in the attempt to have it dance with its martial *mu,* so too the general transformation of authoritarian structures relative to cultural practices may require an irony and self-critique similar to that which Hwang's art music tried to cast on the martial art in the opening ceremonies.

A particularly astute participant at the hub of these interactions took the long view on internal and external evaluations of the ceremonies. After the ceremony, he said, they had received a lot of criticism from Koreans who did not participate.

> That happens in any country; if those people had been in charge, they, too, would have received criticism. The opening ceremony, on the surface, looked like a success. Foreigners enjoyed the Korean things and were surprised scene by scene. But to be honest, such mass games (*nori*) are not important since they can be done even better by Communist countries. What was unique about the music of the Seoul Olympics is that in presenting the culture of Korea we used music created by our own composers. Therefore, when the world's people hear the music of the

ceremonies they may be surprised that a developing country can have such high-quality music and they will perhaps reconsider Korea.

When I asked him how he would personally evaluate the ceremonies, as usual he demurred, but with an addition: "Since we prepared the ceremonies we cannot praise ourselves. Foreigners thought they were well done, but we felt we could have done better." Whenever I encounter this kind of self-diffidence in Koreans, especially in relation to a task so well accomplished, I realize how much an outsider I am to understanding their experience. When I asked the planners for their overall evaluation of the ceremonies and the music, they would often turn the question back to me: what was my opinion?

In a contest between forces of diffusion and cohesion in the ceremony process, creativity played on both sides. The dialectical insight into Korea provided by the central image of wall was responsible for giving both depth and universality to the scenario, which held everything together. The commitment to keep tradition alive by creating it anew and the entrusting of the music to current composers were both signs of belief in culture as malleable material. However, creative individuals felt constrained by both the format and certain procedures; they cooperated with the multiple elements at risk to their artistic independence. I am reminded here of a correction to my Western favoring of the individual artist over the demands of group solidarity and approval. When Han Manyŏng, my principal informant, spotted this bias in an earlier paper, he remarked, "But if the individual artist had prevailed, the ceremonies would have gone to chaos." Perhaps, given the present social and historical circumstances. But I am also sobered by remembering that the "Chaos" scene of the opening ceremony was brought to order by the taekwondo enactment of "Beyond All Barriers," a scene and a process reminiscent of Korea's military tradition. Conquering forces of chaos by depicting mass synchronization was a look to the past. Creative shaping of tradition through collaboration, the major thrust of the ceremony process, augured well for the future.

I see and hear the Seoul ceremonies—and the process by which they came to final form before the world—as a dynamic cultural performance. While depicting the cosmic ritual of interacting forces between heaven, earth, and humans, the final production provides a single if elaborate time cut in the drama of cultural, social, and political ambiguities within contemporary Korea, an unrehearsed and open-ended version of the world-historical process envisioned in the scenario. From the triple replay of the event presented in this study, only one thing is unambiguous: the future of Olympic ceremonies in relation to those of 1988. When other countries now consider how to create their own Olympic ceremonial representations of themselves and of humanity, they will have to listen to Seoul for a new model of meaning and sheer beauty for the genre.

References

Kim Munhwan. 1988. "Kae-p'yehwoeshik ŭi mihakchŏk sŏnggyŏk" [The aesthetic character of the opening and closing ceremonies]. In *Son-e son chapko, pyŏk-ŭl nŏmŏsŏ* [Hand in hand, beyond all barriers]. Seoul: Han'guk pangsong saŏptan.

MacAloon, John J., and Kang Shinbyo. 1990. *"Uri Nara:* Korean Nationalism, the Seoul Olympics, and Contemporary Anthropology." In *Toward One World, Beyond All Barriers: The Seoul Olympiad Anniversary Conference,* 117–59. Seoul: Poong Nam Publishing.

Marcuse, Herbert. 1978. *The Aesthetic Dimension: Towards a Critique of Marxist Aesthetics.* Boston: Beacon Press.

MBC (Munhwa Broadcasting Company). 1989. "Masterpiece Theatre: Modern Music Composer, Kang Sŏkhŭi." MBC-TV documentary, June 13.

Mulling, Craig. 1990. "Dissidents' Perspective of the 1988 Seoul Olympics." In *Toward One World, Beyond All Barriers: The Seoul Olympiad Anniversary Conference,* 394–407. Seoul: Poong Nam Publishing.

Pak, Sejik. 1989. "Seoul Olympic Memorial Address." Paper delivered at the Seoul Olympiad Anniversary Conference "Toward One World, Beyond All Barriers," September 12–16.

———. 1990. "The Story of the Seoul Olympics." *Chosŏn ilbo,* January 12, 25.

SLOOC (Seoul Olympic Organizing Committee). 1988a. *Opening Ceremony Program.* Seoul: SLOOC.

———. 1988b. *Opening-Closing Ceremonies Administration Team Report Number 4.* Foreword by Yi Kiha. Seoul: SLOOC.

Yi, Ŏryŏng. 1988. "Beyond All Barriers: The Making of the Opening and Closing Ceremonies of the Seoul Olympics." In *Opening Ceremony Program.* Seoul: SLOOC.

APPENDIX A: Individuals Cited in the Text

Pak Yonggu	First chairman of the Scenario Planning Committee
Yi Ŏryŏng	Member of the Scenario Planning Committee and Executive/Steering Committee; drafter of the final scenario
Kim Munhwan	Member of the Executive/Steering Committee; co-drafter of the final scenario; translator of the official song into Korean
Han Manyŏng	Member of six advisory committees related to music in the ceremonies
Pak Sejik	President of the Seoul Olympic Organizing Committee (SLOOC)
Yi Kiha	Director-general of the Ceremonies Operations Unit
Yi Kangsuk	Music adviser on the ceremonies Executive/Steering Committee
Yi Sangman	Member of the Music Advisory Committee
Kim Hŭijo	Member of the Music Advisory Committee; composer
Kim Ch'igon	Assistant secretary-general of the SLOOC for Culture and Ceremonies
Kim Kyŏngshik	SLOOC staff liaison between Ceremonies Unit and musicians
Kim Chŏnggil	Music director for the opening ceremonies; composer
P'yo Chaesun	Director and general producer of the ceremonies
Hwang Pyŏnggi	Composer
Kim Unyong	Vice-president of the SLOOC; member of the IOC; president of the national and international taekwondo associations
Kang Sŏkhŭi	Music director of the closing ceremony; composer

APPENDIX B: Draft Versions of the Opening and Closing Ceremonies

Draft	Familiar title	Official title	Date
1	Report no. 1	Same	December 5, 1
2	Scenario	Same	January 1987
3	Report no. 2	Same	February 2, 1⁹
4	Production script	*Changpyŏk-ŭl hŏmulgo* (Breaking down the walls)	February 198?
5	Working script	*Pyŏk-ŭl nŏmŏsŏ* (Over the wall)	April 1987
6	Final program	*Pyŏk-ŭl nŏmŏsŏ* (Beyond all barriers)	September 19.

Index-Glossary

aewan ch'ŏng 애완청 (sad voice), 163
ajaeng 牙箏 (8-stringed bowed zither), 18, 85
ajaeng sanjo 牙箏散調 (*sanjo* for 8-stringed bowed zither), 19
Akchang kasa 樂章歌詞 (Song texts of *akchang*; literary source for *kasa*), 9
Akhak kwebŏm 樂學軌範 (Treatise on music), 101–2, 102n, 104, 106, 116
Akkŭk arirang 樂劇아리랑 (Music and theater *arirang*; theater production), 151
An Kiok 安基玉 (1905–48; *kayagŭm sanjo* master), 19
an majayo 안맞아요 (did not match), 224
An Minyŏng 安玟英 (coauthor of *Kagok wŏllyu*), 8
An Sain 안사인 (shaman, holder of asset no. 71 *Cheju ch'ilmŏri tang kut*), 159n
An Suksŏn 安淑善 (b. 1949; *p'ansori* singer), 47n, 165
aniri 아니리 (speech in *p'ansori*), 128, 134, 135–36, 138–45
anjinban 안진반 (rhythmic cycle used in shamanistic dance), 19
anjŭnban 앉은반 (seated form of *samul nori*), 62n
"Arirang" 아리랑 (traditional folk song), 80–82, 93, 149–52, 193–94, 196, 198n
Austin, Major Herbert H., 27

Bishop, Isabelle Bird, 26n

chaech'angjo 再創造 (re-creation), 174n
chaedam 才談 (witty talk), 28
chaedam kwangdae 재담광대 (singers who tell witty stories), 130

chaehaesŏk 再解釋 (reinterpretation), 174n
Chaeinch'ŏng 才人廳 (Office of Entertainers), 10
chaeng 箏 (zither), 97n
chagi hŭisaengjŏk shilch'ŏllyŏk 自己犧牲的實踐力 (power of self-sacrifice in practice), 221
"Chajin arari" 자진 아라리 (song for transplanting rice), 88
chajin salp'uri 자진살푸리 (rhythmic cycle used in shamanistic dance), 19
chajinmori 자진모리 (fast 4-beat rhythmic cycle), 14, 19, 136, 143
chakp'um 作品 (artistic work), 226
ch'amsŏn 參禪 (meditation in taekwondo), 200, 205
ch'an 禪 (C.: Buddhist meditation), 205
ch'ang 唱 (*p'ansori*), 31
chang 醬 (bean paste), 181–82, 196
Chang Chabaek 張子伯 (*p'ansori* singer), 13
Chang Kyech'un 張桂春 (1868–1946; *chapka* singer), 15
Chang P'an'gae 張判介 (*p'ansori* singer), 15
Chang Sahun 張師勛 (1916–91; scholar), 107
"Changbuhan" 丈夫恨 (Hero's grudge; *tan'ga*), 15
changbyŏk-ŭl hŏmulgo 장벽을 허물고 (breaking down the wall), 178, 235
changdan 長短 (rhythmic pattern or cycle), 8–9, 12, 14, 18, 56, 91
changgo 杖鼓 (hourglass-shaped drum), 9–10, 18, 20, 57, 84–85, 90–91, 159, 165

changgo ch'um 장고춤 (*changgo* drum dance), 198, 198n

changgu 장구 (linguistic variant of *changgo*), 20, 57

ch'anggŭk 唱劇 (lit., "singing drama"; musical theater form), 22–49, 132

Ch'anggŭk chŏngnip wiwŏnhoe 唱劇定立委員會 (Committee for the Establishment of Ch'anggŭk), 35–40, 46

Ch'anggŭksa yŏn'gu 唱劇史研究 (Study of the history of *ch'anggŭk*), 25

"Changkki t'aryŏng" 장끼타령 (Song of the cock-pheasant; one of the 12 *p'ansori* stories), 11

ch'angu chiptan 唱優集團 (singing troupes), 42

chapka 雜歌 (lit., "miscellaneous song"; vocal genre of folk music), 6–7, 14–15

"Chapka" 雜歌 (song for weeding), 88

chapsaek 雜色 (actors), 57

"Chat'an'ga" 自嘆歌 (Grieving song; aria from "Ch'unhyangga"), 13

"Chebiga" 제비가 (Swallow song; aria from "Hŭngbuga"), 12

Cheju ch'ilmŏri tang kut 濟州칠머리堂굿 (shamanistic ritual from Cheju island), 159n

Cheju minyo 濟州民謠 (folk songs of Cheju island), 156–58

Chen Shou 陳壽 (233–97; Chinese historian), 97

Chesŏk 제석 (Buddhist spirit), 163

Chi Sunja 지순자 (daughter of Sŏng Kŭmyŏn), 107

Chi Yonggu 池龍九 (*haegŭm sanjo* master), 19

Chi Yŏnghŭi 池瑛熙 (*haegŭm sanjo* master), 19, 162

chilgut 질굿 (lit., "road ritual"; rhythmic pattern), 71

chinbŏp 陳法 (ground formation), 56

Chinch'an ŭigwe 進饌儀軌 (Court writings on Chinch'an banquets), 101

"Chindo arirang" 珍島아리랑 (folk song *arirang* from the island of Chin), 152

Chindo ssikkim kut 珍島씻김굿 (shamanistic purification ritual of the island of Chin), 158

ching 징 (large hand-held gong), 18, 20, 57, 126, 152

"Chin'guk myŏngsan" 鎭國名山 (The famous Mount Chin'guk; *tan'ga*), 15

Chinju Samch'ŏnp'o Nongak 晋州三千浦農樂 (cultural asset percussion band), 56n

chinyang 진양 (slow 6-beat rhythmic cycle), 12, 14, 19, 138, 144

chirŭm shijo 지름시조 (lit., "high-pitch *shijo*"; variation of *p'yŏng shijo*), 9

cho/-jo 調 (mode), 14

Cho Kijun 曹基俊 (*Kyŏnggi chapka* singer), 15

Cho Kongnye 曺功禮 (1930?–96; cultural asset holder of *Namdo tŭllorae*), 157, 157n, 159–60, 160n

Cho Sanghyŏn 조상현 (*p'ansori* singer), 45n

Cho Ŭlsŏn 趙乙善 (b. 1915; cultural asset holder of *Cheju minyo*), 157–59

Cho Yong Pil (Cho Yongp'il) 조용필 (b. 1950; popular singer), 162, 205

Cho Yŏngbae 조영배 (arranger, composer), 160

ch'odan 初段 (black belt), 202n

Ch'oe Kyŏngshik 崔景植 (1874–1949; *chapka* singer), 115

Ch'oe Oksan 崔玉山 (*kayagŭm sanjo* master), 19

Ch'oe Sŏndal 崔先達 (*p'ansori* singer), 11

Ch'oe Sŏngho 최성호 (popular singer), 165

Ch'oe Soshim 崔小心 (1908–91; cultural asset holder of *Kanggangsullae*), 160, 160n

Ch'oe Tokkyŏn 최독견 (*p'ansori* singer), 31

ch'ojang 醋醬 (soy sauce with vinegar), 145

ch'ŏk 尺 (old standard of measurement), 102

"Chŏkpyŏkka" 赤壁歌 (Song of the red cliffs; *p'ansori*), 11, 13, 131–32

"Chŏksŏngga" 赤城歌 (Song of the red wall; aria from "Ch'unhyangga"), 14

Cholchangmallok 拙庄漫錄 (old *kayagŭm* notation of 1796), 112

Chŏlla province 全羅道 (one of 8 provinces in Chosŏn period), 10, 12, 19, 55–56, 61, 64–65, 72, 126, 146, 166

Chŏn Hwang 전황 (dancer, choreographer), 47n

"Ch'ŏnando samgŏri" 천안도 삼거리 (folk song), 161

ch'ŏn-chi-in 天地人 (heaven, earth, and humans), 176n

Chŏndaehyŏp 全大協 (radical national association of university students), 221n

Chŏng Chaeguk 鄭在國 (*p'iri sanjo* master), 19

Chŏng Ch'angŏp 丁昌業 (*p'ansori* singer), 13

Chŏng Ch'unp'ung 鄭春風 (*p'ansori* singer), 13

Chŏng Kwŏnjin 鄭權鎭 (*p'ansori* singer), 121–22, 128n

Chŏng Noshik 鄭魯湜 (scholar, author of *Chosŏn ch'anggŭksa*), 29

Chŏng Tŭkman 鄭得晚 (*chapka* singer), 15

chŏngak 正樂 ("elegant music"; court music), 103, 111–13, 116

chŏngak kayagŭm 正樂伽倻琴 (alternate name for *p'ungnyu kayagŭm*), 111–12

chŏngbon 定本 (standard text), 37

chŏngga 正歌 (proper song), 6, 8

Ch'ŏnggu yŏngŏn 靑丘永言 (Eternal songs of Korea; anthology of *kagok* texts), 8–9

chŏnghyŏng shijo 定型時調 (standard text *shijo*), 8

chŏngnip 定立 (establishment), 35

Ch'ŏngp'a-dong 靑坡洞 (county of Yongsan district, Seoul), 15

chŏngshim chŏngŭm 正心正音 (correct mind, correct sound), 128

chŏngt'ong sŏng 正統性 (orthodox quality), 42

chŏngt'ong yŏn'gŭk 正統演劇 (legitmate drama), 42

Chŏn'guk minsok yesul kyŏngyŏn taehoe 全國民俗藝術競演大會 (National Folk Arts Competition), 20

"Ch'ŏnja p'uri" 千字풀이 (Song of the thousand Chinese characters), 14

"Ch'ŏnja twip'uri" 千字뒤풀이 (Finishing song of a thousand Chinese characters), 13

ch'ŏnjang 天障 (ceiling), 145

Chŏnju 全州 (capital of North Chŏlla province), 64–65, 166

ch'ŏnmin 賤民 (lowest people), 155

chŏnt'ong sŏng 傳統性 (traditional quality), 42

chŏnt'ong ŭmak 傳統音樂 (traditional music), 22

Chŏnt'ong yesulwŏn 傳統藝術院 (School of Korean Traditional Arts), 20

chŏnt'ong yŏn'gŭk 傳統演劇 (traditional drama), 35

chŏnt'ongjŏgin ŭmak 傳統的인 音樂 (music with an air of tradition about it), 20

"Chŏnyŏk kido" 저녁기도 (The evening prayer; composition by Yi Sŏngch'ŏn), 115

ch'orani 초라니 (cross-dressed actor), 137

"Ch'ŏsaga" 處士歌 (Song of the hidden scholar; *kasa*), 9

Chōsen min'yō shū 朝鮮民謠集 (J.: Collection of Korean folk songs), 150

Chosŏn 朝鮮 (period of Korean history; 1392–1910), 5–6, 9–10, 15–20, 101, 111

Chosŏn ch'anggŭksa 朝鮮唱劇史 (History of Korean *p'ansori*), 29
Chosŏn minyo chip 朝鮮民謠集 (Collection of Korean folk songs), 150
Chosŏn sŏngak yŏn'guhoe 朝鮮聲樂研究會 (Korean Vocal Music Association), 29–32
Chosŏn ŭmnyul hyŏphoe 朝鮮音律協會 (Korean Music Association), 29
"Ch'osudaeyŏp" 初數大葉 (first "Saktaeyŏp"; *kagok*), 7
chŏttae 젓대 (large transverse flute), 18
Ch'u Kyoshin 秋教信 (*chapka* singer), 15
Chu Tŏkki 朱德基 (*p'ansori* singer), 11, 13
ch'uimsae 추임새 (calls of encouragement), 36
ch'ujinryŏk 推進力 ("can-do" spirit), 221
ch'uk 筑 (zither), 97, 97n
"Chukchang manghye" 竹杖芒鞋 (Bamboo stick and straw sandals; *tan'ga*), 15
"Chukchisa" 竹枝詞 (Song of bamboo branch; *kasa*), 9
Chulp'ungnyu 줄風流 (alternate title for *Hyŏnak yŏngsan hoesang*), 17
"Chulp'uri No. 2" '줄풀이' 제2반 (composition by Yi Haeshik), 109
Chun Doo Hwan (Chŏn Tuhwan) 全斗煥 (past military leader and South Korean president, 1980–87), 169
Ch'ungch'ŏng province 忠清道 (one of 8 provinces in Chosŏn period), 10, 12, 140, 163
"Chungdaeyŏp" 中大葉 (Medium song; forerunner of present-day *kagok*), 7
chunggoje 中高制 (upper-central style *p'ansori* singing), 12–13
chunggŭm 中笒 (medium transverse flute), 99
Chunggwangjigok 重光之曲 (alternate title for *Hyŏnak yŏngsan hoesang*), 17

ch'unggyŏksŏng 衝擊成 (shock; impact), 183
chungjungmori 중중모리 (fast moderate tempo rhythmic cycle), 14, 19, 91, 142, 144, 146
chungmori 중모리 (medium-tempo 12-beat rhythmic cycle), 14, 19, 91–92, 140, 140n
"Chungnyŏngsan" 中靈山 (piece from *Yŏngsan hoesang*), 17–18
chungyo muhyŏng munhwajae 重要無形文化財 (important intangible cultural asset), 34, 55, 123, 127
Chungyo muhyŏng munhwajae chosa pogosŏ 重要無形文化財調查報告書 (Cumulative Research Reports on Important Intangible Cultural Assets), 154
Ch'unhyang 春香 (heroine of "Ch'unhyangga/Ch'unhyang-jŏn"), 14, 38, 45
"Ch'unhyangga" 春香歌 (Song of Ch'unhyang; *p'ansori*), 10–14, 131–32, 132n
"Ch'unhyang-jŏn" 春香傳 (Story of Ch'unhyang), 30–31, 35, 38, 46
"Ch'unmyŏn'gok" 春眠曲 (Song of spring sleep; *kasa*), 9
ch'uu odong 秋雨梧桐 ("autumn rain falling on paulownia leaves"), 131
chwajilgut 左질굿 (lit., "left road ritual"; rhythmic pattern), 71

di 笛 (C.: flute), 151
do (*to/-do*) 道 (way or art), 199, 201, 219, 230
Dongki Hong (Hong Tonggi) 홍동기 (b. 1967; pianist and composer), 168
DPRK (Democratic People's Republic of Korea [North Korea]), 87, 109, 151, 165, 178
"Duo" Op. 13 (composition by Yi Sŏngch'ŏn), 109
Ha Handam 河漢潭 (*p'ansori* singer), 11

Index-Glossary

Ha Kyuil 河圭一 (1867–1937; *kagok* singer), 9

Ha Sunil 河順一 (*kagok* singer), 15

Haedong kayo 海東歌謠 (Songs of the eastern sea; anthology of *kagok* texts), 8

haegŭm 奚琴 (2-stringed bowed fiddle), 18, 84–85, 169

haegŭm sanjo 奚琴散調 (*sanjo* for 2-stringed bowed fiddle), 19

haengsa 行事 (event), 226

"Haessal hana na hana" 햇살하나 나하나 (One for the sunlight, one for me; composition by Yi Sŏngch'ŏn), 117

"Hahyŏn hwanip" 下絃還入 (piece from *Yŏngsan hoesang*), 17–18

Hakp'o kŭmbo 學圃琴譜 (Hakp'o's *kŏmun'go* manuscript), 8, 18

Ham Tongjŏngwŏl 咸洞庭月 (*kayagŭm sanjo* master), 19

hamkke p'asang kyŏkp'a 함께 波狀 擊破 (final breaking of the boards in taekwondo), 200

han 恨 (grievance; unrequited desire; regrets; resentment; grudge), 125, 163, 163n, 228

Han Chuhwan 韓周煥 (*taegŭm sanjo* master), 19

Han Ilsŏp 한일섭 (*ajaeng sanjo* master), 19

Han Kaptŭk 韓甲得 (b. 1918; *kŏmun'go sanjo* master), 19

Han madang 한마당 (One world; scene from the Seoul Olympics), 188, 205

Han Manyŏng 韓萬榮 (scholar), 177, 177n, 183n, 188n, 197, 222, 223n, 231, 233

Han Nongsŏn 韓弄仙 (*p'ansori* singer), 132n, 136

Han Pŏmsu 韓範洙 (*taegŭm sanjo* master), 19

Han Sŏnggi 韓成基 (*kayagŭm sanjo* master), 19

Han Songhak 韓松鶴 (*p'ansori* singer), 13

Han Sŏngjun 韓成俊 (*p'ansori* drummer [*kosu*]), 13

Han Sukku 韓淑求 (*kayagŭm sanjo* master), 19

Han Yangsun 한양순 (Olympic ceremony planner), 176n

Han Yü 韓愈 (786–824; Chinese poet), 11

hanbŏn kyŏrugi 한번겨루기 (fighting stance[s] in taekwondo), 200

"Hand in Hand" (official song of the Seoul Olympics), 189, 191–93, 195–96, 216–18, 222

Han'guk ŭmak 韓國音樂 (Korean music), 76

Han'guk yesul chonghap hakkyo 韓國藝術綜合學校 (Korean National University of Arts), 20

han'gŭl 한글 (Korean writing/alphabet), 123

Han'gŭm shinbo 韓琴新譜 (Han's new *kŏmun'go* manuscript; old *kŏmun'go* manuscript), 7, 17

Hanyang 漢陽 (present-day city of Seoul), 10

Hŏ Kyu 허규 (writer, director), 38–41

Hŏ Tŭksŏn 許得善 (*Sŏdo chapka* singer), 15

Hoam Art Hall, 151

Hodori 호도리 (lit., "tiger boy"), 185, 185n

"Hoeshimgok" 회심곡 (shaman-and-Buddhist-influenced song), 163

hojŏk 胡笛, 號笛 (double-reed wind instrument), 57, 65, 126

Honam chwado 湖南左道 ("left-side" style Chŏlla province *nongak/p'ungmul*), 65

"Honam karak" 호남 가락 (Rhythmic patterns of Chŏlla province), 61, 67

Honam udo 湖南右道 ("right-side" style Chŏlla province *nongak/p'ungmul*), 56

"Honam udo kut" 호남우도굿 (Chŏlla province "right-side" ritual/performance), 61, 71

"Honam udo p'ungmulgut karak" 호남 우도 풍물굿가락 (*P'ungmulgut* rhythmic patterns of the "right-side" [western] counties of Chŏlla province), 65, 71, 72
Hondon 混沌 (Chaos; scene from the Seoul Olympics), 186n
Hong Haesŏng 홍해성 (*p'ansori* singer), 31
Hong Sŏngdŏk 홍성덕 (leader of all-female *ch'anggŭk* troupe), 32
horangi 虎狼이 (tiger), 185n
Hosuni 호순이 (lit., "tiger girl"), 185, 185n
hŏt'ŭn karak 허튼가락 (lit., "scattered melodies"; Korean term for *sanjo*), 19
Hŭkpaek sajin 흑백사진 (Black and white photographs; album), 165
Hulbert, Homer B. (journalist), 150
Hŭngbu 흥부 (younger brother of Nolbu), 136, 138–44
"Hŭngbuga" 興夫歌 (Song of Hŭngbu; *p'ansori*), 11–12, 14, 131–32, 136
Hunmongjahoe 訓蒙字會 (old textbook), 97
"Hwach'o sagŏri" 花草사거리 (Song of flowering plants; *chapka*), 15
hwach'ojang 花草欌 (antique chest), 144–45
hwagwanmu 花冠舞 (flower crown dance), 198n
Hwang Haech'ŏng 黃海淸 (*p'ansori* singer), 11
Hwang Pyŏnggi 黃秉冀 (b. 1936; composer, performer, scholar), 111, 118, 199–200, 200n, 201n, 202, 202n, 203–5, 212, 220, 222–25, 230–31, 233
"Hwanggyegok" 還界樂 (Song of yellow cock; *kasa*), 9
"Hwanghwa mannyŏnjigok" 皇化萬年之曲 (Ode to his majesty the emperor), 77
hwangjong 黃鍾 (central pitch), 112n
"Hwan'gyerak" 還界樂 (*kagok* piece), 8
"Hwaryongdo" 華容道 (Song of the Hua-yung road; alternate title for "Chŏkpyŏkka"), 11
hwimori 휘모리 (fast 4-beat rhythmic cycle), 14, 19, 139–41
hyang pip'a 鄕琵琶 (5-stringed long-necked lute), 99
Hyangdan 향단 (character from "Ch'unhyang-jŏn"), 38
hyangje shijo 鄕制時調 (country-style *shijo*), 10
"Hyodoga" 孝道歌 (Song of filial piety), 128
Hyŏl ŭi nu 血의 淚 (Tears of blood; 1906 novel by Yi Injik), 26
Hyŏnak yŏngsan hoesang 絃樂靈山會相 (string version of *Yŏngsan hoesang*), 16–18
hyŏnch'im 絃枕 (lit., "the strings' pillow"; one end of the *kayagŭm*), 99, 101, 107
Hyŏn'gŭm oŭm t'ongnon 玄琴五音通論 (Introduction to the 5 tones of the *kŏmun'go*; old *kŏmun'go* manuscript), 18
Hyŏn'gŭm tongmun yugi 玄琴東文類記 (Classified records on the *kŏmun'go* in Korean literature; old *kŏmun'go* manuscript), 7

"Ibyŏlga" 離別歌 (Farewell song; aria from "Ch'unhyangga"), 12
"*Il kosu i myŏngch'ang*" 一鼓手二名唱 (first the drummer, second the singer), 13
Il Won (Wŏn Il) 원일 (b. 1967; oboist, percussionist, composer), 168–69
Im Kijun 林基俊 (1868–1940; *kasa* singer), 9
Im Pangul 林芳蔚 (1904–61; *p'ansori* singer), 129
IMF (International Monetary Fund), 125, 138
imjong 林鍾 (pitch in the *kyemyŏn* mode), 112, 112n
Imshil P'ilbong Nongak 任實筆峰農樂 (cultural asset percussion band), 56n

Index-Glossary

imyŏn kŭrigi 裏面 그리기 (drawing the picture within), 128
in 人 (human), 176n
in'gan munhwajae 人間文化財 (human cultural asset), 85, 124n, 155
In'gong wisŏng 인공 위성 (a capella singing group), 161
inmul 人物 (appearance; presence), 134n
International Folk Music Council, 153
IOC (International Olympic Committee), 179, 189, 202, 222, 228n
ipch'ang 立唱 (lit., "standing song"; vocal genre of folk music), 15
ipch'ech'ang 立體唱 (concrete singing), 43
Iri Nongak 裡里農樂 (cultural asset percussion band), 55–56, 56n, 57, 59, 61, 71
"Ishibihyŏn kayagŭm-ŭl wihan hyŏpchugok 'Sae sanjo' " 22현 가야금을 위한 협주곡 '새산조' (Concerto for 21-stringed *kayagŭm* 'New sanjo'; composition by Pak Pŏmhun), 118
"Isudaeyŏp" 二數大葉 (second "Saktaeyŏp"; *kagok*), 7–8
isuja 履修子 (master student), 157n

Jang Sun Woo (U Changsŏn) 우장선 (film director), 169

kabuki 歌舞伎 (Japanese traditional theater), 25, 35
kaein ch'angjak 個人創作 (individual creative work), 226
kaejo 改造 (to be modified), 103n
kaeryang 改良 (to be improved), 103n
kagaek 歌客 (*kagok* singer), 6, 8
kagok 歌曲 (long lyric song), 5–10, 200, 200n, 202–6, 218, 220, 222
Kagok wŏllyu 歌曲原流 (Fundamental styles of *kagok*; anthology of *kagok* texts), 8
kamyŏn'gŭk 假面劇 (masked dance-dramas), 29

"Kanan t'aryŏng" 가난타령 (Poor song; aria from "Hŭngbuga"), 14
Kang Hanyŏng 姜漢永 (scholar, librettist, head of the National Ch'anggŭk Troupe), 45–47, 48n, 134n
Kang Hojung 강호중 (b. 1960; founder of Seulgidoong), 166–67
Kang Namjung 姜南中 (*Namdo chapka* singer), 16
Kang Paekch'ŏn 姜白川 (*taegŭm sanjo* master), 19
Kang Sŏgyŏn 姜石鳶 (singer), 150
Kang Sŏkhŭi 강석희 (music director, composer), 207–8, 208n, 209, 209n, 210–13, 223–24, 226, 234
Kang T'aehong 姜太弘 (1894–1968; *kayagŭm sanjo* master), 19
Kang Yonghwan 姜龍煥 (*p'ansori* singer), 25
"Kanggangsullae" 강강술래 (folk song; women's song-and-dance genre), 86, 156, 159–60
Kangnŭng 江陵 (city in Kangwŏn province), 88
"Kangnŭng maehwajŏn" 江陵梅花傳 (Tale of the Kangnŭng plum; one of the 12 *p'ansori* stories), 11
Kangnŭng Nongak 江陵農樂 (cultural asset percussion band), 56n
kangsanje 江山制 (alternate term for *sŏp'yŏnje*), 12
Kangwŏn province 江原道 (one of 8 provinces in Chosŏn period), 88, 150, 152
karak 가락 (rhythmic pattern or cycle; melody), 12, 56
Karak hwanip 加樂還入 (version of *Yŏngsan hoesang* found in the *Hyŏn'gŭm oŭm t'ongnon*; piece from *Yŏngsan hoesang*), 18
"Karak tŏri" 가락더리 (piece from *Yŏngsan hoesang*), 17–18
"Karojigi" 가로지기 (alternate title for "Pyŏn Kangsoe t'aryŏng," or "Song of Pyŏn Kangsoe"), 40
Karpeles, Maud (scholar), 153

kasa 歌詞 (narrative song), 6, 8–10, 14
"Katcha shinsŏn t'aryŏng" 가짜神仙打令 (Song of the false hermit; one of the 12 *p'ansori* stories), 11
Kaya 加耶 (kingdom), 97, 97n, 99
kayago 가야고 (older Korean zither), 97n, 101–3
kayagŭm 伽倻琴 (12-stringed plucked zither), 18–19, 84–85, 96–118, 124, 166n, 199, 202n, 205, 209n
kayagŭm sanjo 伽倻琴散調 (*sanjo* for 12-stringed plucked zither), 19
KBS (Korean Broadcasting System) Hall, 111
KBS Traditional Music Orchestra (KBS kugak kwanhyŏn aktan) KBS 國樂管絃樂團, 166
ki 氣 (vitality; vital force), 200, 203
kibon tongjak 基本動作 (basic techniques in taekwondo), 200
"Kil kunak" 길軍樂 (Road military music; *kasa*; rhythmic pattern), 9, 72
killori 길놀이 (lit., "road play" or "procession"), 176
Kim Ch'angjo 金昌祖 (1865–1920; *kayagŭm sanjo* master), 19, 101n
Kim Chat'ap 김자탑 (theater producer), 151
Kim Ch'igon 김치곤 (member of Seoul Olympic Organizing Committee), 176n, 190, 190n, 192–94, 233
Kim Ch'ilsŏng 金七星 (*Sŏdo chapka* singer), 15
Kim Chiyŏn 김지연 (scholar), 150
Kim Chonggi 金宗基 (*kŏmun'go sanjo* master), 19
Kim Chŏnggil 金正吉 (music director; composer), 198n, 223n, 225, 233
Kim Chonggŭn 金宗根 (*p'ansori* singer), 13
Kim Chŏngmun 金正文 (*p'ansori* singer), 15
Kim Ch'ŏnt'aek 金天澤 (author of *Ch'ŏnggu yŏngŏn*), 8

Kim Chukp'a 金竹坡 (*kayagŭm sanjo* master), 19
Kim Ch'uwŏl 金秋月 (*Namdo chapka* singer), 16
Kim Duk Soo (Kim Tŏksu) 金德洙 (b. 1952; founding member of SamulNori, teacher), 60–61, 61n, 62, 64–67, 69, 71–72
Kim Hŭijo 김희조 (b. 1920; composer), 85, 188n, 202–3, 223, 223n, 233
Kim Hyŏngsun 金炯淳 (b. 1933; cultural asset holder of *nongak*, leader of Iri Nongak), 55
Kim Ilgu 김일구 (*p'ansori* teacher, singer), 41, 43–45
Kim Kirim 김기림 (b. 1927; cultural asset holder of *kanggangsullae*), 160n
Kim Kisu 金琪洙 (1917–86; scholar, composer), 77
Kim Kwangŏk 김광억 (popular singer), 165
Kim Kwangshik 金光植 (1911–72; *taegŭm sanjo* master), 19
Kim Kwanjun 金寬俊 (*Sŏdo chapka* singer), 15
Kim Kyech'ŏl 金啓喆 (*p'ansori* singer), 11–12
Kim Kyedal 김계달 (*p'ansori* singer), 12
Kim Kyohwan 김교환 (scholar), 150
Kim Kyŏngshik 김경식 (Seoul Olympic Organizing Committee staff liaison), 198, 198n, 201, 204, 233
Kim Min'gi 김민기 (b. 1951; dissident popular singer and poet), 164–65
Kim Munhwan 김문환 (Seoul Olympic Organizing Committee member), 177, 181, 193, 226, 233
Kim Myŏnghwan 金命煥 (1913–89; *p'ansori* drummer), 121
Kim Ogyŏp 金玉葉 (*chapka* singer), 15–16
Kim Okshim 金玉心 (*chapka* singer), 15

Kim Oksŏn 金玉仙 (*Sŏdo chapka* singer), 15
Kim Pyŏngsŏp 金炳燮 (*nongak changgo* performer), 126
Kim Sejong 金世鍾 (*p'ansori* singer), 13
Kim Sohŭi 金素姫 (1917–95; *p'ansori* singer), 129, 132
Kim Sŏnggi 金聖器 (*kŏmun'go* master), 8
Kim Suchol (Kim Such'ŏl) 김수철 (contemporary composer), 164, 165n
Kim Sujang 金壽長 (1690–?; author of *Haedong kayo*), 8
Kim Sunt'ae 金順泰 (*chapka* singer), 15
Kim T'aeun 金泰運 (1897–1963; *Sŏdo chapka* singer), 15
Kim Unyong 김운용 (Seoul Olympic Organizing Committee and International Olympic Committee member, president of national and international taekwondo associations), 202–3, 205–6, 222, 234
Kim Yongbae 김용배 (1953–86; founding member of SamulNori), 60–1, 61n
Kim Yŏngim 김영임 (folksinger), 85
Kim Young Dong (Kim Yŏngdong) 김영동 (b. 1951; contemporary composer), 164, 164n, 167
Kim Youngsam (Kim Yŏngsam) 金泳三 (South Korean president, 1992–98), 124
"Kimch'i t'aryŏng" 김치 打令 (Ballad of Korean pickled cabbage), 165
"Kimmaegi sori" 김매기소리 (Weeding song; example of *t'osok minyo*), 16
"Kin sarangga" 긴사랑가 (Long love song; aria from "Ch'unhyangga"), 14
King Chabi 慈悲王 (reigned 458–79), 97
King Chinhŭng 眞興王 (reigned 540–76), 96–97
King Kashil 가실王 (king of Kaya), 97

King Kojong 高宗王 (reigned 1864–1907), 13, 15
King Mich'u 味鄒王 (reigned 261–84), 101
King Naehae 奈解王 (reigned 196–230), 97
King Sejong 世宗王 (reigned 1418–50), 123
King Yŏngjo 英祖王 (reigned 1724–76), 7–9, 13
kisaeng 妓生 (female entertainer), 28, 126, 143, 156, 164
kkach'i 까치 (magpie), 220n
"Kkŏgŭm odokttegi" 꺽음 오독떼기 (song for weeding), 88
kkoktugakshi 꼭두각시 (puppet plays), 24
Kkonip 꽃잎 (A petal; film), 169
kkwaenggwari 꽹과리 (small hand-held gong), 20, 57
ko 고 (zither), 97n
Ko Hŭnggon 고홍곤 (instrument maker), 109, 111
Ko Sŏlbong 고설봉 (actor, writer), 26n, 30–31
Ko Sugwan 高壽寬 (*p'ansori* singer), 11–12
koch'ojang 고초장 (chili pepper paste), 145
Kogŭm kagok 古今歌曲 (Past and present *kagok*; anthology of *kagok* texts), 9
kohaeng 苦行 (self-discipline; asceticism), 201
Koji ruian 古事類苑 (J.: Ancient garden), 99
kŏlgung 걸궁 (see *kŏllip kut*)
kŏllip kut 걸립굿 (fund-raising performance by a *p'ungmul/nongak* band), 20, 162n
kŏmun'go 거문고 (6-stringed plucked zither), 6, 8–9, 16–17, 84, 97n, 99, 107, 209n
kŏmun'go sanjo 거문고산조 (*sanjo* for 6-stringed plucked zither), 19
kongdong ch'angjak 共同創作 (cooperative creative work), 226

konori 고놀이 (knot game), 176, 182, 198n, 199, 220n
Korean Music Orchestra of the Korean Broadcasting System, 77
Korean War (1950–53), 122
Koreana (popular vocal group), 191, 195–96, 196n, 197, 217–18
Koryŏ 高麗 (period of Korean history; 918–1392), 10, 99
Koryŏsa 高麗史 (History of the Koryŏ dynasty), 10, 99
kosŏn 고선 (pitch in *p'yŏng* mode), 112n
kossaum nori 고싸움놀이 (competitive folk art), 203
kosu 鼓手 (drummer and accompanist in *p'ansori*), 13–14
koto 箏 (J.: zither), 97n, 99, 209
koyusang 固有狀 (specific), 181
Ku Hyesŏn 구혜선 (interior designer), 41
Ku Taegam 具大監 (*Sŏdo chapka* singer), 15
kudŭlchang 구들장 (hypocaust), 145
kugak 國樂 (court music; classical music; national music; Korean music), 1, 33, 76, 123, 157
kugak kayo 國樂歌謠 (folk songs based stylistically on *p'ansori*), 166
kugaksa 國樂師 (musician), 33n
kugaksajang 國樂師長 (head musician), 33n
kugŭk 舊劇 (old drama), 28n
"*kujŏn shimsu*" 口傳心授 (imparted by lips, taken in by heart), 6, 16
kukkŏri 굿거리 (regular 4-beat rhythmic cycle in moderate tempo), 19, 71, 91, 159
kukkŭk 國劇 (national drama), 32
kŭm 琴 (zither), 97, 97n, 99
Kŭm hapchabo 琴合字譜 (*Kŏmun'go* tablature; an old *kŏmun'go* manuscript), 7
kŭmbagap shillagŭm 金箔押新羅琴 (older version of the *kayagŭm*), 99n, 111
"Kŭmbing" 금빙 (Ice strings; composition by Pak Ilhun), 109

Kŭmbo shinjŭng karyŏng 琴譜新證假令 (Newly revised *kŏmun'go* handbook; an old *kŏmun'go* manuscript), 7, 17
kŭmni shillagŭm 金泥新羅琴 (older version of the *kayagŭm*), 99n
"Kŭmp'uri" 금풀이 (Exorcism of strings; composition by Yi Haeshik), 117
"Kun pam t'aryŏng" 군밤 打令 (Roast chestnut song), 161–62
"Kunak" 軍樂 (Military music; piece from *Yŏngsan hoesang*), 17–18
kungjung ŭmak 宮中音樂 (court music), 5
Kungnip kugagwŏn 國立國樂院 (National Center for Korean Traditional Performing Arts), 20, 33, 42–45, 61, 85–86, 87n, 93, 103, 161n, 177n
Kungnip Kugagwŏn Samulnori 國立國樂院四物놀이 (*samul nori* group of the National Center for Korean Traditional Performing Arts), 71
Kungnip kugagwŏnbo 國立國樂院譜 (Notation of the National Center for Korean Traditional Performing Arts), 112
Kungnip kŭkchang 國立劇場 (National Theater), 34, 39–42, 44, 111
Kungnip kukkŭktan 國立國劇團 (National Drama Troupe), 34
kunsa munhwa 軍事文化 (military culture), 221
Kunsan 群山 (city in North Chŏlla province), 64
kup'a 舊派 (old school), 28
Kura ch'ŏlsa kŭmjabo 歐邏鐵絲琴字譜 (Manuscript for the Western dulcimer; an old *yanggŭm* manuscript), 9
Kurye 求禮 (town in Chŏlla province), 12
kut 굿 (shaman[istic] ritual and/or performance; alternate term for *nongak*), 20, 56, 124, 162n, 178n, 198

Index-Glossary

kutp'an 굿판 (shamanistic religious ritual), 18
kuŭm 口音 (oral mnemonics), 57n, 169
kuyŏn'gŭk 舊演劇 (old drama), 28
Kwanak yŏngsan hoesang 管樂靈山會相 (wind version of *Yŏngsan hoesang*), 17
kwangdae 廣大 (professional folk entertainer), 6, 10–11, 13, 18, 156, 164
Kwangdaech'ŏng 廣大廳 (Office of *Kwangdae*), 10
Kwangdaega 廣大歌 (Song of the *kwangdae*; *tan'ga*), 10–12, 14, 134
Kwangju 光州 (capital of South Chŏlla province), 12, 97–98, 169
Kwangju shirip kukkŭktan 光州市立國劇團 (Kwangju Municipal Ch'anggŭk Troupe), 45, 47n
Kwang-Soo Lee (Yi Kwangsu) 이광수 (b. 1952; lead small-gong player from original SamulNori group), 152, 162–63
Kwansŏ akpu 關西樂府 (Music section of the western province; chapter of *Sŏkpukchip*), 9
Kwanuhŭi 觀優戲 (Viewing actor's performance; literary source for *p'ansori*), 11
kwoeroe 傀儡 (actor), 10
Kwŏn Sain 權士仁 (*p'ansori* singer), 11
Kwŏn Samdŭk 權三得 (1771–1841; *p'ansori* singer), 11–14
"Kwŏnjuga" 勸酒歌 (Drinking song; *kasa*), 9
Kyego 階古 (minister of Shilla), 97
kyemyŏnjo 界面調 (*kyemyŏn* mode), 12, 14, 19, 105, 112, 125
"Kyerak" 界樂 (*kagok*), 8
kyŏngdŭrŭm 경드름 (melodic style of Kyŏnggi province), 12, 14
kyŏnggi 競技 (competition), 184
Kyŏnggi chapka 京畿雜歌 (*chapka* of Kyŏnggi province), 15
Kyŏnggi ipch'ang 京畿立唱 (*ipch'ang* of Kyŏnggi province), 15

Kyŏnggi minyo 京畿民謠 (folk songs from the central region), 156, 161
Kyŏnggi province 京畿道 (one of 8 provinces in Chosŏn period), 12, 14, 82–84, 158
Kyŏngje p'yŏng shijo 京制平時調 (regional *shijo* of the Seoul area), 9–10
Kyŏngjŏngsan kadan 敬亭山歌壇 (Music salon of respected arbor mountain; one of the famous music salons in the capital Hanyang [Seoul]), 8
kyŏngju 競走 (competition), 184
Kyŏngju 慶州 (city in Kyŏngsang province), 101
Kyŏngsang province 慶尙道 (one of 8 provinces in Chosŏn period), 10, 83–84, 126, 146

Lee, Bo-hyung (see Yi Pohyŏng)
Lee Jung Hyun (Yi Chŏnghyŏn) 이정현 (singer), 169
Lee, Kang Sook (see Yi Kangsuk)
Li Po 李白 (701–62; revered Chinese poet), 11

madang 마당 ([village] meeting ground; repertories; movement), 7, 40, 56, 124
madang nori 마당놀이 (ritual ceremony), 176
madanggŭk 마당劇 (open-air theater), 124
madanghwa 마당化 (return to *madang*-style traditional performance), 38, 40
"Madengi" 마뎅이 (rice-threshing song), 88
maedoji 매도지 (cadential rhythmic pattern), 71
maegu 매구 (alternate term for *nongak*), 20
maegut 매굿 (alternate term for *nongak*), 162n
"Maehwagok" 梅花曲 (Plum song; *kasa*), 9

"Mandaeyŏp" 慢大葉 (Slow song; forerunner of present *kagok*), 7

Mandŏk 萬德 (minister of Shilla), 97

"Man'go kangsan" 萬古江山 (The old mountain and river; *tan'ga*), 15

Manhwajip 晚華集 (Essay collection by Manhwa; literary source for *p'ansori*), 10–11

Masan 馬山 (city in Kyŏngsang province), 127

"Matpoegi" 맛뵈기 (A taste; composition by Yi Sŏngch'ŏn), 109

maŭl kut 마을굿 (village ritual performance; type of *nongak*), 20

MBC (Munhwa Broadcasting Company), 193

McQuain, Jan (Peace Corps volunteer, American *nongak* performer), 126–27

Meari 메아리 (Echo; music protest association), 164, 164n

Meng Chiao 孟郊 (751–814; Chinese poet), 11

Midnight's Children (novel by Salman Rushdie), 48

"Mikkuraji nondurŏng-e ppajida" 미꾸라지 논두렁에 빠지다 (Mudfish falls into a rice paddy; composition by Yi Sŏngch'ŏn), 116

"Mikkuraji ŭi sesang" 미꾸라지의 세상 (The world of a mudfish; composition by Yi Sŏngch'ŏn), 116

Millima iyagi hara 밀림아 이야기 하라 (Tell the story, forest; revolutionary opera), 151

minjung munhwa 民衆文化 (culture of the masses), 157, 167

minsogak 民俗樂 (folk music), 1, 5, 123

minsok chujŏm 民俗酒店 (ethnic tavern), 122

minsok ŭmak 民俗音樂 (folk music), 5

minsok yenŭngin 民俗藝能人 (folk entertainer), 5

minyo 民謠 (folk song[s]), 6–7, 14, 16, 76–93, 152, 198

"Miryang arirang" 密陽아리랑 (*Arirang* of Kyŏngsang province), 83

Mo Hŭnggap 牟興甲 (*p'ansori* singer), 11–12

Mo Manhwan 모만환 (b. 1885?; hat weaver), 159

Mongŭn temple 夢恩寺 (scene from "Shimch'ŏngga"), 13

"Mongyuga" 夢遊歌 (Dreaming song; aria from "Ch'unhyangga"), 13

"Mori for Three Kayagŭm" 3 대의 가야금을 위한 '모리' (composition by Pak Pŏmhun), 109

"Moshimnŭn sori" 모심는소리 (Sowing song; example of *t'osok minyo*), 16

mu 武 (military), 201, 219, 230

mudang 巫堂 (shaman), 18

muhyŏng munhwajae 無形文化財 (intangible cultural assets), 154

Muk Kyewŏl 墨桂月 (b. 1921; cultural asset holder of *Kyŏnggi minyo*, *chapka* singer), 15, 161

Mulgyeja 勿稽子 (196–229; *kŭm* performer), 97

"Mulle sori" 물레소리 (Spinning song; example of *t'osok minyo*), 16

Mun Yŏngsu 文泳洙 (*chapka* singer), 15

Munhwa kongbobu 文化公報部 (Korean Ministry of Culture and Information), 150

Munhwa kwan'gwangbu 文化觀光部 (Korean Ministry of Culture and Tourism), 150n

munhwa undong 文化運動 (cultural movement), 29

munhwajae 文化財 (cultural asset), 127, 131

Munhwajae kwalliguk 文化財管理局 (Office for Cultural Asset Management), 154, 156, 157n

Munhwajae pohobŏp 文化財保護法 (Cultural Asset Preservation Law), 34, 154, 181n

Munhwajae wiwŏnhoe 文化財委員會 (Cultural Assets Committee), 154

Index-Glossary 247

"Musugi t'aryŏng" 무숙이타령 (Song of Musugi; one of the 12 *p'ansori* stories), 11
myŏngsang ŭmak 瞑想音樂 (music for meditation), 164

"Na hana" 나하나 (One for me; composition by Yi Sŏngch'ŏn), 115, 117
Na Un'gyu 羅運奎 (1902–37; film producer, director, actor), 81, 150, 155
nabal 나발 (valveless long trumpet), 20
Naep'oje shijo 內浦制時調 (regional *shijo* of Ch'ungch'ŏng province), 10
Naju 羅州 (town in Chŏlla province), 12
nak 樂 (song type of *kagok*), 8
nallari 날라리 (double-reed wind instrument with a funnel), 20
naltangp'ae 날당패 (folk entertainer's group of P'yŏngyang), 15
Namdaemun 南大門 (South gate; one of city gates to the capital Hanyang [Seoul]), 15
Namdo chapka 南道雜歌 (*chapka* of the southern province; *chapka* of Chŏlla province), 15
Namdo tŭllorae 南道들노래 (rice-planting songs of the southwest provinces), 156–57
Namhun t'aep'yŏngga 南薰太平歌 (Namhun's peaceful song; anthology of *kagok* texts), 9
namryŏ 南呂 (pitch in *p'yŏng* mode), 112, 112n
namsadang 男寺黨 (itinerant performing troupes), 60
namul 나물 (steamed vegetable dish), 142
National Ch'anggŭk Troupe (Kungnip ch'anggŭktan) 國立唱劇團, 23, 25, 33–39, 41–45, 47–48, 132
NBC (National Broadcasting Company), 213
Nihon kōki 日本後記 (J.: Postscript of Japan), 99

"Nilli riya" 닐리리야 (folk song), 83
"Nodŭl kangbyŏn" 노들강변 (Beautiful riverside of the Han River), 82
nogoja 노고자 (someone who falls behind), 184n
noh 能 (traditional Japanese theater), 35
"Nojŏnnŭn sori" 노젓는소리 (Rowing song; example of *t'osok minyo*), 16
Nolbu 놀부 (elder brother of Hŭngbu), 14, 136, 138, 141–42, 144–45, 165
nong 弄 (song type of *kagok*), 8
nongak 農樂 (farmers' music; farmer's band music; percussion band music and dance), 2, 16, 20, 56, 56n, 58, 60–61, 65, 67, 69, 124, 162, 162n, 198
nongaktan 農樂團 (farmers' band troupe), 126
"*nongja ch'ŏnhaji taebon*" 農者天下之大本 (agriculture is the foundation of a nation), 87
nongyo 農謠 (farming songs), 16, 87–88, 156
"Nongyŏp" 弄葉 (Rolling song; *kagok* found in the *Yuyeji*), 8
nonjaeng 論爭 (argue; contend), 225n
norae undong 노래 운동 (song movement), 164
nori 놀이 (mass games), 230
norip'an 놀이판 (communal village meeting ground), 57
Nŭngna Island 陵羅島 (island on Taedong River near P'yŏngyang), 12

O Pongnyŏ 吳福女 (b. 1913; cultural asset holder of *Sŏdo sori*), 157
"Ŏbuga" 漁夫歌 (Song of fisherman; *kasa*), 9
och'ae chilgut/"Och'ae chilgut" 五채질굿 (lit., "5 stroke road ritual"; rhythmic pattern; piece; movement), 54, 56, 61, 64–65, 67, 69–71

"Odokttegi" 오독떼기 (song for weeding), 88
Oga chŏnjip 五歌全集 (Complete collection of 5 *p'ansori* songs), 11
ogwibang 五鬼方 (most unnatural and ominous of all directions), 136, 137n
"Ŏllak" 言樂 (*kagok*), 8
"Ŏllong" 言弄 (*kagok*), 8
om 옴 (wisdom sound), 200, 202
onggi 甕器 (traditional storage jar), 197
"Onggojipchŏn" 甕固執傳 (Tale of a stubborn person; one of the 12 *p'ansori* stories), 11
Ongnumong 玉樓夢 (Dream of the jade chamber; novel), 32
ŏnmori 엇모리 (rhythmic cycle in 5/8 meter), 14, 19
"Ŏnp'yŏn" 言編 (*kagok*), 8, 10
"Ŏsa-wa ch'odong" 御使와 草童 (The royal inspector and the woodcutter), 45
ŏtchungmori 엇중모리 (rhythmic cycle in moderate tempo), 14
Ŏŭnbo 漁隱譜 (Ŏŭn's manuscript; old *kŏmun'go* manuscript), 17
Ou-yang Hsiu 歐陽修 (1007–72; Chinese poet), 12
ŏyo 漁謠 (fishing songs), 16

"Pada" 바다 (The sea; composition by Yi Sŏngch'ŏn), 109, 115
"Paebijangjŏn" 배비장전 (Story/Tale of Officer Pae; one of the 12 *p'ansori* stories), 11, 31–32, 132, 132n
Paegunam kŭmbo 白雲庵琴譜 (Paegunam's *kŏmun'go* manuscript; old *kŏmun'go* manuscript), 7
Paek Ch'angu 백창우 (popular singer), 165
Paek Hyŏnmi 白賢美 (*p'ansori* scholar), 25, 32, 35n
Paek Nakchun 白樂俊 (1884–1934; *kŏmun'go sanjo* founder and master), 19
Paek Taeung 白大雄 (composer), 109

"Paekkusa" 白鷗詞 (Song of the seagull; *kasa*), 9
Paekkyŏl 百結 (*kŭm* performer), 97
"Paennorae" 뱃노래 (Boat song; example of *t'osok minyo*), 16
paennori 뱃놀이 (boat songs), 198
Pak Chin 박진 (*p'ansori* singer), 29, 31, 39, 48
Pak Chonggi 朴鍾基 (1880–1947; *taegŭm sanjo* master), 19
Pak Ch'owŏl 朴初月 (*p'ansori* singer), 129
Pak Ch'un'gyŏng 朴春景 (*Kyŏnggi chapka* singer), 15
Pak Ch'unjae 朴春載 (1877–1948; *chapka* singer), 15
Pak Hwang 朴晃 (*p'ansori* scholar), 25, 28n
Pak Hyogwan 朴孝寬 (*kagok* singer, coauthor of *Kagok wŏllyu*), 8
Pak Hyŏngsŏp 박형섭 (scholar), 109n
Pak Ilhun 박일훈 (performer, composer), 109
Pak Mansun 朴萬順 (*p'ansori* singer), 13
Pak Nokchu 朴綠珠 (1905–79; *p'ansori* and *Namdo chapka* singer), 16, 129, 136
Pak Pŏmhun 박범훈 (scholar, composer, performer), 107n, 109, 111, 118
Pak Pyŏngch'ŏn 朴秉千 (b. 1933; cultural asset holder of *Chindo ssikkim kut*), 158
Pak Sanggŭn 朴相根 (1905–49; *kayagŭm sanjo* master), 19
Pak Sejik 박세직 (Seoul Olympic Organizing Committee president), 183, 192, 192n, 193n, 194–95, 206, 216, 216n, 217, 220, 220n, 221–22, 224, 226–27, 233
Pak Sŏkki 朴錫紀 (*kŏmun'go sanjo* master), 19
Pak Sŏnggi 박성기 (instrument maker), 111
Pak Sŏnghwa 박성화 (Confucian scholar), 199

Pak Sŏngok 박성옥 (instrument maker), 107
"Pak t'aryŏng" 박타령 (Song of the gourd; alternate title for "Hŭngbuga"), 11
Pak Tongjin 朴東鎭 (b. 1916; *p'ansori* singer), 132
Pak Yonggu 박용구 (Seoul Olympic Organizing Committee member), 176n, 199, 226, 233
Pak Yujŏn 朴裕全 (*p'ansori* singer), 12–13
p'an 판 (communal meeting space; performance space), 56, 127, 134–35
p'an kut 판굿 (entertainment-oriented *nongak/p'ungmul* performance), 20, 56–57, 61, 65, 162n
pangjang 方丈 (abbot), 145
Pangjang 방장 (old name for Chiri mountain), 146
Pangsanhanssi kŭmbo 芳山韓氏琴譜 (String notation by Han of Pangsan), 112
p'ansori 판소리 (narrative song; musical storytelling; folk dramatic song), 2, 6, 10–15, 18–20, 22–48, 121–46, 158, 165–67, 197
"Panyŏp" 半葉 (Half song; *kagok*), 8
para ch'um 바라춤 (cymbal dance), 201, 220n
Park Chung Hee (Pak Chŏnghŭi) 朴正熙 (South Korean president, 1961–79), 34, 48, 154
Peking opera (Chinese traditional opera), 25, 35
"Pet'ŭlga" 베틀가 (Loom song; example of *t'osok minyo*), 16
pibimbap 비빔밥 (traditional dish), 182, 182n
Pihl, Marshall (*p'ansori* scholar), 134n
piho p'umsae 비호품새 (lit., "flying tiger" action in taekwondo), 200, 224
p'iri 피리 (double-reed wind instrument), 18, 84–85
p'iri sanjo 피리산조 (*sanjo* for double-reed wind instrument), 19

Po Chu-i 白居易 (772–831; Chinese poet), 11
pŏdŭl p'iri 버들피리 (small wind instrument), 185
Pokhŭi 복희 (legendary emporer of ancient China), 146, 146n
"Pŏlgŏbŏkkin Sŏul" 벌거벗긴 서울 (Naked Seoul; composition by Yi Sŏngch'ŏn), 115–16
Polygram (recording company), 191–96, 196n, 197, 217–18
"Pongjiga" 봉지가 (hat-weaving folk song), 158–60
pongmi 鳳尾 (lit., "phoenix's tail"; one end of the *kayagŭm*), 101
"Ponjo arirang" 本調 아리랑 (Original *arirang*), 80
"Ponyŏngsan" 本靈山 (Fundamental *yŏngsan*; piece from *Yŏngsan hoesang*), 18
Pŏpchi 法知 (minister of Shilla), 97
pŏpkŭm 法琴 (lit., "law zither"; alternate term for *p'ungnyu kayagŭm*), 99
"Poryŏm" 報念 (Recompensing song; *chapka*; shaman-and-Buddhist-influenced song), 15, 163
"Poshint'ang chip-e ungk'ŭrin kaegirŭm shinsa" 보신탕집에 웅크린 개기름 신사 (Greasy man in a dog-soup restaurant; composition by Yi Sŏngch'ŏn), 116
Posŏng 寶城 (town in Chŏlla province), 12
poyuja 保有者 (holder), 124, 154
pudŭl 부들 (cords on a *kayagŭm*), 107, 109, 111
puk 북 (barrel drum), 20, 28, 32, 57, 168
"Pullim" 불림 (rice-mowing song), 88
punch'ang 分唱 (divided singing), 43
p'ungjang 풍장 (alternate term for *nongak*), 20
p'ungmul(gut) 風物굿 (percussion band music and dance; alternate term for *nongak*), 2, 20, 56, 56n, 58, 60–61, 65, 67, 69, 162, 162n, 198
"P'ungnyŏn'ga" 豊年歌 (folk song), 91–92

p'ungnyŏn'gut 풍년굿 (see *p'ungnyugut*)
p'ungnyu 風流 (elegant music), 99, 107
p'ungnyu kayagŭm 風流伽倻琴 (12-stringed plucked zither), 99, 101–3, 105–7, 109, 111, 116, 118
p'ungnyubang 風流房 (music salon), 5, 10
p'ungnyugaek 風流客 (music salon participant), 6, 7, 17
p'ungnyugut 風流굿 (lit., "*p'ungnyu* ritual"; rhythmic pattern), 71
Puri (P'uri) 푸리 (neo-traditional percussion ensemble), 168n
Puschnig, Wolfgang (leader of Red Sun Group), 68
pusoe 副쇠, 副釗 (second small-gong [*soe*] player), 57
P'yo Chaesun 표재순 (director and producer of Olympic ceremonies), 198, 198n, 200, 203, 205, 225, 233
"Pyŏbegi sori" 벼베기소리 (Harvesting song; example of *t'osok minyo*), 16
P'yojŏngmanbangjigok 表正萬方之曲 (alternate title for *Kwanak yŏngsan hoesang*), 17
pyŏk 벽 (wall), 178
Pyŏk-ŭl nŏmŏsŏ 벽을 너머서 (scene titled "Beyond All Barriers" from the Seoul Olympics), 179, 188, 235
"Pyŏl hana na hana" 별하나 나하나 (One for the star, one for me; composition by Yi Sŏngch'ŏn), 115
"Pyŏljubu-jŏn" 별주부傳 (alternate title for "Sugung-ga," or "Song of the underwater palace"), 27
"P'yŏllak" 編樂 (Weaving song; *kagok*), 8, 10
p'yŏn 編 (song type of *kagok*), 8
Pyŏn Chongha 변종하 (artist), 176n
p'yŏng shijo 平時調 (ordinary *shijo*), 9
"Pyŏn'gangsoe t'aryŏng" 변강쇠타령 (Song of Pyŏn Kangsoe; one of the 12 *p'ansori* stories), 11, 40
p'yŏngjo 平調 (*p'yŏng* mode), 14, 19, 105, 112

P'yŏngjo hoesang 平調會相 (*Yŏngsan hoesang* in the *p'yŏng* mode; another ensemble version of *Yŏngsan hoesang*), 17
P'yŏngt'aek Nongak 平澤農樂 (cultural asset percussion band), 56n
P'yŏngyang 平壤 (present capital of North Korea), 12, 15, 87
pyŏn'gyŏng 變更 (to be modified), 103n
Pyŏnjin 변진 (the combined kingdoms of Pyŏn and Chin), 97, 97n
"P'yŏnshich'un" 片時春 (Short spring; *tan'ga*), 15
"P'yŏnsudaeyŏp" 編數大葉 (Weaving *saktaeyŏp*; *kagok*), 8, 10

qin 琴 (C.: plucked-string zither), 209n

Red Sun Group (West German jazz/avant-garde ensemble), 68, 68n, 71, 162
"Reach Out" (official song of the Los Angeles Olympics), 193
Roh Tae Woo (No T'aeu) 盧泰愚 (South Korean president, 1988–93; Seoul Olympic Organizing Committee president), 192n

sabimmak 揷入幕 (interpolated scene), 45
sadangp'ae 社堂牌 (performing group of folk entertainers), 15
"Sae sanjo" 새 산조 (*kayagŭm* composition by Pak Pŏmhun), 111
"Sae t'aryŏng" 새타령 (Bird song; aria from *p'ansori*), 13
saekkal 색깔 (color), 214
"Saeya saeya" 새야 새야 (folk song), 91–92
"*Sagong-i manŭmyŏn, pae-ka san-ŭro kanda*" 사공이 많으면 배가 산으로 간다 (lit., "If there are too many sailors, the boat goes to the mountain"; too many cooks spoil the broth), 229n

Index-Glossary 251

"Saktaeyŏp" 數大葉 (Fast song; forerunner of present *kagok*), 7
salp'uri 살풀이 (shamanist dance of purging; rhythmic cycle in moderate tempo), 19, 130, 130n, 182
sam t'aegŭk sasang 三太極思想 (idea of the threefold ultimate), 177, 177n
samch'ae 三채 (lit., "three strokes"; rhythmic pattern), 71
samgang oryun 三綱五倫 (three bonds and five relations), 13
Samguk sagi 三國史記 (History of the three kingdoms), 96–97, 99
"Samhyŏn hoeip" 三絃回入 (*kŏmun'go* piece in the *Yuyeji*), 18
"Samhyŏn hoeip ijang tu" 三絃回入 2 章頭 (*kŏmun'go* piece in the *Yuyeji*), 18
"Samhyŏn hoeip sajang tu" 三絃回入 4 章頭 (*kŏmun'go* piece in the *Yuyeji*), 18
"Samhyŏn hwanip" 三絃還入 (piece from *Yŏngsan hoesang*), 17–18
samhyŏn samjuk 三絃三竹 (3 stringed and 3 wind instruments), 99
samjae sasang 三財思想 (idea of triple foundation), 177
Samjuk kŭmbo 三竹琴譜 (Samjuk's *kŏmun'go* manuscript; old *kŏmun'go* manuscript), 8–9, 18
samsalbang 三煞方 (direction that invites three kinds of damnation), 136, 136n
"Samsudaeyŏp" 三數大葉 (third "Saktaeyŏp"; *kagok*), 7
samul nori/Samulnori/SamulNori 四物놀이 (urbanized "traditional" percussion quartet), 60–61, 61n, 62, 62n, 63–67, 68n, 72, 77, 152, 162
Samulnori Chŏnsoe 사물놀이 전쇠 (subquartet under Kim Duk Soo's umbrella organization), 65, 71
"San t'aryŏng" 山打令 (Mountain song; *chapka*), 15
san t'aryŏng p'ae 山打令牌 (performing group of folk entertainers), 15

sandae nori 山臺놀이 (court variety show), 24
sandaehŭi 山臺戲 (court variety show), 24
Sangdŏk 상덕 (pen name of *p'ansori* singer Ch'oe Tokkyŏn), 31
"Sanghyŏn hwanip" 上絃還入 (piece from *Yŏngsan hoesang*), 18
sangmo 象毛 (twirling hat), 182
"Sangnyŏngsan" 上靈山 (piece from *Yŏngsan hoesang*), 17
"Sangsa pyŏlgok" 相思別曲 (Song of mutual love; *kasa*), 9
sangsoe 上쇠, 上釗 (lead small-gong [*soe*] player), 57, 152
Sanguo zhi 三國志 (C.: History of the three kingdoms), 97
"Sangyŏ sori" 상여소리 (Bier song; example of *t'osok minyo*), 16
sanjo 散調 (lit., "scattered melodies"; solo instrumental suites; solo instrumental music), 2, 6, 16, 18–19, 86, 101, 101n, 102, 112, 114
sanjo kayagŭm 散調伽倻琴 (smaller version of the *p'ungnyu kayagŭm*), 101–3, 105–7, 109, 111–13, 116, 118
saram 사람 (human), 176n
"Sarangga" 사랑가 (Love song; aria from "Ch'unhyangga"), 12
"Sarirang" 사리랑 (song for weeding), 88
sasŏl 辭說 (words), 134
sasŏl shijo 辭說時調 (narrative *shijo*), 8–10
"Segye-nŭn Sŏul-lo, Sŏul-ŭn segye-ro" 세계는 서울로, 서울은 세계로 (The world to Seoul, Seoul to the world; slogan of the 1988 Seoul Olympics), 174n
Sejong Cultural Center, 190n
semach'i 세마치 (rhythmic cycle), 91
Seo Taiji (Sŏ T'aeji) 서태지 (popular singer, dancer, composer), 162, 162n
Seoul Norimadang 서울놀이마당 (outdoor performance venue in Seoul), 57, 59
Seoul Olympics (1988), 132, 173–235

Seoul shirip kugak kwanhyŏn aktan 서울市立國樂管絃樂團 (Seoul City Korean Music Orchestra), 77, 85
"Seryŏngsan" 細靈山 (piece from *Yŏngsan hoesang*), 17–18
Seulgidoong (Sŭlgidung) 슬기둥 (popular music group), 166–69
shakuhachi 尺八 (J.: end-blown bamboo flute), 151
shamisen 三味線 (J.: 3-stringed lute), 151
Sharp, Cecil (British folklorist), 153
shibi kasa 十二歌詞 (literati lyric song style), 157
shigimsae 시김새 (melodic embellishment or figuration), 84
shijo 時調 (short lyric song; poetry), 6, 8–10, 14, 200n, 201–3, 205
Shilla 新羅 (kingdom and period of history), 96–97, 97n, 99
shillagŭm 新羅琴 (old zither), 99, 99n, 100, 116
Shim Ch'angnae 沈昌來 (*kayagŭm sanjo* master), 19
Shim Ch'ŏng 沈淸 (heroine of "Shimch'ŏngga"), 43
"Shim Ch'ŏng-jŏn" 沈淸傳 (Story of Shim Ch'ŏng), 30–31, 39
Shim Sanggŏn 沈相健 (1889–1965; *kayagŭm sanjo* master), 19
Shim Usŏng 沈雨晟 (folklorist), 166
"Shimch'ŏngga" 沈淸歌 (Song of Shim Ch'ŏng; *p'ansori*), 11–13, 39, 43, 131–32, 132n
shimpa geki 新派劇 (J.: new-school dramas), 26
Shin Chaehyo 申在孝 (1812–84; *p'ansori* ethnographer, theorist, patron), 7, 10–11, 13–15, 39
Shin Kŭmhong 申錦紅 (*Namdo chapka* singer), 16
Shin K'waedong 申快童 (1910–78; *kŏmun'go sanjo* master), 19
Shin Kwangsu 申光洙 (1712–75; author of *Sŏkpukchip*, a literary source for *shijo*), 9

Shin Manyŏp 申萬葉 (*p'ansori* singer), 11
shin minyo 新民謠 (new-[style] folk song), 78–85, 93
Shin Nakt'aek 申洛澤 (founder of *Kyŏnggi ipch'ang*), 15
"Shin paennorae" 신 뱃노래 (New boat song), 168
Shin Pangch'o 申芳草 (*Namdo chapka* singer), 15
shinawi 시나위 (instrumental ensemble for shamanistic rituals), 18–19, 130, 130n
Shinjak kŭmbo 新作琴譜 (Newly compiled manuscript for the *kŏmun'go*; old *kŏmun'go* manuscript), 7
"Shinje ip'al ch'ŏngch'un'ga" 新制二八 青春歌 (New-style song for the blooming of youth at 16 years), 78
"Shinje nongbuga" 新制 農夫歌 (New-style farmers' song), 78
"Shinje sanyŏmbul" 新制 山念佛 (New-style Buddhist song), 78
"Shinshik yangsando" 新式 陽山道 (New-style *yangsando*), 78
shinsosŏl 新小說 (new novel), 27
shinyŏn'gŭk 新演劇 (lit., "new drama"; *ch'anggŭk*), 27
"Shipchangga" 十杖歌 (Song of whipping by ten sticks; aria from "Ch'unhyangga"), 12
shiragi koto しらぎこと, 新羅琴 (Japanese pronunciation for *shillagŭm*), 99
shirhak 實學 (practical learning), 7
Shōsōin 正倉院 (repository in Japan), 99–100, 102, 106, 111, 116
SLOOC (Seoul Olympic Organizing Committee), 174n, 188n, 189–96, 196n, 197, 198n, 202, 204, 206–7, 211–12, 216–18, 220–22, 226, 228, 228n, 229–30
Sŏ Hangsŏk 서항석 (chairman of Ch'anggŭk chŏngnip wiwŏnhoe), 36
So Wanjun 蘇完俊 (*chapka* singer), 15

Index-Glossary

Sŏ Yŏnho 徐淵昊 (drama historian, scholar), 26n, 37, 40
Sŏ Yugu 徐有榘 (1764–1845; author of *Yuyeji*, an old *kŏmun'go* manuscript), 8, 9, 17
Sŏdo chapka 西道雜歌 (*chapka* of western provinces; *chapka* of Hwanghae and P'yŏngan provinces), 15
Sŏdo ipch'ang 西道立唱 (*ipch'ang* of western provinces; *ipch'ang* of Hwanghae and P'yŏngan provinces), 15–16
Sŏdo sori 西道소리 (folk songs from the northwest), 156
soe 쇠, 釗 (small hand-held gong), 57
sogak 俗樂 (folk music), 1
sogo 小鼓 (small hand-held drum), 57
sogŭm 小笒 (small transverse flute), 99
soju 燒酒 (inexpensive Korean hard liquor), 137, 137n, 145
Sŏkpukchip 石北集 (Literary collection by Sŏkpuk; literary source for *shijo*), 9
sŏlchanggo 설장고 (*changgo* drum dance), 126
Sollisŭt'ŭ 솔리스트 (a capella singing group), 161
sŏllŏngje 설렁제 (melodic type of *p'ansori*), 12, 14
sŏlmyŏngch'ang 說明唱 (narrative singing in *ch'anggŭk*), 36
sŏm 섬 (straw sack of grain), 139, 139n
Sŏmjin River 蟾津江 (river of Chŏlla province), 12
sŏn 禪 (Buddhist meditation), 205
"Sonata in C# minor, Op. 27, no. 2, 1st movement" (arrangement by Yi Sŏngch'ŏn), 117
sŏnban 선반 (standing form of *samul nori*), 62
Sŏng Ch'angsun 成昌順 (b. 1934; *p'ansori* singer), 85–86
Song Hŭngnok 宋興祿 (*p'ansori* singer), 11–13
Song Hyejin 宋惠眞 (scholar), 24n
Sŏng Kŭmyŏn 成錦鳶 (instrument maker, *kayagŭm* performer), 107, 114, 162n
Song Kwangnok 宋光祿 (*p'ansori* singer), 11–13
Sŏng Kyŏngnin 成慶麟 (scholar), 27n, 35n
Song Manjae 宋晚載 (1769–1847; author of *Kwanuhŭi*, a literary source for *p'ansori*), 11
Sŏng Tongho 성동호 (actor), 150
Sŏng Uhyang 成又香 (*p'ansori* singer), 132n
Song Uryong 宋雨龍 (*p'ansori* singer, son of Song Kwangnok), 13
Sŏngho sasŏl 星湖僿說 (Essay collection by Sŏngho; literary source for *kagok*), 7
songjang 송장 (corpse), 145
"Sŏngju p'uri" 성주푸리 (*Namdo chapka*), 15
sŏnsori 선소리 (lit., "standing song"; vocal genre of folk music), 15
Sŏnsori san t'aryŏng 선소리山打令 (songs by itinerant bands), 156
sŏp'yŏnje 西便制 (western-style *p'ansori* singing), 12–13
Sŏp'yŏnje 西便制 (*p'ansori* film), 125
sori 소리 (singing in *p'ansori*), 128, 134–35
"Sosang p'algyŏng" 蕭湘八景 (Eight landscapes of the Hsio-hsian region; *tan'ga*), 13, 15
sōshi geki 壯士劇 (J.: political dramas), 26
Sŏul ollimp'ik chŏngshin kyesŭng palchŏn undong 서울올림픽정신계승발전운동 (Seoul Olympic Spirit Enhancement Movement), 216, 216n
"Soyongi" 搔聳伊 (*kagok*), 8
Space Theater, 60
"Ssadae sori" 싸대 소리 (weeding song), 88
ssaum 싸움 (fight), 203, 225n
"Sugungga" 水宮歌 (Song of the underwater palace; alternate title for "T'okki t'aryŏng"), 11, 131–32

"Sujech'ŏn" 壽齊天 (court banquet music), 210
sŭl 瑟 (zither), 97
Sunch'ang 淳昌 (town in Chŏlla province), 12
Sunjong 純宗 (1874–1926; Korea's last monarch), 33n
susŏng karak 수성가락 (extemporaneous accompanying technique), 44
"Suyangsan'ga" 首陽山歌 (Song of Mt. Suyang; kasa), 9
Synnara (Shinnara) 신나라 (recording company), 150

"Tae-ak" 대악 (composition for the kŭm), 97
Taeborŭm 大보름 (seasonal festival), 88
taech'wit'a 大吹打 (military music), 197
Taedong kagŭktan 大同歌劇團 (variety-acts troupe), 129
Taedong River 大洞江 (river of P'yŏngan province), 12
t'aegŭk 太極 (the Great Absolute), 227
taegŭm 大笒 (large transverse flute), 18, 84–85, 99, 152
taegŭm sanjo 大笒散調 (sanjo for large transverse flute), 19, 87
taehak kayoje 大學歌謠祭 (university song festival), 166
taejanggunbang 大將軍方 (one of the 8 directions in ancient Korean cosmology), 136, 136n
taekwondo (t'aegwŏndo) 跆拳道 (Korean martial art), 179, 199–201, 201n, 202, 202n, 203–4, 206, 212, 218–20, 220n, 222, 224–25
taenama 大奈麻 (tenth degree rank), 97, 97n
Taep'ungnyu 대풍류 (alternate title for Kwanak yŏngsan hoesang), 17
"T'aep'yŏngga" 太平歌 (Song of great peace), 82
t'aep'yŏngso 太平簫 (double-reed wind instrument with a funnel; alternate term for nallari), 18, 20, 57
taesa 大舍 (twelfth degree rank), 97, 97n
Taewŏn'gun 大院君 (prince regent; King Kojong's father), 149
t'al ch'um 탈춤 (masked dance-drama; mask dance), 24, 29, 124
"Tal hanop'igom" 달하노피곰 (Oh the moon, rise high and shine brightly; composition by Hwang Pyŏnggi), 118
"Talgujil sori" 달구질소리 (Pounding song; example of t'osok minyo), 16
"Tamsŏngga" 담성가 (weeding song), 88
tan'ga 短歌 (lit., "short song"; p'ansori warm-up song), 13–15, 128, 167
tangsan 堂山 (local deity's shrine), 20
tangsan kut 당산굿 (village ritual performance; alternate term for nongak), 20
tanjŏm 短點 (drawbacks), 221
Tano 端午 (seasonal festival), 88, 161n
tanso 短簫 (small bamboo flute), 159, 166
tao 道 (C.: way or art), 199
"T'aryŏng" 打令 (piece from Yŏngsan hoesang), 17–18
tchamppong 짬뽕 (Chinese-Korean stew), 46
"Tcholbudŭl nŏ chalnatta" 쫄부들 너 잘났다 (The overnight millionaires, yeah you!; composition by Yi Sŏngch'ŏn), 115
Three Kingdoms era 三國時代 (37 B.C.E.–C.E. 668), 129, 150
"Three Variations on 'Sangju moshimgi norae' for Three Kayagŭm" 3대의 가야금을 위한 3개의 변주곡 '상주 모심기 노래' (composition by Paek Taeung), 109
toch'ang 導唱 (lit., "lead singer"; ch'anggŭk narrator), 28, 31, 36, 38, 43, 46–47
toenjang 된장 (soy bean paste), 145

Index-Glossary

"T'okki t'aryŏng" 토끼타령 (Song of the rabbit; alternate title for "Sugungga"), 11, 13
tolgwae 돌괘 (wooden peg on the kayagŭm), 107
t'omak sori 토막소리 (performance by piece), 131
tŏngdŏkkungi 덩덕궁이 (rhythmic cycle used in shamanistic dance), 19
Tonghak 東學 (Eastern learning), 165
"T'ongil arirang" 통일 아리랑 (Unification *arirang*), 149, 157, 161
tongp'yŏnje 東便制 (eastern-style *p'ansori* singing), 12–13, 136
t'ongso 洞簫 (long end-blown flute), 18
t'ongsok minyo 通俗民謠 (folk song by professional singers), 16
tongyang 東洋 (Eastern), 180
Tongyang Theater 東洋劇場, 30–31
tŏnŭm 더늠 (singing quality or technique of musical characteristics of *p'ansori*), 12–13
"T'o-saengwŏn-kwa Pyŏljubu" 토생원과 별주부 (alternate title for "Sungung-ga," or "Song of the Underwater Palace"), 44–45
tosalp'uri 도살풀이 (rhythmic cycle used in *shinawi*), 19
t'osok minyo 土俗民謠 (folk song by commoners in daily life), 16
t'ou 토우 (terra cotta figure), 99, 101–3
toyŏn 導演 (leader), 36
"Tto chŏnom ŭi sori" 또 저놈의 소리 ("That damned noise!"), 125
ttorang kwangdae 또랑광대 (wishy-washy singers), 130
Tu Fu 杜甫 (712–70; Chinese poet), 11
Tu Mu 杜牧 (803–52; Chinese poet), 11
tugŏ 頭擧 (male singer in *kagok*), 10
"Tŭngjim sori" 등짐 소리 (rice-carrying song), 88
ture p'ungjang kut 두레풍장굿 (communal labor performance; a style of *nongak*), 20

U Ch'undae 禹春大 (*p'ansori* singer), 11
Ŭi T'aegi 의택이 (founder of *Kyŏnggi ipch'ang*), 15
ujilgut 右질굿 (lit., "right road ritual"; rhythmic pattern), 71
ujo 羽調 (*u* mode), 12, 14, 19
"Ulsan agassi" 蔚山 아가씨 (Young lady of Ulsan), 83
Unbong 雲峰 (town in Chŏlla province), 12
"Ŭnsegye" 銀世界 (Silver world; *ch'anggŭk* play by Yi Injik), 27
"Urak" 羽樂 (*kagok*), 8
uri nara 우리나라 (lit., "our country"; Korea), 211
Urŭk 于勒 (musician), 97

wanch'ang 完唱 (*p'ansori* narrative in its entirety), 132
Wang Wei 王維 (669–739; Chinese poet), 12
Wanje shijo 完制時調 (*shijo* of Chŏlla province), 10
wanp'an 完版 (complete *ch'anggŭk* text), 38
wŏlgŭm 月琴 (4-stringed lute), 107
Wŏn Okhwa 元玉花 (*kayagŭm sanjo* master), 19
Wŏn'gaksa 圓覺社 (first indoor Korean theater; royal theater of the late Chosŏn dynasty), 15, 26–27
wŏnhyŏng 原型 (original form; archetypes), 34, 37, 131, 152

yaksok 約束 (contract), 40
yangban 兩班 (aristocrat), 138
yangban kwangdae 兩班廣大 (aristocrat *kwangdae*), 6, 13
Yanggŭm shinbo 梁琴新譜 (Yang's new *kŏmun'go* handbook; old *kŏmun'go* manuscript), 7
yangidu 羊耳頭 (lit., "sheep's horn"; one end of the *kayagŭm*), 99, 99n, 101, 106, 109, 111, 116
yangsando 양산도 (rhythmic pattern), 71

"Yangyangga" 襄陽歌 (Song of Yangyang; *kasa*), 9
Ye Yonghae 예용해 (journalist), 155, 159
Yesul p'yŏngnon'ga hyŏbŭihoe 藝術評論家協議會 (Art Critics Association), 176n
Yesul ŭi chŏngdan 藝術의 展堂 (Seoul Arts Center), 42
Yi Byung Uk (Yi Pyŏnguk) 이병욱 (b. 1951; contemporary composer), 165
Yi Ch'asu 李且守 (*kayagŭm sanjo* master), 19
Yi Chinbong 李眞鳳 (*chapka* singer), 15
Yi Chinsun 이진순 (*ch'anggŭk* director), 24n, 35
Yi Chŏngbŏm 이정범 (*nongak* performer), 126
Yi Chŏnghwa 李正華 (*chapka* singer), 15
Yi Ch'ŏngjun 李清俊 (novelist), 125
Yi Ch'ungsŏn 李忠善 (*p'iri sanjo* master), 19
Yi Haeshik 李海植 (composer), 109, 117
Yi Hwajungsŏn 李花中仙 (1898–1943; *p'ansori* and *Namdo chapka* singer), 16, 129
Yi Ik 李瀷 (1681–1763; author of *Sŏngho sasŏl*), 7
Yi Injik 李仁稙 (1862–1916; writer, politician), 26–28, 31, 39, 48
Yi Kangsuk 李康淑 (scholar, music adviser to Olympic committee), 166, 188n, 212, 222–23, 223n, 224, 233
Yi Kiha 이기하 (director of Olympic ceremonies), 187n, 206, 213–15, 233
Yi Kŏnyong 이건용 (b. 1947; composer and critic), 166
Yi Kŭmok 李錦玉 (*chapka* singer), 15
Yi Kyugyŏng 李圭景 (1788–?; author of *Kura ch'ŏlsa kŭmjabo*), 9
Yi Manik 이만익 (architect), 186n

Yi Mongnyong 李夢龍 (character in "Ch'unhyangga"), 45
Yi Nalch'i 李捺致 (*p'ansori* singer), 13
Yi Ŏryŏng 이어령 (Seoul Olympic Organizing Committee member), 174n, 176, 177n, 180–81, 205, 233
Yi Pohyŏng 李輔亨 (b. 1935; folk scholar), 42–43, 45, 150
Yi Sangman 李相萬 (music adviser), 188n, 233
Yi Sech'un 李世春 (*shijo* singer), 9
Yi Sŏngch'ŏn 李成千 (composer), 109, 111, 115–17
Yi Sŏnyu 李善裕 (1872–?; *p'ansori* singer), 11
Yi Sora 이소라 (musicologist, staff member at Office for Cultural Assets), 156
Yi Sujŏng 李秀晶 (scholar), 30n
Yi T'aemun 李泰文 (*chapka* singer), 15
Yi Tongbaek 李東柏 (*p'ansori* singer), 25, 129
Yi Toryŏng 李道令 (hero of "Ch'unhyangga"), 14
Yi Ŭnju 李恩珠 (b. 1922; cultural asset future holder of *Kyŏnggi minyo*), 161
Yi Wŏn'gyŏng 이원경 (director), 40
Yi Yanggyo 李良敎 (b. 1928; cultural asset holder of *shibi kasa*), 157
Yi Yŏngsanhong 李暎山紅 (*chapka* singer), 15
yin-yang 陰陽 (cosmic harmony), 68, 138, 175, 180, 198, 219
yŏksagŭk 歷史劇 (historical dramas), 32
Yŏm Kyedal 廉季達 (*p'ansori* singer), 12
"Yŏmbul" 念佛 (piece from *Yŏngsan hoesang*), 17–18
"Yŏmbul hwanip" 念佛還入 (*kŏmun'go* piece in the *Yuyeji*), 18
"Yŏmbul t'aryŏng" 念佛打令 (*kŏmun'go* piece in the *Yuyeji*), 18
yŏnch'ang 連唱 (economical type of *ch'anggŭk* performance), 35

Index-Glossary

yŏnch'ul 演出 (director), 36
Yŏndae sojang kŭmbo 延大所藏琴譜 (*Kŏmun'go* manuscript preserved at Yonsei University Library), 7
Yong Woo Kim (Kim Yongu) 김용우 (b. 1968; popular singer), 149, 157, 157n, 158–61, 161n, 162–64, 166, 168
yŏngga 令歌 (ancient vocal music with body movements), 199
Yŏngje shijo 嶺制時調 (*shijo* of Kyŏngsang province), 10
"Yŏngnam karak" 영남가락 (Rhythmic patterns of Kyŏngsang province), 67
Yŏngsan hoesang 靈山會相 (orchestral suite of nine pieces), 6, 16–18, 199
"Yŏngsan hoesang" 靈山會相 (piece in the *Yuyeji*), 17
Yŏngsan hoesang cheji 靈山會相除指 (variation of *Yŏngsan hoesang* in the *Ŏŭnbo*), 17
Yŏngsan hoesang hwanip 靈山會相還入 (variation of *Yŏngsan hoesang* in the *Ŏŭnbo*), 17
"Yŏngsan hoesang ich'ŭng cheji" 靈山會相二層除指 (*kŏmun'go* piece in the *Yuyeji*), 18
Yŏngsan hoesang kapt'an 靈山會相甲彈 (variation of *Yŏngsan hoesang* in the *Ŏŭnbo*), 17
"Yŏngsan hoesang pulbosal" 靈山會相佛菩薩 (Buddha and bodhisattvas meet at Spirit Vulture Peak), 17
"Yŏngsan hoesang samch'ŭng cheji" 靈山會相三層除指 (*kŏmun'go* piece in the *Yuyeji*), 18

Yongsan-gu 龍山區 (district of Seoul), 15
"Yŏngsanhong" 映山紅 (song that refers to a kind of azalea), 88
yŏn'gŭk sori 演劇소리 (play singing), 32, 39
yŏnswaegŭk 連鎖劇 (kino-drama), 32
yŏsŏng kukkŭk 女性國劇 (women's national drama), 23, 32–33
Yu Chinhan 柳振漢 (1711–91; author of *Manhwajip*, a literary source for *p'ansori*), 10
"Yu Ch'ungnyŏl-jŏn" 유충렬전 (Story of Yu Ch'ungnyŏl), 32
Yu Kaedong 柳開東 (1898–?; *chapka* singer), 15
Yu Minyŏng 柳敏榮 (theater historian), 26n, 30n
Yuch'oshinjigok 柳初新之曲 (poetic name for the *P'yŏngjo hoesang* suite), 17
yuhaengga 流行歌 (old-style popular song form), 165
"Yukcha yŏmbul" 六字念佛 (*kŏmun'go* piece in the *Yuyeji*), 18
yulgaek 律客 (instrumentalist), 6, 8
Yun Yonggu 尹用求 (1853–1939; author of *Hyŏn'gŭm oŭm t'ong-non*), 8
Yuyeji 遊藝志 (Section on amusing arts; literary source for *kŏmun'go* music in Sŏ Yugu's essay collection *Imwŏn shimyukchi*), 8–9, 17

zen 禪 (J.: Buddhist meditation), 205
zheng 箏 (C.: plucked-string zither), 209

Contributors

Margaret Dilling was assistant professor of music (ethnomusicology) at the University of California, San Diego. A member of the Religious of the Sacred Heart, she received her Ph.D. in ethnomusicology from the University of California, Berkeley, where her primary area of research was the music of Korea. In addition to being a founding member and officer of the Association for Korean Music Research, her articles appeared in *Asian Music, College Music Symposium, Ethnomusicology, Olympic Message,* and *Korean Culture.* While at UCSD she taught courses in world music, music of East Asia, music of ethnic Americans, and ethnomusicology.

Nathan Hesselink is assistant professor of ethnomusicology at Illinois State University. He received his Ph.D. in ethnomusicology (Korean music) from the University of London, School of Oriental and African Studies, and was a postdoctoral research fellow in Korean studies at the University of California, Berkeley. His ongoing research focuses on the Korean percussion ensemble tradition known by the names *p'ungmul* and *nongak,* in both its urban and rural settings. He has studied Korean percussion with Ch'oe Pyŏngsam and Pak Ŭnha (*samul nori*), as well as with Kim Hyŏngsun, Pak Hyŏngnae, and Yi Sangbaek (*p'ungmul/nongak*), was a performing member of Iri Nongak, and competed in Kim Duk Soo's International SamulNori Drumming Competition as a representative of England. An officer of the Association for Korean Music Research and an editorial board member of the interdisciplinary journal *Music and Culture,* he has published in the *British Journal of Ethnomusicology, Kyoto Journal, Korea Journal, Han'guk ŭmak yŏn'gu, Tongyang ŭmak, Ŭmak-kwa munhwa,* and *Asian Music.*

Keith Howard is senior lecturer in music, School of Oriental and African Studies, University of London. His publications include *True Stories of the Korean Comfort Women* (London:

Cassell, 1995), *Korean Musical Instruments* (Hong Kong: Oxford University Press, 1995), *Korea: People, Country and Culture* (London: SOAS, 1996), and *Korean Shamanism: Revivals, Survivals, and Change* (Seoul: Royal Asiatic Society, 1998). The author/editor of eight further volumes, he also wrote *The 1999 State Visit of Her Majesty Queen Elizabeth II to Korea* (Seoul: Foreign and Commonwealth Office and the British Embassy, 1999) and has written more than eighty articles on Korean music, Korean culture, shamanism, and ethnomusicology in such journals as *Ethnomusicology, Cahiers de Musique Traditionelles, World of Music,* and *Journal of Ritual Studies.*

Serra Miyeun Hwang is instructional assistant professor of theory and composition at Illinois State University. Born and raised in Seoul, Korea, she received her D.M.A. in composition from the University of Michigan, Ann Arbor, with a minor in ethnomusicology. She was formerly at Chŏnju University (Korea), Bradley University, and Illinois Wesleyan University. She has conducted research on Korean folk music, and her own music has been performed in England, Korea, Mexico, and Costa Rica.

Andrew P. Killick is assistant professor of ethnomusicology at The Florida State University and president of the Association for Korean Music Research. His dissertation from the University of Washington is the first monograph in a Western language on the Korean opera form *ch'anggŭk,* on which topic he has also published articles in *Korean Studies, Korea Journal, Korean Culture, Review of Korean Studies,* and *Asian Music* (forthcoming 2002). He is an associate editor and contributing author for the East Asia volume of *The Garland Encyclopedia of World Music* (New York: Garland, 2002) and has contributed chapters to *Taboo: Sex, Identity, and Erotic Subjectivity in Anthropological Fieldwork* (London: Routledge, 1995) and *Soundtrack Available: Essays on Film and Pop Music* (Durham, N.C.: Duke University Press, 2001).

Kim Jin-Woo is currently a Ph.D. candidate in musicology at the University of Michigan, Ann Arbor, where she also received her M.M. in music education and M.A. in musicology. She studied the *kayagŭm* with Lee Chaesuk and Kim Chongja at Seoul National University, where she received her B.M. in Korean music.

Lee Chaesuk is professor of Korean music at the College of Music, Seoul National University, where she received both her B.A. and M.A. in Korean traditional music (*kayagŭm*). After graduation, she began a ten-year period of research into all the major forms of *kayagŭm sanjo*. Learning directly from the masters themselves, she became the first Korean to gain a performing knowledge of the six most famous types of *sanjo*. She then published the results of her research, making this genre generally available in transcription for the first time. She has also been visiting professor at Lucy Cavendish College, Cambridge, and Andrews Chair of the University of Hawai'i School of Hawaiian Asian and Pacific Studies. She serves or has served as head of the Asian Music Research Institute, board member of the Korean Musicological Society and the Society for Korean Music Educators, adviser for the National Center for Korean Traditional Performing Arts, and president of the Korean Zither Musicians' Association.

Chan E. Park is associate professor of Korean language and literature at The Ohio State University. An accomplished *p'ansori* performer, she received her Ph.D. in East Asian languages and literature from the University of Hawai'i and was a postdoctoral research fellow in Korean studies at the University of California, Berkeley. She is the co-author of *Ch'anggŭk of Korea: Song of Ch'unhyang; Song of Shim Ch'ŏng* (Seoul: National Theater of Korea, 1995) and has contributed chapters to *Perspective on Korea* (Sydney: Wild Peony, 1998), *Traditional Storytelling Today: An International Sourcebook* (Chicago: Fitzroy Dearborn, 1999), and *Folktales from Korea*, World Folklore Series (Libraries Unlimited, 1999). Her articles have appeared in the *Journal of American Folklore* and *Korean Studies*.

Sheen Dae-Cheol is associate professor of music at Kangnung National University. He received his B.A. and M.A. from Seoul National University and his Ph.D. from the Academy of Korean Studies. He is the author of *Uri ŭmak, kŭ mat-kwa sorikkal* (Korean music, its flavor and tone color) (Seoul: Kyobo mun'go, 1993) and has contributed historical studies on Korean music, Chinese music, and organology to *Minjok ŭmakhak* (Journal of Asian music research), *Han'guk ŭmak yŏn'gu* (Studies in Korean music), and *Kugagwŏn nonmunjip* (Journal of the National Center for Korean Traditional Performing Arts).

Song Bang-Song, former director of the National Center for Korean Traditional Performing Arts and dean of the College of Music at Yeungnam University, is professor of music at the Korean National University of Arts, Seoul. Educated at Seoul National University, he pursued further studies at the

University of Toronto, Canada, and at Wesleyan University, where he received his Ph.D in ethnomusicology. He has served as assistant professor at McGill University, Montreal, Canada, as president of the Society for Korean Historico-Musicology, and as a member of the Cultural Assets Committee. He is the author of a number of English works, including *An Annotated Bibliography of Korean Music* (1971), *The Korean-Canadian Folk Song* (1974), *The Sanjo Tradition of Korean Kŏmun'go Music* (1986), and *Korean Music: Historical and Other Aspects* (2000).

INSTITUTE OF EAST ASIAN STUDIES PUBLICATIONS SERIES

CHINA RESEARCH MONOGRAPHS (CRM)

36. Suzanne Pepper. *China's Education Reform in the 1980s: Policies, Issues, and Historical Perspectives*, 1990
sp. Phyllis Wang and Donald A. Gibbs, eds. *Readers' Guide to China's Literary Gazette, 1949–1979*, 1990
38. James C. Shih. *Chinese Rural Society in Transition: A Case Study of the Lake Tai Area, 1368–1800*, 1992
39. Anne Gilks. *The Breakdown of the Sino-Vietnamese Alliance, 1970–1979*, 1992
sp. Theodore Han and John Li. *Tiananmen Square Spring 1989: A Chronology of the Chinese Democracy Movement*, 1992
40. Frederic Wakeman, Jr., and Wen-hsin Yeh, eds. *Shanghai Sojourners*, 1992
41. Michael Schoenhals. *Doing Things with Words in Chinese Politics: Five Studies*, 1992
sp. Kaidi Zhan. *The Strategies of Politeness in the Chinese Language*, 1992
42. Barry C. Keenan. *Imperial China's Last Classical Academies: Social Change in the Lower Yangzi, 1864–1911*, 1994
43. Ole Bruun. *Business and Bureaucracy in a Chinese City: An Ethnography of Private Business Households in Contemporary China*, 1993
44. Wei Li. *The Chinese Staff System: A Mechanism for Bureaucratic Control and Integration*, 1994
45. Ye Wa and Joseph W. Esherick. *Chinese Archives: An Introductory Guide*, 1996
46. Melissa Brown, ed. *Negotiating Ethnicities in China and Taiwan*, 1996
47. David Zweig and Chen Changgui. *China's Brain Drain to the United States: Views of Overseas Chinese Students and Scholars in the 1990s*, 1995
48. Elizabeth J. Perry, ed. *Putting Class in Its Place: Worker Identities in East Asia*, 1996
sp. Phyllis L. Thompson, ed. *Dear Alice: Letters Home from American Teachers Learning to Live in China*, 1998
49. Wen-hsin Yeh, ed. *Landscape, Culture, and Power in Chinese Society*, 1998
50. Gail Hershatter, Emily Honig, Susan Mann, and Lisa Rofel, comps. and eds. *Guide to Women's Studies in China*, 1999
51. Wen-hsin Yeh, ed. *Cross-Cultural Readings of Chineseness: Narratives, Images, and Interpretations of the 1990s*, 2000
52. Marilyn A. Levine and Chen San-ching. *The Guomindang in Europe: A Sourcebook of Documents*, 2000
53. David N. Keightley. *The Ancestral Landscape: Time, Space, and Community in Late Shang China*, 2000
54. Peter M. Worthing. *Occupation and Revolution: China and the Vietnamese August Revolution of 1945*, 2001.

KOREA RESEARCH MONOGRAPHS (KRM)

13. Vipan Chandra. *Imperialism, Resistance, and Reform in Late Nineteenth-Century Korea: Enlightenment and the Independence Club*, 1988
14. Seok Choong Song. *Explorations in Korean Syntax and Semantics*, 1988
15. Robert A. Scalapino and Dalchoong Kim, eds. *Asian Communism: Continuity and Transition*, 1988
16. Chong-Sik Lee and Se-Hee Yoo, eds. *North Korea in Transition*, 1991
17. Nicholas Eberstadt and Judith Banister. *The Population of North Korea*, 1992
18. Hong Yung Lee and Chung Chongwook, eds. *Korean Options in a Changing International Order*, 1993
19. Tae Hwan Ok and Hong Yung Lee, eds. *Prospects for Change in North Korea*, 1994
20. Chai-sik Chung. *A Korean Confucian Encounter with the Modern World: Yi Hang-no and the West*, 1995
21. Myung Hun Kang. *The Korean Business Conglomerate: Chaebol Then and Now*, 1996